DATE DUE

MAR 09 2011			
	DISCARDED		

Demco, Inc. 38-293

Offender Profiling in the Courtroom

The Use and Abuse of Expert Witness Testimony

Norbert Ebisike

Westport, Connecticut
London

Library of Congress Cataloging-in-Publication Data

Ebisike, Norbert.
    Offender profiling in the courtroom : the use and abuse of expert witness testimony /
Norbert Ebisike.
      p. cm.
    Includes bibliographical references and index.
    ISBN 978-0-313-36210-1 (alk. paper)
    1. Evidence, Expert—United States. 2. Forensic psychology—United States.
3. Criminal behavior, Prediction of—United States. I. Title.
    KF8965.E25 2008
    347.73'67—dc22   2008022561

British Library Cataloguing in Publication Data is available.

Library of Congress Catalog Card Number: 2008022561
ISBN: 978-0-313-36210-1

First published in 2008

Praeger Publishers, 88 Post Road West, Westport, CT 06881
An imprint of Greenwood Publishing Group, Inc.
www.praeger.com

Printed in the United States of America

The paper used in this book complies with the
Permanent Paper Standard issued by the National
Information Standards Organization (Z39.48-1984).

10 9 8 7 6 5 4 3 2 1

Excerpt from The Complete Jack the Ripper by Donald Rumbelow, published by W.H. Allen.
Reprinted by permission of The Random House Group, Ltd. 111 (1975), and with permission of
Curtis Brown Group Ltd, London on behalf of Donald Rumbelow. Copyright © Donald Rumbelow
1975.

Contents

Preface

This book examines the use of offender profiling evidence in criminal cases—its meaning, history, approaches, and legal admissibility. The introduction of offender profiling into the courtroom has been controversial, problematic, and full of inconsistencies. This book therefore, examines the central problems with offender profiling evidence, and answers questions such as: Is offender profiling impermissible character evidence? Who is qualified to give expert profiling evidence? Is offender profiling too prejudicial? Is offender profiling an opinion on the ultimate issue? Is offender profiling sufficiently reliable as to be admissible? This book has noted that in United States, there are inconsistencies in the court decisions on offender profiling evidence as a result of three conflicting rules governing the admissibility of expert evidence. After a critical examination of the three rules, the adoption of one rule has been suggested. The *Frye* test standard combined with the *Federal Rules of Evidence* 702 provides the best admissibility standard.

Many people are confused as to the definition of offender profiling. This book has therefore, presented a step-by-step analysis of the history and development of offender profiling. Offender profiling is a multidisciplinary practice, which, at the moment, is best described as an art with the potential of becoming a science. This book concludes that offender profiling is not sufficiently reliable as to be admissible. It is more prejudicial than probative. This book also concludes that there is an uneasy relationship, lack of unity, and absence of information sharing among the different segments of the criminal justice system involved with offender profiling, and that this problem has limited the potential of offender profiling. Hence, some courts are not convinced as to the reliability and validity of this technique. I make several recommendations throughout the work to address these issues.

Many people provided me with great support and strength that enabled me to bring this book to fruition. First of all, I would like to thank my parents for their continued belief that education is a good investment that opens many doors. I also take this opportunity to express my appreciation to my brothers and sisters for their encouragement and understanding throughout the various stages of this book.

I would also like to express my sincere gratitude to Dean Emeritus and Professor Peter Keane, Distinguished Professor Emeritus Sompong Sucharitkul and Professor Christian Okeke, of Golden Gate University School of Law, for their support and encouragement. I would like to thank them for sharing their knowledge and for showing me the "light." My sincere gratitude goes to all the staff of Golden Gate University Center for Advanced International Legal Studies and Golden Gate University Law Library for their assistance. My special thanks also go to the Greenwood Publishing Group staff for doing excellent work. Finally, I would like to thank the many people who assisted me in one way or the other throughout this work. Many thanks to the offender profiling experts who assisted me by sharing their knowledge and information.

Norbert Ebisike

Introduction

In spite of the ever-increasing media interest in the use of offender profiling in criminal trials, this technique is still not well understood by a lot of people, including judges, lawyers, and jurors. Some people see offender profiling as mystical and others simply see it as a fiction. It is the aim of this book to demystify offender profiling and try to raise the general level of knowledge and understanding of this crime investigation technique. This book has two hypotheses. The first is that offender profiling is not widely accepted in courts because its reliability and the scientific basis has not been established, and second, that there are inconsistencies surrounding the admission of offender profiling as a result of the conflicting rules and standards governing its admissibility in various jurisdictions. The central thesis of this book is that offender profiling is not sufficiently reliable as to be admissible (in proving the guilt or innocence of an accused); its prejudicial effect substantially outweighs its probative value; and that there is an uneasy relationship, lack of unity, cooperation, and absence of information sharing among the different segments of the legal system that has limited the potential of offender profiling. There is also the problem with the existence of three rules governing the admissibility of expert evidence in United States. This has led to inconsistencies in the decisions to admit or exclude offender profiling and its derivatives. There have also been many conflicting court decisions on this technique.

This book examines the central problems of offender profiling evidence. Two questions provided the impetus for this book. First: Is offender profiling sufficiently reliable as to be admissible? Offender profiling involves gathering information from the crime scene; witness and victim statements; autopsy reports; offender's physical descriptions, race, age, and criminal records; and so on. The second question then is: How accurate is information gathered in this manner? Should it be tendered in court as proof of guilt or innocence? Offender profiling does not point to specific offenders. It does not determine whether a given defendant committed a specific act. This question arises because in several cases the reliability and accuracy of offender profiling has been at issue. Second, is offender profiling more prejudicial than probative? I conclude that offender profiling is too prejudicial to the accused. Offender profiling only provides an indication of the type of person likely to have committed a type of crime. It does not point to a specific individual. This question arises because in several cases examined, courts have been inconsistent in their decisions on this issue.

In Chapter 1, I discuss the meaning and nature of offender profiling. The goals of offender profiling are also discussed. Offender profiling is an innovative but worrisome technique of crime investigation. In order to have a better understanding of this technique, its history and development are discussed in detail.

Offender profiling is mainly used by the police to narrow down a suspects' list in cases where no physical evidence was left at the crime scene. In recent times however, this technique has been introduced into the courtroom as evidence and there has been a lot of controversy surrounding it. Hence, there have been conflicting court decisions on its status as admissible evidence. In several cases, the reliability, validity, and scientific basis of this technique have been at issue. Chapter 2 therefore, introduces the principles and practice of offender profiling. The different approaches to profiling are discussed, as well as their various strengths and weaknesses.

In Chapter 3, the general rules and principles governing the admissibility of scientific evidence are discussed. As I mentioned earlier, there are many inconsistencies surrounding the admission of offender profiling in criminal cases. One reason has been identified and it relates to the fact that there are three main rules governing the admissibility of scientific evidence. The three rules are as follows: the *Frye* test standard, the *Federal Rules of Evidence,* and the *Daubert* decision. Each state in United States has adopted one of these rules/standards. Some states use *Frye,* some have adopted the *Daubert* criteria, while others have adopted *Frye* plus their own rules of evidence. It should be noted that the *Daubert* criteria is the main rule applied at the federal courts. This leads us to the question: Is it possible to adopt one particular rule? This question will be fully examined.

This book also aims to provide a critical analysis of the use of offender profiling in criminal cases. Hence, Chapter 4, covers the central problems of offender profiling evidence and critically examines cases that involved offender profiling. Chapter 4 also discusses different aspects of challenging offender profiling, answering such questions as:

1. Is offender profiling impermissible character evidence?
2. Who is qualified to give expert offender profiling testimony?

3. Is offender profiling more prejudicial than probative?
4. Is offender profiling an opinion on the ultimate issue?
5. Is offender profiling sufficiently reliable as to be admissible?

Another aim of this book is to provide a comparative analysis of the use of offender profiling in various jurisdictions. Chapter 5 discusses the admissibility of offender profiling in England and Canada, as well as the state of offender profiling in other countries.

In concluding, I offer some recommendations, look at the future of offender profiling, and suggest areas where further research is needed. This book argues the point that offender profiling is a specialized area of knowledge, but one which has not yet reached a sufficient level of reliability as to be admissible. I remain critical of the continued admission of offender profiling in criminal trials and conclude that offender profiling is a technique based on assumptions, suspicion, stereotypes, and probabilities.

This book differs from other previously published studies in many ways. First, this work has presented an interdisciplinary and nonsegmental approach to the understanding of offender profiling. The nature, theory, practice, and the legal aspects of offender profiling are presented in one study. This book goes further with supporting the theory that offender profiling can be used as a tool in developing crime prevention measures. This book also examines offender profiling in a comparative perspective. Above all, none of the previously published studies examine the uneasy relationship among the different segments or approaches to offender profiling, which has limited the potential of this technique. It is my hope that this work demystifies offender profiling.

What is Offender Profiling?

DEFINITION OF OFFENDER PROFILING

Offender profiling has been defined in many ways by various scholars based on their backgrounds. Similarly, offender profiling is known by various names such as psychological profiling, criminal profiling, criminal investigative analysis, crime scene analysis, behavioral profiling, criminal personality profiling, socio-psychological profiling and criminological profiling. In this book, however, the term "offender profiling" will be used. Put simply, offender profiling is a crime investigation technique whereby information gathered from the crime scene, witnesses, victims, autopsy reports, and information about an offender's behavior is used to draw up a profile of the sort of person likely to commit such crime. It is a complementary technique and is usually taken up when no physical traces have been left at the crime scene. Offender profiling does not point to a specific offender. It is based on the probability that someone with certain characteristics is likely to have committed a certain type of crime. An examination of the behavioral and personality characteristics exhibited by an offender at the scene of crime may assist investigators in narrowing down the suspects' list to those persons who match those characteristics.

There are two operating words in offender profiling: 1) *modus operandi* (method of operation), and 2) behavior. There is the idea that an offender is likely to commit a particular type of crime in a particular or similar pattern. Thus, the *modus operandi* may lead to clues about the perpetrator and the crime scene characteristics may point to the personality of the perpetrator. An offender's behavior helps to predict the personality type or the motives for the crime. Therefore, the single most important thing that a profiler looks for at a scene of crime is anything that may point to the offender's personality.

The process of offender profiling involves an examination of the individual traits, physical features, behavior, verbal utterances, and all the actions taken by the offender before, during, and after the attack. Offender profiles typically include information about the offender's likely age, gender, race, occupation, and criminal background. Detailed information about the steps taken by the offender to avoid detection, the method of killing, and information about the victim are also noted when profiling.

GOALS OF OFFENDER PROFILING

Offender profiling is mainly used when the offender did not leave any physical trace at the crime scene. It is used to narrow down the suspects list. It is generally believed that the crime scene characteristics can reveal the offender's personality type. Three major goals of profiling have been outlined:[1]

1. Social and psychological assessments of offenders. This involves an evaluation of the social and psychological characteristics of the offender. A typical profile contains such information as the perpetrator's age, race, educational attainment, employment type, marital status, and religion.[2]
2. Psychological evaluations of belongings found in the possession of suspected offenders. This involves the evaluation of any items found at the suspect's home, such as souvenirs taken from the crime scenes, pictures, videos, books, magazines, or other items that might point to the background and motives for the crimes, as well as link the suspect to the crime. Jerome Brudos, a sadistic serial killer in the United States had such a fetish about his victims' high-heeled shoes that he took their shoes, wore them, and stored them at his home.[3]
3. Suggestions and strategies for interviewing suspected offenders when they are apprehended. As there are different types of offenders, one interrogation strategy may not be suitable for all the different types, especially when dealing with rapists. It has been noted that serial killers, for instance, may kill for several reasons and consequently one interviewing strategy may not be appropriate for all serial killers.[4]

It has been observed that offender profiling is usually taken up late in an investigation. Offender profiling normally tends to be taken up as an alternative when physical evidence, such as DNA, is impossible to collect because there were no samples left at the crime scene. There are obviously certain dangers with this approach. It is therefore, suggested that in major crimes, offender profiling should be used at the onset, along with the other techniques. It should not be left till later in the investigation when we have come to realize that no physical trace has been left at the crime scene, bearing in mind the issue of "staged crime scenes." Important details might be lost later in the investigation and as we know, crime scenes can be tampered with, by both weather conditions and human tampering.

CRIME SCENE STAGING

"Crime scene staging" occurs when the offender alters the crime scene in order to conceal the original intent. For instance, the offender may stage signs of burglary in order to conceal a homicide, or set the murder scene on fire in order to make it look like arson. Arguably, staging is mainly done by an organized offender as opposed to a disorganized offender. Crime scene staging is a calculated attempt by an offender to frustrate investigators. In fact, any conscious criminal action by an offender to mislead the investigators and to thwart an investigation can be described as crime scene staging.[5]

MODUS OPERANDI OR METHOD OF OPERATION

An offender's method of operation (MO) includes such things as the type of victim chosen, location of attack, time of attack, type of weapon used, as well as the method of gaining entry. The method of operation is very important in linking cases, but needs to be examined with caution.

It should be noted that the method of operation can change. In fact, as an offender commits more crime, he or she learns new ways that will help avoid detection. Hence, the method of operation can change. For instance, an offender who normally strangles the victims with bare hands may change and start strangling the victims with stockings or start suffocating the victims with pillows. Similarly, an offender may change from attacking at night to attacking during the daytime, or the offender may change from choosing females to males, young victims to older victims, blacks to whites, or blondes to brunettes. Several things can affect the method of operation that an offender uses. For instance, the victim's response during an attack may lead the offender into changing the MO; the effects of imprisonment may also affect an offender's future MO.[6]

OFFENDER'S SIGNATURE OR CALLING CARD

It should be noted that *modus operandi* is different from the "signature aspects" of a crime. An offender is revealing his or her signatures when there is evidence that the offender exhibited certain behavior or carried out certain actions that where not really necessary to commit the crime. These actions or behaviors may include torturing the victims in a particular way, mutilation, using a particular weapon, constantly inflicting the same kind of injury, or some sort of ritualistic activity.[7]

The signature aspects of a crime, which can also be called the "mark" of the perpetrator, are elements in an offender's behavior that in most cases may be present and recognizable at the scene of crime; but these can change.

They are the overriding psychological need of an offender. It is what drives a killer to engage in an attack and the particular method of carrying out that attack. Signature aspects of a crime reveal the deep emotional needs that have to happen in order for the offender to fulfill his fantasy. Put simply, the signature aspect of a crime refers to the specific thing(s) that an offender tends to do at the crime scene. It could be cutting off a specific part of the victim's body and taking it as a souvenir, cutting the victims' throats, or putting the victims inside the bath tub after killing them, and so on. Hence, signature can be described as the "mark" of a killer, which may distinguish one killer from another. It should be noted that there are various things that can affect signature; therefore, signatures are not a conclusive or a reliable indicator that a particular offender carried out a particular attack. Offenders learn from other offenders, from television crime series, and from their experience; they develop new fantasies and they also read or learn from books on crime investigations and forensic science, and so their signature may change.

The motive of a crime is different from the signature aspects of a crime and refers to the reason why a particular crime was committed. An offender can have different motives for different crimes.

LINKAGE ANALYSIS

Linkage analysis refers to the method whereby behavioral patterns, wound patterns, crime scene characteristics, victimology, and other aspects of two or more crimes committed at different crime scenes are examined in an attempt to ascertain whether the crimes were committed by one offender. Linkage analysis has faced much criticism. It has been argued that linkage analysis is not a means of identification but rather "a means of obtaining either the admission of other crimes evidence which might not otherwise be admitted, or a means to convince the jury that the other crimes evidence was more meaningful than they otherwise might believe, or both."[8] Linkage analysis is one of the most contentious issues when offender profiling is being introduced into the courtroom as evidence.

TYPES OF CRIME SUITABLE FOR PROFILING

It has been recognized that not all types of crime are suitable for profiling. In fact, there is general agreement that crimes most suitable for profiling are:

1. Crimes where there were signs of psychopathology,
2. Crimes believed to be part of a series,

3. Violent crimes,
4. Attacks on strangers, and
5. Contact crimes—crimes where the offender engaged in long conversations and communications with the victim.

Serial murders, serial rapes, sexual homicides, ritual crimes, arson, and hostage taking have been viewed as suitable for profiling. Research by Ronald Holmes and Stephen Holmes has shown that the types of crimes most suitable for profiling include sadistic torture in sexual assaults, evisceration, postmortem slashing and cutting, motiveless fire setting, lust and mutilation murder, rape, satanic and ritualistic crime, and pedophilia.[9] It has also been noted that assaults, property crimes, and drug-induced crimes are not suitable for profiling because the true personality of the offender cannot be properly deduced; the personality may have been altered.[10]

"Contact crimes" are suitable for profiling. These are crimes where the underlying motives for the crime are most likely to be revealed by examining the manner and nature of the attacks.[11] "Serial killers are the most frustrating and disturbing of all violent predators, but they are the most profilable. Why? When they kill, they are filling complex psychological needs. Sometimes, they may steal when they kill, but from my experience of studying serial predators for twenty years and interviewing over twenty-five of them, their motivations are in their heads, not their wallets. Because they kill for psychological reasons, many times, they leave a lot of clues for profilers."[12]

HISTORY AND DEVELOPMENT OF OFFENDER PROFILING

Offender profiling goes as far back as 1876 when the Italian criminologist, physician and psychiatrist, Cesaro Lombroso (1835–1909), published his work *L'Uomo Delinquente* (The Criminal Man), in which he argued that there are certain physical characteristics that are indicative of a born criminal. He maintained that by comparing information about similar offenders such as race, age, sex, physical characteristics, education, and geographic location, the origins and motivations of criminal behavior could be better understood and subsequently predicted. Lombroso, basing his ideas on Darwin's theory of evolution, maintained that there are six types of criminals: 1) the born criminal, 2) the insane criminal, 3) the criminal by passion, 4) the habitual criminal, 5) the occasional criminal, and 6) and the criminaloid.

Lombroso had the idea that there is a born criminal and argued that criminality is inherited and could be identified by physical defects. For him, criminals have certain physiognomic deformities. He saw criminals as savage and atavistic. In his theory of atavism, he measured the heads of living and executed criminals against the skulls of apes and prehistoric humans and came up with the idea that criminals were victims of atavism. He maintained that "born criminals" have the following physical characteristics/deformities[13]:

- Deviation in head size and shape from type common to race and region from which the criminal came,
- Asymmetry of the face,
- Eye defects and peculiarities,
- Excessive dimensions of the jaws and cheek bones,
- Ears of unusual size, or occasionally very small, or standing out from the head as do those of the chimpanzee,
- Nose twisted, upturned, or flattened in thieves, or aquiline or beak-like in murderers, or with a tip rising like a peak from swollen nostrils,
- Lips fleshy, swollen, and protruding,
- Pouches in the cheek like those of some animals,
- Peculiarities of the palate, such as are found in some reptiles, and cleft palate,
- Chin receding, or excessively long, or short and flat, as in apes,
- Abnormal dentition,
- Abundance, variety, and precocity of wrinkles,
- Anomalies of the hair, marked by characteristics of the hair of the opposite sex,
- Defects of the thorax, such as too many or too few ribs, or supernumerary nipples,
- Inversion of sex characters in the pelvic organs,
- Excessive length of arms,
- Supernumerary fingers and toes, and
- Imbalance of the hemispheres of the brain (asymmetry of cranium).

Lombroso maintained that the insane criminals were the type of criminals who suffered from mental illnesses and also had some physical deformities. The habitual criminals according to Lombroso are those who commit crimes as a result of poor socialization. The occasional criminals commit crimes to protect family honor and as self-defense. The criminaloids are those who commit crimes when the opportunities arise in their environment. Lombroso maintained that criminaloids are usually left-handed, which he said was common among swindlers, are also characterized by early baldness and grayness and insensitivity to pain and that a large number of them abuse alcohol.

Lombroso believed that the study of individuals should involve the utilization of measurements and statistical methods in compiling anthropological, social, and economic data. He was against capital punishment and argued in favor of rehabilitation. He also contended that there should be humane treatment for criminals because their criminality is inherited.

Lombroso's views were undoubtedly criticized. The greatest criticism came from Charles Goring, an Englishman, who carried out a study of 3,000 English convicts and compared them with groups of university students, hospital patients, and British soldiers. Using statistical methodology, Goring compared measurements of 37 specific physical characteristics of the groups and observed that "in fact, both with regard to measurements and the presence of physical anomalies in criminals, our statistics present a startling conformity with similar statistics of the law-abiding classes. Our inevitable conclusion must be that there is no such thing as a physical criminal type."[14] Goring also observed some differences between criminals and noncriminals in terms of sexual profligacy, alcoholism, and epilepsy, and concluded that "the one vital mental constitutional factor in the etiology of crime is defective intelligence."

It should be noted that two of Lombroso's students—Enrico Ferri (1856–1929) and Raffaelo Garofalo (1852–1934), later took a different approach to the explanations of criminal behavior. For instance, Garofalo, in his theory of moral degeneration, maintained that degeneration resulted from retrogressive selection and caused the individual "to lose the better qualities which he had acquired by secular evolution, and has led him back to the same degree of inferiority whence he had slowly risen. This retrogressive selection is due to the mating of weakest and most unfit, of those who have become brutalized by alcohol or abased by extreme misery against which apathy has prevented them from struggling. Thus are formed demoralized and outcast families whose interbreeding in time produces a true face of inferior quality."[15]

Following the criticisms of his work and after further research, Lombroso later revised his work and admitted that social, economic, and environmental factors also played significant roles in criminal behavior. He still maintained, however, that at least 40 percent of criminality is a result of biological heredity. Nevertheless, Lombroso's early explanation of criminality, using measurements, is undoubtedly the beginning of the attempts to find a scientific basis for the idea of predicting crimes and criminals.

Following the work of Goring, Earnest Hooton, an American anthropologist, in 1939, carried out a study of 13,873 male criminals in 10 states and compared it with a civilian group of 3,023 and found out that "criminals are organically inferior. Crime is the resultant of the impact of environment upon low grade human organisms. To eliminate crime, the physically, mentally, and morally unfit must be exterminated or segregated completely in a "socially aseptic environment."[16]

Hooton claimed that certain morphological characteristics were more common in criminals than among civilians. These characteristics include thin lips, straight hair, thin beards and body hair, thick head hair, long thin necks, sloping shoulders, low and sloping foreheads, compressed jaw angles, blue-gray and mixed eyes, protruding and small ears, tattooing, and nasal bridges and tips varying to both extremes of breadth and narrowness.[17] Hooton also believed that criminals were inferior to noncriminals, and that inferiority could be explained by heredity, arguing that physical inferiority indicates mental inferiority. Furthermore, Hooton claimed that murderers and robbers tend to be tall and thin; burglars and thieves tend to be undersized. and that short and heavily built men tend to be involved in sexual offenses and assaults.

Hooton's arguments were seen as fundamentally flawed. It has been noted for instance, that more than 50 percent of the prisoners used in the study had served previous prison sentences and that the majority of the sentences were for offenses different from the ones they were serving at the time of the study.[18] Hooton used prisoners to represent all criminals, the control group was too small, and the study included firemen and militiamen who had already passed physical examinations before they were recruited. This led to an exaggeration in the physical differences between offenders and nonoffenders in the study.[19]

Dr. Hans Gross, an Austrian judge and criminologist also made important contributions toward attempts to explain criminality and the prediction of criminals. In fact, he is widely regarded as the first person to write about offender profiling *per se*. In 1893 he published his work *Criminal Investigation: A Practical Textbook for Magistrates, Police Officers, and Lawyers*, in which he maintained that criminals can be better understood by studying their crimes. Gross argued that:

In nearly every case the thief has left the most important trace of his passage, namely the manner in which he has committed the theft. Every thief has in fact a characteristic style or modus operandi which he rarely departs from, and which he is incapable of completely getting rid of; at times this distinctive feature is so visible and so striking that even the novice can spot it without difficulty; but on the one hand the novice does not know how to group, differentiate, or utilize what he has observed, and on the other hand the particular character of the procedure is not always so easy to recognize.[20]

Gross also maintained that by examining the character and beliefs of an offender we can know more about the offender's criminal actions. He believed that "every deed is an outcome of the character of the doer" and noted that "a certain character predisposes to determinate deeds; another character makes them unthinkable and unrelatable with this or that person."[21]

In 1888 there were several murder cases in the Whitechapel area of East London, England. In fact, between August 31 and November 9, 1888, five female prostitutes were murdered, and the police had no clues as to the identity of the killer. On August 31, 1888 Mary Ann Nichols was found brutally murdered. This was followed by the discovery of the viciously mutilated body of Annie Chapman on September 8, 1888. On September 30, 1888 was the discovery of the double murder of Elizabeth Stride and Catherine Eddowes. On November 9, 1888 another murder occurred and this time Mary Jane Kelly was the victim. At this point Dr. Thomas Bond, a police surgeon, was asked to perform an autopsy on Kelly. The killer, after strangling the women, would cut their throats and then remove some of their internal organs. This prompted the police to think that the killer might be somebody with anatomical or surgical knowledge like a surgeon or a butcher.

Hence, Bond was also instructed to give an opinion on this issue. After the autopsy on Kelly, Bond also studied the medical reports of the other victims as well as the police reports, and he decided to do a crime scene reconstruction to see if he could find any behavioral patterns that could lead investigators to the possible killer. He believed that the mutilations of the five victims suggested that one person was responsible for all five murders. Above all, the five murders all shared similar characteristics: All the victims were left in open places, where their bodies were found soon after they were killed; all the victims were female prostitutes; all the victims were viciously mutilated and internal organs were removed from their bodies. Bond produced a profile that he sent to the head of the Criminal Investigation Division (CID) in London. In his profile, Bond wrote that:

The murderer must have been a man of great physical strength and of great coolness and daring. There is no evidence that he had an accomplice. He must in my opinion be a man subject to periodical attacks of homicidal and erotic mania. The character of the mutilations indicates that the man may be in a condition sexually, that may be called satyriasis. It is of course possible that the homicidal impulse may have developed from a revengeful or brooding condition of the mind, or that religious mania may have been the original disease but I do not think either hypothesis is likely. The murderer in external appearance is quite likely to be [a] quiet inoffensive-looking man probably middle-aged and neatly and respectably dressed. I think he must be in the habit of wearing a cloak or overcoat or he could hardly have escaped notice in the streets if the blood on his hands and clothes were visible.

Assuming the murderer to be such a person as I have just described, he would be solitary and eccentric in his habits, also he is most likely to be a man without regular occupation, but with some small income or pension. He is possibly living among respectable persons who have some knowledge of his character and habits and who may have grounds for suspicion that he isn't quite right in his mind at times. Such persons would probably be unwilling to communicate suspicions to the police for fear of trouble or notoriety, whereas if there were prospects of reward it might overcome their scruples.[22]

The unknown killer was referred to as the "Leather Apron" killer, but in a letter he sent to the police he called himself "Jack the Ripper." As of today, the identity of this killer is still a mystery; hence, the five murders still remain unsolved. Therefore, the accuracy or usefulness of Bond's profile cannot be evaluated; however, his efforts constitute another major contribution toward the history and development of offender profiling.

In 1943 the U.S. Office of Strategic Services (OSS) asked Dr. Walter C. Langer, a psychiatrist based in New York to produce a psychological profile of Adolf Hitler. This was for military intelligence purpose, and not for criminal investigation. The OSS was the arm of the U.S. Army responsible for gathering intelligence. The Central Intelligence Agency (CIA) took over in 1945 when the OSS was disbanded. The OSS wanted a personality profile of Hitler in order to know the best interrogative strategy to be used if he was captured. Langer studied and analyzed Hitler's speeches, studied Hitler's book, *Mein Kampf*, and interviewed those who knew Hitler and he came up with a psychodynamic personality profile. Langer stated that the OSS asked him to provide "a realistic appraisal of the German situation. If Hitler is running the show, what kind of person is he? What are his ambitions? How does he appear to the German people? What is he like with his associates? What is his background? And most of all, we want to know as much as possible about his psychological make-up—the things that make him tick."[23]

Among other things, Langer predicted that Hitler might possibly be killed in battle, might possibly be assassinated, or might go insane and was likely to commit suicide, because "Hitler has already envisaged a death of this kind, for he has said to Rauschning: 'Yes, in the hour of supreme peril I must sacrifice myself for the people.'"[24]

Langer's profile was seen to be correct, as Hitler committed suicide in a bunker when he found out that the Allies were winning.

In 1949, William H. Sheldon, a psychologist came up with his "somatotype" theory in which he argued that physique or body type is related to certain temperaments. During an eight-year period, Sheldon tested his theory on delinquent boys and normal college students and found out that there is a link between the mesomorphic body type and crime, which explained why some juveniles are delinquent. His three body types are as follows[25]:

1. Endomorphs: These are individuals whom he said are soft, round or fat physiques, and plump;
2. Mesomorphs: These people are muscular and hard, with heavy chest and heavy bones; and
3. Ectomorphs: These are people who are thin/lean, fragile, with droopy shoulders and small faces.

Sheldon's three temperaments are as follows:

1. Viscerotonia—The individuals with this type of temperament tend to be relaxed, comfort-loving, greedy for affection and approval, slow in reaction, even in emotions, and tolerant.
2. Somatotonia—This type of temperament is associated with individuals who are assertive, adventure-loving, psychologically callous, energetic, compulsive, and ruthless.
3. Cerebrotonia—Individuals with this type of temperament are tight in posture, physiologically overresponsive, emotionally restrained, unpredictable in attitude, and mentally overintense.

Sheldon maintained that endomorphs tend to have viscerotonia temperaments, mesomorphs tend to be somatotonic, and ectomorphs have cerebrotonia type of temperament. In his study of 200 delinquent boys (aged 15–21) in a rehabilitation center, he found out that delinquent youths tend to be mesomorphs. Sheldon used statistical correlations and ranked individuals on a subject scale of 1 to 7 to indicate the predominant temperament in each individual. Using what he called an "index of delinquency" or "index of disappointingness," Sheldon tried to provide a quantitative account of an individual's psychiatric problems and residual delinquency, as well as shortcomings in IQ insufficiency. He concluded that delinquents are mainly mesomorphs. As we have seen, Sheldon made a great contribution towards the attempts to predict criminals and criminal behavior. In fact, his study was later supported by Sheldon and Eleanor Glueck. In 1956, the Gluecks, using Sheldon's somatotype system, studied 500 boys considered to be persistently delinquent and compared them to 500 nondelinquent boys in public schools in Boston Massachusetts, and they also found out that mesomorphic boys have higher delinquency level/potential than the other body types.[26]

In 1955, Ernst Kretschmer (1888–1964), a German criminologist, came up with a body types theory in which he argued that there is a high degree of correlation between body types, personality types, and criminal potential. Kretschmer studied 260 insane people in Swabia (a southwestern German town), and in his work *Physique and Character*, he contended that there are four body types and that each is linked to a person's personality, character, and criminal potential. His four body types are as follows:[27]

1. Leptosome or asthenic: Tall and thin, and mainly involved in fraud and thievery. He said that schizophrenics fall into this group;
2. Athletic: Very muscular, flat stomachs, and usually involved in violent crimes;

3. Pyknic: Short, fat, broad faces, and usually involved in fraud, deception, and sometimes violent crimes, and that manic-depressives fall into this category; and
4. Dysplastic or mixed: These are individuals who fit into more than one body type and who are generally involved in some violent crimes and indecency. Generally, these individuals are very emotional, lack self-control and are mostly involved in sexual offenses and crimes of passion.

Dr. James Brussel, an American psychiatrist, is arguably the father of modern offender profiling. In 1956, Brussel who was in private practice and was also the assistant commissioner of mental hygiene for the State of New York, was approached by police investigators to help them investigate a series of bomb explosions in New York City. It should also be noted that Brussel was the chief of neuropsychiatry in the U.S. Army (at Fort Dix) prior to going into private practice. Later he was the head of U.S. Army neuropsychiatry during the Korean War.

In 1956, Brussel came up with a psychological profile which led to the identification of George Metesky. Metesky was known as the New York "Mad Bomber." He caused 32 explosions in New York City between 1940 and 1956. Using crime scene information, Brussel was able to make psychodynamic inferences. He studied the crime scene photos and the letters that the bomber wrote and he produced a profile of the likely offender.

In his psychological profile, Brussel urged the investigators to look for a single, middle-aged man, heavy-built, Roman Catholic, foreign-born and who lives with a brother or sister, is currently or formerly employed by Consolidated Edison Company, and probably suffering from progressive paranoia.[28] He also stated that there was a chance that the offender would be wearing a buttoned double-breasted suit.[29] In general, Brussel's profile also asked the police to look for, "single man, between 40 and 50 years, introvert. Unsocial but not antisocial. Skilled mechanic. Cunning. Neat with tools. Egoistical of mechanical skill. Contemptuous of other people. Resentful of criticism of his work but probably conceals resentment. Moral. Honest. Not interested in women. High school graduate. Expert in civil or military ordinance. Religious. Might flare up violently at work when criticized."[30]

Brussel's profile proved to be accurate. Metesky was a former employee of Consolidated Edison, and most interesting of all, when the police went to arrest him at his house, they asked him to get changed and he came out dressed in a double-breasted suit, just as Brussel predicted. Metesky confessed to having committed the crimes.

The police also asked Brussel to help them in the case of the "Boston Strangler." In Boston, Massachusetts, between June 1962 and January 1964,

13 sexually motivated murders occurred and the police had no suspects. In what became known as the "Boston Strangler" case, Brussel was asked to produce a psychological profile of the likely offender. Initially, the investigators believed that the murders were committed by two killers. This was based on the fact that the victims were of two age groups—young women and older women, aged 19 to 85. Brussel believed that only one person was responsible for the 13 murders, and he produced a profile. Albert DeSalvo was arrested in November 1964 in connection with another rape and murder known as the "Green Man Sex Crimes." He fitted the profile drawn up by Brussel. He was detained and he later confessed to his psychiatrist that he was the "Boston Strangler." While in prison awaiting trial for the other murders, DeSalvo was stabbed to death by a fellow inmate; hence, he was not tried for the "Boston Strangler" murders. The accuracy or otherwise of Brussel's profile therefore cannot be evaluated on this case.

Suffice it to say, however, that Brussel used his practical psychiatric knowledge and experience, personal intuition, and police and medical records to come up with the profiles. Such an approach is therefore, subjective and should be used with caution. In fact, Brussel admitted that he made mistakes in some of his cases, analyzed facts incorrectly or incompletely; and he wrote: "The only thing that I have done to get my name in the papers has been to apply some common psychiatric principles in reverse, using my own private blend of science, intuition, and hope. With this approach, I've been able to help the police solve some bizarre criminal cases and I've been summoned as an expert witness in some famous criminal trials."[31]

Following the work of Brussel, the FBI in the 1970s started to expand on offender profiling and in 1974 established the Behavioral Science Unit at the FBI training academy in Quantico, Virginia, with the aim of studying serial rape and homicide cases. Howard Teten and Pat Mullany were the first instructors at this unit, however, in 1975, Robert Ressler, Dick Ault, and John Douglas joined and expanded the unit. It should be noted that in 1983 Pierce Brooks founded the FBI's VICAP (computer reporting system) and the unit was made up of Anna Boudea, Ken Handfland, David Icove, and Jim Howlett. In 1984, the National Center for the Analysis of Violent Crimes (NCAVC) was created and charged with the responsibility of identifying and tracking serial killers.

During the 1970s there were several murder cases that the FBI was unable to solve. They became increasingly frustrated with the fact that physical evidence—even when present at the scene of crime—could not provide clues as to the sort of person they should be seeking. The FBI needed a technique that would help focus on the most likely offenders rather than focusing on a large number of suspects. The FBI conducted in-depth interviews with

36 convicted serial killers and found that their crimes were almost all sexually motivated. Their main aim of carrying out the interviews was to identify the personality and behavioral characteristics of these offenders.

Following the interviews, the FBI then developed the concept of organized and disorganized offenders. The FBI noted that there are several differences between the organized and the disorganized offenders in terms of their personality and social characteristics. The organized offender is likely to be intelligent and probably an underachiever, socially skilled, sexually competent, and likely to follow news report about the attack.[32] The disorganized offender on the other hand is likely to live near the crime scene, live alone, be generally of low intelligence, likely to be suffering from some form of mental illness, likely to have been sexually and physically abused as a child, and more likely to attack in a state of panic.[33]

The first case in which the FBI used offender profiling occurred in June 1973 when a seven-year-old girl, Susan Jaegar, went missing while on a camping holiday with her parents. She was abducted from her tent while her parents were sleeping. For a year, the Montana police could not find the missing girl. Then in January 1974, police discovered the charred body of an 18-year-old girl in the woodlands near the camp where Jaegar had been abducted. The police suspected that one killer was responsible for both murders and they decided to call in the FBI to assist them with the investigation. The FBI drew up a profile of the likely killer, which among other things stated that the offender was a young white male, a loner who lived near the camp, likely to have been arrested before, and likely to have kept souvenir from the victims.

Their profile fitted David Meirhofer who was already on the FBI suspects list. He was named by an informant, arrested, and questioned but then released as there was no physical evidence linking him to the murders. As part of its investigation, the FBI kept a telephone recorder at the home of Susan Jaeger's mother. "When, as predicted, an anonymous caller telephoned and said that he has abducted Susan, her mother was able to record his voice. It was identified as that of Meirhofer. A search of his home revealed the gruesome body parts, kept as 'souvenirs.' He later admitted to both murders as well as two others of local boys, before hanging himself in his cell."[34]

It should be noted that the FBI in the 1970s carried out another series of interviews with 41 convicted serial rapists and they came up with four types of rapists: 1) power reassurance, 2) power assertive, 3) anger-retaliatory, and 4) anger excitation.

In Britain, on the other hand, Paul Britton, a British criminal psychologist was approached by the police in 1984 to assist them with the case of a 33-year-old woman, Caroline Osborne, from Leicestershire, England.

Osborne's body was found with seven stab wounds and her hands and feet were bound with string. There were no signs of robbery or sexual assault. It should be noted that a piece of paper containing a drawing of a pentagram in a circle was found at the crime scene. This image is usually linked to black magic or "satanism." In order to draw up a profile of the likely killer, Britton studied the crime scene photographs and autopsy reports and he predicted that the killer was:

1. Male in his mid-teens to early twenties,
2. Sexually immature,
3. Lacked social skills to maintain relationships,
4. Lived at home either with both parents or one parent,
5. Liked to keep to himself,
6. Probably lived near the area where the body was found,
7. Was a manual worker,
8. Had a strong and athletic build, and
9. Had forensic awareness or kept souvenirs.

Another murder occurred 14 months later in the area, with similar patterns and Britton was called in again to assist with the investigation. Britton said that even though there were a few differences in the two murders that they were committed by the same person. Following Britton's profile, Paul Kenneth Bostock was arrested. Britton suggested to the police the interviewing strategies to be used and Bostock later confessed to the two murders. In June 1986, he was sentenced to life imprisonment by the Leicester Crown Court. Britton believed that there were sexual motives for the murders and he wrote: "Caroline Osborne's murder was an expression of a corrupt lust. The bindings, control, and choice of victim suggested a killer whose sexual desire had become mixed with anger and the need to dominate. He would have rehearsed the scene in his mind beforehand—fantasizing about a woman being taken, restrained, bound, dominated, mutilated, and killed with a knife."[35]

Paul Britton was also involved in the controversial case of Rachel Nickell, a 20-year-old model who was murdered on July 15, 1992 on Wimbledon Common, London, while walking her dog with her 2-year-old son. Following the initial investigation, police had a suspect, Colin Stagg, but he was released because there was no physical evidence to charge him. The police, on Britton's advice, decided to organize a sting operation whereby an undercover policewoman codenamed "Lizzie James" would begin a relationship with the suspect. The aim of the operation was to link their suspect to the crime. "Lizzie James" started to exchange letters with Stagg and swapped sexual fantasies. Britton's idea was to see if the suspect would implicate himself. Hence, through letters, meetings, and telephone calls over a seven-month undercover operation, "James" encouraged Stagg to develop his fantasies that matched the profile characteristics drawn up by Paul Britton. It should be noted that Stagg's replies to the James letters led to him being charged with the murder of Rachel Nickell. In one of their meetings, James told Stagg that she enjoyed hurting people and always "wants blood, buckets of it." She also described to Stagg how in her teenage years she was involved in satanism and had murdered a mother and her baby. She told Stagg that she was looking for a meaningful and long-lasting relationship with a man with similar experience and desires. In order to impress James and carry on with their relationship, Stagg told her that he murdered a woman in New Forest. Police records and investigations showed that there was no such murder and that Stagg lied to impress "James." Britton at this point advised James to go back to Stagg and tell him that she did not believe the New Forest story and asked if he committed the Wimbledon Common murder. Stagg told her that he was not involved in that murder, yet because he fitted some of the characteristics in the profile drawn up by Britton, he was charged with the murder.

During the trial the defense argued that the undercover police operation was unfair and constituted a breach of a defendant's right not to incriminate himself. Gisli Gudjonsson, a psychologist representing the accused, argued that Britton's profile was mere speculation and based only on his own personal intuition. It was also argued that the offender profiling used is an unreliable technique that had not achieved general acceptance as a science.

On September 14, 1994, Justice Harry Ognall acquitted Colin Stagg of the murder. The judge was very critical of the seven-month undercover police operation and the role of Paul Britton in the case. The judge ruled that the whole operation was unfair, a breach of a defendant's right not to incriminate himself and was "misconceived." Justice Ognall said: "I am afraid this behavior betrays not merely an excess of zeal, but a blatant attempt to incriminate a suspect by positive and deceptive conduct of the grossest kind. Any legitimate steps taken by the police and the prosecuting authorities to bring perpetrators to justice are to be applauded, but the emphasis must be on the word legitimate. A careful appraisal of the material demonstrates a skillful and sustained enterprise to manipulate the accused, sometimes subtly, sometimes blatantly."[36]

It should be noted that because of his role in this case, Paul Britton faced charges of professional misconduct by the British Psychological Society; however, the disciplinary committee of the society met on October 29 and 30, 2002 and dismissed the charges. The committee maintained that due to the delays that occurred during the process of the case, it believed that Britton would not receive a fair hearing. The committee stated that "the disciplinary process was originally subject to four years delay, due to the likelihood

of private civil proceedings, then latterly it was delayed by the need to gather extensive evidence and agree on a date when all parties would be available. All of this has had a bearing on whether Mr. Britton could receive a fair hearing after so long."[37]

Robert Napper, aged 41, was charged with the murder of Rachel Nickel on November 28, 2007. He is a convicted sex offender and currently awaiting trial for Rachel's murder.

Canter and Alison were also very critical of the work of Britton. They described Britton's work as mere intuitive personal opinion, arguing that there was no reference to any process or psychological theories from which Britton drew his conclusions.[38] "Thus despite an advert for Britton's book that boasts, 'if you did it he'll get you' we are no clearer by the end of the book of how 'he will get you'."[39]

Paul Britton as we have seen has assisted the police in several cases in Britain, but David Canter is undoubtedly the father of offender profiling in Britain. Between 1982 and 1986 a series of rapes and murders occurred in London and the Home Counties and the police were not making any progress in apprehending the offenders. Police sought the help of David Canter, a professor of psychology, presently at the University of Liverpool. In July 1985, three women were raped and the police launched "Operation Hart" to find the rapist. John Duffy was arrested a month later and charged with violent offenses but was released on bail. Immediately after Duffy was released, a 19-year-old girl, Alison Day, was dragged from an East London train and taken to a garage where she was raped and killed. Another girl, 15-year-old Maartje Tamboezer was also raped and killed three months later on her way to the shops in West Horley. Her body was set on fire; however, semen traces were found. Another attack occurred on May 18, 1986 when Anne Lock was abducted on her way to work.

Having found semen traces on one of the bodies, the investigations intensified. Duffy was rearrested and interviewed, but he refused to give a blood sample. Duffy was again released on bail and he later bribed one of his friends to "mug" him. He reported to the police that he had been mugged and voluntarily checked himself into a psychiatric hospital claiming that he was suffering from trauma and amnesia as a result of the mugging. John Duffy attacked and raped another girl, a 14-year-old.. The girl survived the attack. She was blindfolded during the attack but a caught a glimpse of Duffy when his mask fell off. She later identified Duffy as her attacker at the identification parade.

The profile that Canter compiled matched Duffy's characteristics and he was placed under surveillance.[40] A few weeks later, he was arrested at his mother's house. The police found overwhelming physical evidence linking Duffy to the attacks. It should be noted that his blood sample matched the

semen traces found on Tamboezer's body. Some fibers found on Duffy's clothing also matched those found on one of the victims. Strings found at Duffy's house also matched the strings used to bind the victims. Thus, there was enough evidence to charge Duffy with the murders and rapes. He received seven life sentences.

Approaches to Offender Profiling

There are three main approaches to offender profiling: the diagnostic evaluation or clinical approach, criminal investigative analysis or the FBI approach, and the investigative psychology or environmental psychology approach. In recent times some scholars have developed other "approaches" such as geographic profiling, behavioral evidence analysis, and crime action profiling.

DIAGNOSTIC EVALUATION OR CLINICAL APPROACH

Diagnostic evaluation (DE) or clinical approach is the oldest approach to offender profiling, adopted mainly by psychiatrists and clinical psychologists. Diagnostic evaluation approach looks at offenders from a mental illness point of view and tries to examine crimes and crime scenes from that perspective. Based on their clinical practice experience, their knowledge of mental health processes, and their knowledge of psychological disorders, these practitioners try to predict the type of offenders who are likely to be responsible for certain types of criminal behavior. These practitioners try to provide insights into the motivations underlying an offender's criminal behavior.

The DE approach involves an analysis of the behavior exhibited at the scene of crime, an analysis of information that can be deduced from a mental reconstruction of what happened at the crime scene and why it happened. Then an attempt is made to put together the mental and reasoning abilities of the likely offender. There is general agreement that some forms of mental illness may predispose certain individuals to commit certain crimes. This is why psychiatrists and clinical psychologists play a very important role in offender profiling. Their knowledge of mental disorder, for instance, puts them in a better position to produce a profile of the individuals likely to commit certain types of crime, especially crimes showing elements of psychopathology, paraphilias, and sadomasochistic behavior. Indeed, it has been noted that mental disorders such as psychoses, sociopathic personality disorder, and drug and alcohol additions may be linked to certain offenses.[1]

The diagnostic evaluation approach was very useful and in fact seen to be accurate in the New York "Mad Bomber" case in 1956, when James Brussel produced a psychological profile of the bomber using this approach. This approach was also used by Thomas Bond in profiling "Jack the Ripper." In spite of the above noted successes of the diagnostic evaluation approach, it is not without criticism. The scientific basis of this approach is still in question. This is an approach that relies heavily on the personal clinical experience and knowledge of an individual practitioner. As such it is subjective and cannot be empirically tested.

Another criticism leveled against this approach is that it is undertaken by psychiatrists and psychologists who have no law enforcement background.[2] This approach has been criticized for its individualistic nature which "also prevents adequate comparative assessments of validity, utility, and process."[3]

In the final analysis, it should be noted that all other approaches to offender profiling originated from diagnostic evaluation, and as we have seen it has proved very useful in several cases. The most important thing about this approach is that it offers a more authoritative insight into the motivations underlying an offender's criminal action.

CRIMINAL INVESTIGATIVE ANALYSIS OR THE FBI APPROACH

The Federal Bureau of Investigation (FBI) defined criminal investigative analysis as "a process of reviewing crimes from both a behavioral and investigative perspective. It involves reviewing and assessing the facts of a criminal act, interpreting offender behavior, and interaction with the victim, as exhibited during the commission of the crime, or as displayed in the crime scene."[4] This approach is based on crime scene analysis and involves an examination of the method of operation and other behavioral patterns that can be deduced from the crime scene characteristics. Having found that the diagnostic evaluation approach proved very helpful in apprehending unknown serial killers, and having been influenced by the work James Brussel, the FBI introduced criminal investigative analysis. It should be noted that the Behavioral Analysis Unit (Behavioral Sciences Unit) of the FBI based in Quantico, Virginia conducts the Bureau's criminal investigative analysis activities This approach is undoubtedly the most popular approach and in fact, is fast becoming synonymous with the term "offender profiling" itself. This does not mean that it is the most reliable approach. This situation exists because those in the law enforcement field see offender profiling as their own exclusive club, and have virtually succeeded in showcasing themselves as the one and only group of people who are better placed to produce the best and most accurate profiles. Are they correct? You will find out for yourself after reading this book.

There is no gainsaying the fact, however, that the FBI has given immense popularity to this crime investigation technique. In line with Kocsis, "this popularization in itself is a significant accomplishment that should not be underestimated or devalued as without these efforts it is debatable to what extent, if at all, the practice of profiling would have evolved beyond the classical circumstance of DE."[5] This technique is undoubtedly the offshoot of diagnostic evaluation and it was after the work and contributions of Dr. James Brussel that the FBI began to embrace and develop this technique.

In the 1970s the FBI used data from serious sexual assault and murder cases and tried to identify the behavioral characteristics of these sorts of offenders. The Bureau also carried out in-depth interviews with 36 convicted serial killers. "A careful recording and analysis of the crimes which these offenders had committed built up a database. Based on this information, the FBI advocated that important information could be gleaned by: 1) a careful examination of the various aspects of the crime scene, 2) a study of the nature of the attacks themselves, 3) consideration of any forensic evidence, 4) careful consideration of the medical examiners report, [and] 5) the identification of the characteristics of the type of victim selected."[6]

Under the FBI approach, an offender is classified according to whether the crime scene appeared to be organized or disorganized. This classification of offenders into organized or disorganized offenders helps investigators to draw conclusions as to the characteristics of the likely offenders. The FBI maintained that the organized and disorganized offenders have different demographic and behavioral characteristics. According to the FBI, the crime scene of an organized offender shows signs of some sort of planning, shows that the offender was in control at the scene, and shows evidence of attempts to destroy physical traces. Ressler et al. maintained that organized offenders tend to:[7]

- Have a high birth order (likely to be the firstborn son),
- Have a father with a generally stable work history,
- Perceive parental discipline as inconsistent,
- Have mobility (have a car),
- Choose a stranger as the victim,
- Be intelligent and possibly an underachiever,
- Be socially skilled,
- Be sexually competent,
- Live with a partner,

- Be depressed and experiencing a great deal of anger around the time of attack, and
- Follow news report about the attack and likely to leave the area after the attack.

On the other hand, the FBI maintained that the crime scene of a disorganized offender tends to show the following features.

- Evidence of little or no planning,
- Signs that the attack was random,
- Evidence that the offender carried out the attack when in a frightened or confused state of mind,
- Evidence of disorganized behavior,
- Signs that the offender chose any weapon available at the scene and was likely to leave the weapons at the scene, and
- Little or no attempt by the offender to conceal any clues at the scene.

It has also been noted that the disorganized offender is likely to:[8]

- Live alone,
- Live near the scene of crime,
- Be socially and sexually inept,
- Be of below average intelligence,
- Suffer from some form of mental illness,
- Have suffered physical or sexual abuse as a child,
- Be of low birth status in the family,
- Have a father with unstable work history,
- Have poor work history.
- Have suffered harsh parental discipline.

This classification into categories of organized and disorganized offenders helps to determine at the outset whether a series of attacks is likely to be the work of one person or more individuals.

The FBI also classified crime scenes into the categories of organized crime scene, disorganized crime scene, mixed crime scene, and the atypical crime scene. The organized crime scene as we have seen shows elements of planning and premeditation, as well as attempts to conceal any physical traces. The disorganized crime scene shows a high level of disorganized and disoriented behavior; appears to be unplanned and random with no attempts made to destroy any physical traces. The mixed crime scene refers to a crime scene that shows the characteristics of both the organized and the disorganized. It has been noted that three reasons may account for this type of crime scene: 1) more than one offender was responsible for the crime, 2) one offender was responsible but changed his or her method of operation, or 3) it could be a case of crime scene staging.[9] The atypical crime scene is one where no classification can be made because of lack of available information.

The FBI has done considerable specific analysis of offenders who rape. They classified rapists into two groups: selfish and unselfish rapists.[10] According to the FBI, the selfish rapist tends to:

- Be violent, with a high level of aggression,
- Show total sexual dominance,
- Be self-confident,
- Make no attempt to establish any form of intimacy with the victim,
- Engage in anal sex, followed by fellatio, and
- Use very offensive, threatening, abusive, profane, demeaning, humiliating, impersonal, and sexually-oriented language.

On the other hand, according to the FBI, the unselfish rapist is:

- Lacking in self-confidence,
- Not likely to be violent in the attack. Tends to use minimal level of force,
- Not likely to cause any physical harm,
- Likely to involve the victim in the sexual act, to establish some sort of intimacy,
- Likely to tell the victim to perform certain sexual acts on him; for instance asking the victim to kiss him, fondle him, and so on, and
- Likely to use language that is personal, reassuring, complimentary, non-profane, concerned, and apologetic.

This classification is useful because it is believed that the things that an offender said during the attack may reveal a lot of information about him or her. Above all, this classification helps in choosing an appropriate interviewing or interrogation strategy.

Expanding on the usefulness of the above classification, the FBI made further classification of rapists. Robert Hazelwood maintained that there are four types of rapists:[11]

1. Power Reassurance Rapist or Compensatory Rapist

This type of rapist sees rape as a way of showing his masculinity and sexual adequacy, and shows the signs of an unselfish rapist. This type of rapist sees rape as a way of removing any doubts about his sexual inadequacy. The power reassurance rapist is likely to keep on attacking until he is caught, most likely to keep a diary of his attacks, and likely to take something belonging to the victim, which he will keep as a souvenir.[12]

It has also been noted that this type of rapist usually attacks in late evenings or early mornings when the victim is likely to be alone or with small children, and chooses a victim about his own age and his own race.[13] It is also believed that this type of rapist likes to think that the victim is enjoying the rape and is most likely to ask the victim to undress on her own.[14] They appear to be concerned about the welfare of the victim, tend to feel some sort of remorse, and are likely to apologize to the victim.[15] This rapist is likely to be single; likely to live with one or both parents; is nonathletic; quiet, and passive; a social loner with limited education; often employed in a menial job; likes to visit adult bookstores; is likely to be a transvestite, a fetishist, or involved in voyeurism, excessive masturbation, and exhibitionism; tends to attack in his own neighborhood; and most likely has been raised by an aggressive, seductive, and dominating mother.[16]

Furthermore, this type of rapist sees himself as a loser and through the rape, believes that he is important by controlling the victim.[17] Ronald Holmes and Stephen Holmes have suggested that when interviewing this type of rapist that the interviewer should adopt the strategy of appealing to the rapist's "sense of masculinity," arguing that "the interviewer might indicate to him that the woman who was raped in the case under investigation has not suffered 'undue' trauma, and that the police realize the rapist had no desire to harm his victim; such a statement could set the stage for a 'sympathetic' relationship that might result in the rapist's sharing information, not only about the rape currently under investigation, but about other suspected connected rapes."[18]

2. Power-Assertive Rapist or Exploitative Rapist

The power-assertive rapist views rape as a way of showing his superiority. This rapist has no doubts or fears about his sexual adequacy and falls under the selfish category. This type of rapist is normally athletic and does not see anything wrong with rape. Date rapes fall into this category and this type of rapist tends to use force.[19] It has been observed that this type of rapist is likely to have been raised in a single-parent family, lived in foster homes, suffered physical abuse as a child, was a high school dropout, has domestic problems, unhappy marriages, likes to visit bars, is likely to be employed in macho occupations—construction or police work—and likely to choose a victim of his own race.[20] It is suggested that the interviewer should "approach the interview session with all the facts in hand: the placement of the suspect at the scene, physical evidence that directly implicates him in the rape (or rapes), and other pertinent information that shows the interviewer is a professional. What the police should communicate is this: We know you did it, and this is how we are going to prove it. If the interviewer is in error about the facts, or if there is some other reason for the rapist to discount the interviewer's competence as a professional, it is unlikely that any cooperation will be gained from the rapist through any means, including intimidation, pleas for aid, and appeals based on the victim's welfare."[21]

3. Anger-Retaliatory Rapist

As the name suggests, this rapist tends to rape as a result of his anger and distaste of women, is extremely violent, derives sexual excitement by hurting women, sees women as the source of his troubles, and so seeks revenge.[22]

Generally speaking, this type of rapist likes to perform degrading sexual acts on the victims. The attack tends to be unplanned, the victim is likely to be someone who closely matches the woman the rapist sees as the source of his troubles.[23] The rapist is likely to be married, has had many affairs, and is likely to choose a victim of his own age.[24] This type of rapist tends to come from a broken home and is likely to have been physically abused as a child.[25] It has been observed that about 80 percent of anger-retaliatory rapists come from a female-headed single-parent family or have been brought up by a single female caregiver, so it is suggested that the interviewer should be male as this type of rapist hates women.[26]

4. Anger-Excitement Rapist or Sadistic Rapist

This type of rapist sees rape as a source of pleasure and likes to torture and inflict pain on the victims, which provides him with sexual excitement.[27] The attack tends to be planned and violent and could result in murder. This rapist is likely to have a "rape kit," which he takes to the location of the attacks.[28] Furthermore, this type of rapist falls under the selfish category and likes to see the victims suffer; likes to instill fear in the victims and most likely chooses the type of victim that will fulfill his inner fantasies and desires.[29] This rapist is likely to come from a single-parent family and have divorced parents; lived in foster homes; is between 30 and 39 years of age; was physically abused as a child; raised in a sexually deviant home; is married, with some college education; employed in white-collar jobs; likely to be a middle-class family man; has compulsive personality; and is ritualistic, likely to stalk and eventually kill victims.[30] It has been noted that there is no interviewing strategy that is effective with this type of rapist.[31]

Having discussed these examples of the FBI's various classifications of rape offenders, we now move on to discussing how a typical criminal profile is produced. Douglas et al. have clearly outlined the various stages involved in the criminal profile generating process as thus: 1) profiling inputs, 2) decision process models stage, 3) crime scene assessment, 4) criminal profile, 5) investigation, and 6) and apprehension.[32]

1. *Profiling Inputs*: This is the initial stage when all information about the crime, such as physical evidence, crime scene photographs, autopsy reports, witness statements, victim statements, and police reports will be put together. Detailed background information about the victim is noted.
2. *Decision Process Models*: At this stage, the profiler organizes "the input into meaningful questions and patterns."[33] Here attempt will be made to ascertain the intent of the attack, length of time taken to carry out the attack, and everything that happened before and after the attack.
3. *Crime Scene Assessment*: This is arguably the most crucial stage and care should be taken to note whether the crime scene is staged or not. The profiler at this stage tries to reconstruct the behavior of the offender and the victim. Here the profiler also tries to classify the crime scene and the likely offender. Also to be determined at this stage is the likely motive of the crime.
4. *Criminal Profile*: At this stage, the profiler formulates an initial description of the most likely suspects. The best methods of apprehending the unknown offender will be suggested.
5. *Investigation*: At this stage a written report will be presented to the investigators and they will focus more on the suspects matching the profile.
6. *Apprehension*: If any suspect is arrested, an interviewing technique will be chosen. The criminal profile is then evaluated to see how it matches the suspect.

The FBI approach has proved to be very useful in many cases, although it has been criticized. It has been argued that the approach is not scientific, that the data samples have been insufficient, that the approach is subjective, and that the FBI declines to share information about its methods, so that other scholars can test their hypothesis. As noted in Peter Ainsworth's *Offender Profiling and Crime Analysis*:

One immediate problem with this [FBI] approach was the fact that the classification arose mainly from interviews with just 36 American, convicted, serial murderers. It was not clear whether the findings applied only to serial murderers, who are after all a type of offender which is still statistically extremely rare, even in the U.S.A. The fact that all the interviewees were convicted murderers also raises the question as to whether more successful murderers (i.e., those who have not been caught) might have provided different information. It is also not clear whether any information obtained from this American sample is directly applicable to offenders in different countries.[34]

The FBI approach has also been criticized for lack of clarity, which "is not helped by the fact that the FBI is reluctant to allow social scientists to test their hypotheses in a systematic and objective way. The situation is confused further when former FBI employees who have written memoirs of their exploits appear to contradict each other." (See for example Douglas and Olshaker, 1995 and Ressler and Shachtman, 1992.)[35]

Canter and Alison were also very critical of the FBI approach. They argued that the profiles generated by the FBI approach make no reference to any generally accepted psychological principles, hence, "their profiles show a severe lack in accounts of any systematic procedures or any substantive theoretical models of behavior."[36]

This approach is primarily based on the personal experience and intuition of the profiler which makes it not amenable to any sort of empirical test.[37] As noted in Damon Muller's *Criminal Profiling*:

Many of the claims of crime scene analysis (CSA) sound much like those of psychoanalysis, with talk of fantasies and sexual motivations; and like psychoanalysis, these claims do not seem to be falsifiable in most cases. Take, for example, the following statement: "Although some of the murderers in our study did not report fantasies in [a] conscious way, their descriptions of the murders they committed reveal hidden fantasies of violence." (Ressler et al.. 1988, p. 52). We may be left wondering when FBI agents became experts in interpreting the unconscious fantasies of others. If one claims that a violent murder is a sign of violent fantasies—even if the murderer does not report any violent fantasies—then how is one to falsify the hypothesis that murderers have violent fantasies?

As it stands, the CSA approach is not a good candidate for falsifiability, primarily due to the nature of the ideas that it is based on. A further problem is that those involved have had little interest in their work being empirically substantiated. One of the problems is that of operationalizing the variables.[38]

The major problem with the FBI approach relates to the fact that there is no method of testing the reliability, validity, or consistency of their methods. This approach is subjective and needs to be used with caution. It should be noted however, that their classification of crime scenes and offenders has been very useful in crime investigations.

THE INVESTIGATIVE PSYCHOLOGY OR ENVIRONMENTAL PSYCHOLOGY APPROACH

I quickly realized that "profiling" lacked any clearly articulated or scientifically based set of procedures, findings, or theories and that many of the people following in my footsteps were doing little more than attempting to live up to a media-created fiction. I therefore set about creating a new discipline that I named "Investigative Psychology" that would offer a real scientific base for the development of our understanding of criminal behavior in ways that are relevant to police investigations. The Centre for Investigative Psychology that I have set up at The University of Liverpool now provides a framework for that activity.[39]

The "investigative psychology" approach was developed by David Canter, currently a professor of psychology at the University of Liverpool, England. This approach started in 1985 when Canter said he was invited by Detective Chief Superintendent Thelma Wagstaff and Detective Chief Inspector John Grieve to their Scotland Yard office to discuss the possibility of using psychology to assist in police investigations. Canter admitted that at the beginning he had no experience of police procedure and had just a little knowledge of criminal behavior. After further contact with the police detectives and police investigations, however, Canter said he "felt a start had to be made somewhere to see whether even elementary psychological principles could be used to help a major police investigation."[40] In 1986, Canter wrote a letter to Detective Chief Superintendent Wagstaff regarding a series of rapes he had read about in the local newspaper. In response to the letter, he was invited to Hendon Police College where an incident room was set up in connection with the rapes (named the Hart inquiry). Canter stated that it was at this meeting that he was formally asked by Detective Chief Superintendent Vince McFadden, the head of the Surrey Criminal Investigation Department (CID), to "use whatever skills I might have as a psychologist to contribute directly to a major inquiry into rape and murder."[41] Canter noted that this was in effect the beginning of his "personal journey to see if a criminal's actions in a crime really could reveal systematically his key identifying characteristics."[42]

Canter maintained that a criminal leaves not only physical traces at a crime scene, but also psychological traces, and that by examining these psychological traces, investigators can have an idea as to the sort of person likely to commit a particular crime.[43] Following in the footsteps of the FBI and drawing from its work, Canter maintained that "the only way open to me to discover what profiling could be, and how it might relate to the psychological theories and methods that I knew, was by working alongside an ongoing investigation, trying out ideas as they occurred to me. This is not the best way to become involved in any area of research, coming up with possible results without the time or resources to test them thoroughly, but it was the only way forward."[44]

Professor Canter came up with what he called a five-factor model of offender behavior. He based his work on the five aspects of the interaction between the victim and the offender. According to Canter, the five aspects of interaction are: 1) interpersonal coherence, 2) significance of time and place, 3) criminal characteristics, 4) criminal career, and 5) and forensic awareness.[45]

Interpersonal Coherence

Canter argued that offenders' criminal activity makes sense to them within their own personal psychology. This involves analyzing an offender's criminal actions to see if they are related to the way he or she deals with other people in noncriminal situations. It is believed that an offender's actions at a crime scene mirror his or her actions in noncriminal day-to-day activities. As such, "the psychologist should be able to determine something about the offender from the victim and the way the offender interacted with the victim (where this can be determined, such as with rape)."[46] Hence, it has been argued that an offender is likely to choose victims that share the characteristics of people who appear to be important to that offender.[47]

Significance of Time and Place

Canter believed that an offender will likely choose to attack at a location that has some personal significance. There is the idea that offenders tend to commit murder and rape in familiar locations, where they feel in control and comfortable. This implies that the offender is most likely to live or work near the area of attack.[48] Furthermore, an examination of the place and time of an attack may lead to clues about the offender's mobility.[49]

Criminal Characteristics

Here attempt is made to classify offenders, the crimes, and the crime scenes. There are various ways of classifying offenders and crimes scenes, for instance, the FBI's classification into organized and disorganized offenders, power-reassurance rapists, power-assertive rapists, anger-retaliatory rapists, and anger-excitement rapists.

Criminal Career

It is believed that many offenders do not change their crime patterns. Therefore, attempts should be made to determine if the likely offender is a career criminal. This involves looking at the possible skills and occupations of the likely offender.

Forensic Awareness

Canter also maintained that if a crime scene reveals that the offender took conscious steps to conceal physical evidence, then such offender is likely to have had previous contact with the police and knows about crime scene investigation techniques. This sort of offender, therefore, is likely to have a criminal record, and so investigators are able to narrow their search to suspects with criminal records.

Drawing ideas from environmental psychology, Canter also came up with what he called the "Circle Theory of Environmental Range."[50] He maintained that there is some sort of relationship between criminal activity range and the home base of serial offenders. Canter argued that serial offenders tend to attack and operate in locations where they feel in control and comfortable. The circle theory emphasizes the study of offenses to find out the offender's home base. It involves the prediction of an offender's residential area by examining the spatial distribution of serial offenses.

In his circle theory, Canter came up with two models: the "marauder" and the "commuter." The marauder is the serial offender who commits crime within his home base, while the commuter travels a distance from his home to commit crime. Canter maintained that there is a causal relationship between the marauder and his home base as opposed to the commuter model where there is no causal relationship.

In order to test the circle theory, Godwin and Canter in 1997 carried out a study in the United States involving 54 male U.S. serial killers.[51] These 54 serial killers were only those who were convicted of at least 10 murders on different dates and at different locations. Godwin and Canter gathered data from various police departments in the United States and also studied 540 victims.

This study was based on the hypothesis that the home is the focus of a serial killer's activities in apprehending victims and where the bodies will be left; that there will be differences in the distances where the serial killer apprehends victims and where the body will be left; and that "the distances serial killers travel to dump the victim's bodies are likely to change systematically over time while the victims' points of fatal encounter locations do not. The counter-intuitive possibility that this change relates to an increasing incorporation of all his killing activities into his domestic area will also be tested."[52]

Their study showed the home as a focus of serial murder, which implies that serial killers are most likely to apprehend nearly all their victims near their home (serial killer's home).[53] This study further showed that: "As the number of murders increases, killers generally cover a narrower area in which to leave the bodies of their victims, until the ninth and tenth offenses where the offender may be disposing of bodies quite close to his home."[54]

In a nutshell, Godwin and Canter concluded that as the series of offenses progresses, the sites where the serial offender dumps the bodies of victims get closer to the offender's home, and that this could be as a result of the serial offender trying to reduce the risks associated with transporting the body, and could also be that the offender has gained more confidence.

This study by Godwin and Canter is very useful for investigators in making decisions as to the first areas to search for suspects. This has to be approached with extreme caution, however. In fact, Godwin and Canter even drew attention to this issue and called for more research to explore this process, arguing that "the systematic changing of locations and distances relative to the home base may be a deliberate ploy to distract police attention from the killer's home base."[55] Above all, no investigator can really be sure of the number of victims and the locations in any serial killing case.

It should be noted that investigative psychology (IP) approach uses a statistical analysis method called multidimensional scaling (MDS). There are different types of MDS and investigative psychology uses the type called "smallest space analysis." Multidimensional scaling (MDS) refers to "a method of statistically analyzing the relationships between multiple variables simultaneously."[56]

Data analyzed using MDS enable the creation of a diagram within which the variables under consideration can be individually plotted. Where these variables appear within a diagram (i.e. plotted) denotes the relationship they hold with each other. Consequently, variables that are plotted in a region of space close together hold a relationship with each other. The closer any variables are plotted together, the stronger their relationship or association. The opposite applies with variables appearing far apart in a MDS diagram, indicating that the variables hold few similarities in that case. Furthermore, variables that appear in a location between other variables can be interpreted as holding some central or common relationship. In addition to the relationship plotted variables may have with each other in MDS diagram, their respective positions also convey some impression of their distinctiveness. Thus, variables that appear closer to the center of a MDS diagram are typically found to be commonly occurring variables, where as those that are plotted in the outlying regions of a MDS diagram, are said to be more distinctive.[57]

Investigative psychology approach seems to have advantage over the other approaches and has been well received by many scholars. Investigative psychology has the advantage that it falls under the established science of psychology or criminology and most of the theories upon which it is based can be falsified.[58] This is in fact where investigative psychology approach appears to be of more value and stronger than the other approaches. One can safely say therefore, that if any approach is capable of becoming genuinely scientific on its own, then it is investigative psychology. On a similar vein, it has been observed that:

While Canter's work shares some commonalities with that developed by the FBI's Behavioral Science Unit, he has tried to place his approach within an accepted psychological framework. Canter believes that as a branch of applied psychology, his work goes beyond what is traditionally thought of as offender profiling. Canter's early work tried to understand the type of crime in which any one individual might be likely to become involved, and he also considered the way in which such a crime might be carried out. Most importantly, Canter tried to establish whether the way in which an offender's behavior while committing a crime mirrored their nonoffending behavior in everyday life. Canter suggested for example, that in their choice of victims, offenders will only select people who, even within nonoffending behavior, are important to them. Canter supports this viewpoint by reference to the fact that the vast majority of serial killers target victims within their own ethnic group.[59]

The investigative psychology approach has undoubtedly been criticized. Investigative psychology practitioners lack police or law enforcement experience; investigative psychology does not make use of interview data of a wide range of offenders, and it relies heavily upon victim information.[60] Furthermore, it has been argued that the circle theory "relies on one being able to draw a circle around all of an offender's crimes. Given some of the arguments presented . . . , we must question how feasible this is. Not all crimes will be reported or recorded, and even those may be recorded inaccurately. Furthermore, in the real world of police investigation it will not be particularly easy to establish whether a series of crimes has been committed by the same individual."[61]

The statistical analysis adopted by investigative psychology can only be useful if it is based on accurate data.

A weakness of Canter's work is that to date it does not necessarily offer anything new, although contributions from the field of environmental psychology do provide new avenues to explore. What it does do is encouch known criminological or psychological principles in ways that can be useful to the crime investigator. It utilizes the same factors as the FBI but places them firmly within psychological theory and methodology. It is not yet clear how well Canter's theories (especially circle theory) will be adapted for use in the United States with its higher rate of serial crime, its greater penchant for mobility, and its more vast urban environment in many regions.[62]

The above criticism of investigative psychology approach seems to be an overreaction. As we mentioned earlier, if any approach to offender profiling has the potential of being generally accepted as scientific, then it is the investigative psychology approach. As we can see from the above discussion, investigative psychology approach is based on psychological theories. Research in the field of psychology is peer reviewed and accepted.

The main difference between the FBI approach and the investigative psychology approach is that the FBI approach is mainly drawn from crime scene analysis while investigative psychology approach goes further with the application of psychological theories and principles.

While sharing some characteristics with the FBI's approach it does differ in a number of ways. For example, Canter and Heritage used statistical analysis in order to establish connections between various elements in rape behavior. Publication of their methods and techniques also allowed other researchers to examine their work. Based on this, those who wished to do so could replicate the study but perhaps varying the method slightly. They may, for example, use different type of statistical analysis in order to test whether the conclusions remained the same under such conditions. The point is that by disclosing their methods and findings in an appropriate journal, researchers such as Canter and Heritage allowed the academic community to scrutinize their work and to comment upon it. One of the reasons why the FBI's work has come in for so much criticism is that such an opportunity has never been afforded those who might wish to test the reliability or validity of their claims.[63]

In the final analysis, one can safely say that even though Canter's investigative psychology approach offers a more scientific basis to offender profiling (based on psychological principles, and the use of statistical analysis), it still does not provide a way of using the profiles to point to specific offenders. Nevertheless, Canter has made and is still continuing to make very important contributions to the understanding of the theory and practice of offender profiling. The main strength of investigative psychology approach lies in the attempts to predict the location of serial offenders, by analyzing the spatial distribution of offenses.

GEOGRAPHIC PROFILING

Geographic profiling was developed in 1995 by D. Kim Rossmo, a former police officer with the Vancouver City Police Department in Vancouver, Canada. Geographic profiling has been described as a strategic information management system for investigating serial violent crimes.[64] Drawing ideas from environmental psychology and investigative psychology, geographic profiling "focuses on the probable spatial behavior of the offender within the context of the locations of, and the spatial relationships between the various crime sites."[65] Geographic profiling uses a computer program to analyze crime scene locations in an attempt to predict the likely residence of the offender. This computerized program is known as criminal geographic targeting (CGT). It is believed that:

By examining the spatial information associated with a series of crime sites, the CGT model produces a three-dimensional probability distribution termed a "jeopardy surface," the "height" of which at any point represents the likelihood of offender residence or workplace. The jeopardy surface is then superimposed on a street of the area of the crimes; ... ; such maps are termed "geoprofiles" and use a range of colors to represent varying probabilities. A geoprofile can be thought of as a fingerprint of the offender's cognitive map.[66]

Geographic profiling is made up of two components—quantitative or objective and qualitative or subjective. The qualitative or subjective aspect involves the reconstruction as well as the interpretation of the perpetrator's mental map.[67]

Geographic profiling approach has been criticized on many grounds. Scholars have argued that geographic profiling is not an approach on its own and indeed, it seems to be more of an aid to the investigative psychology approach. It has also been noted that geographic profiling may not be suitable for a small number of known linked offenses or cases where linked offenses have not yet been identified.[68] "Also, the underlying theories are mostly drawn from databases related to burglaries and other crimes that may not translate well to the serial murderer or rapist, and these theories relate to overall crime patterns, not individual crimes or crime series. Research on the connection between spatial coordinates and offender and victim variables continues, but at present, geographic profiling is probably best viewed as an adjunct to criminal profiling and not as a profiling process in and of itself."[69]

Geographic profiling is clearly a useful aid to crime investigation, but whether it qualifies as an approach on its own is a different matter. It does appear however, that geographic profiling is best construed as an aspect of the investigative psychology approach.

BEHAVIORAL EVIDENCE ANALYSIS APPROACH

Behavioral evidence analysis (BEA), also known as the deductive method of criminal profiling, was developed by Brent E. Turvey, an American forensic scientist. In 1999, and following his interview with Jerome Brudos, an American serial killer, Turvey noted that police case files differed from Brudos's own accounts, and therefore concluded that it was totally wrong to accept the premises on which the earlier profiling approaches based their profiles; thus he came up with his new approach. Behavioral evidence analysis (BEA) is arguably based on the availability of physical evidence. Turvey was critical of the assumptions and inferences made by the other approaches (e.g.. diagnostic evaluation, FBI approach, and investigative psychology), and therefore argued that "a full forensic analysis must be performed on all available physical evidence before this type of profiling can begin."[70] Fundamentally, Turvey maintained that BEA produces a deductive criminal profile as opposed to an inductive one.[71] He also maintained that the information used to argue a deductive criminal profile includes forensic and behavioral evidence (equivocal forensic analysis), victimology, and crime scene characteristics.[72]

Turvey further argued that deductive criminal profiling has two phases: the investigative phase and the trial phase. The investigative phase "involves behavioral analysis of the patterns of unknown offenders for known crimes,"[73] while the trial phase "involves behavioral evidence analysis of known crimes for which there is a suspect or a defendant (sometimes a convicted defendant); this takes place in the preparation for both hearings and trials (criminal, penalty, and/or appeal phases of the trial are all appropriate times to use profiling technique."[74] This approach has been criticized.[75]

There is still debate as to whether BEA can be properly seen as an approach on its own. The point however, remains that BEA still cannot point to a special offender being responsible for a certain crime, and also has not established any scientific basis. Finally, there seems to be an over reliance on the availability of physical evidence by this approach.

CRIME ACTION PROFILING

Crime action profiling (CAP) was developed by Richard N. Kocsis, an Australian forensic psychologist. Based on his clinical knowledge and research literature, Kocsis claimed that profiling has its foundation in forensic psychology. Kocsis maintained that he became fully involved in offender profiling when he was approached by the Australian police to assist them in a high-profile serial murder case.

Crime action profiling is a process of predicting an offender's characteristics through the examination of the offender's criminal actions.[76] Basically, crime action profiling tries to "examine offense behaviors independent of any inferred motivations."[77] In analyzing patterns of crime behaviors, crime action profiling uses the multidimensional scaling (MDS) method of statistical analysis. This approach also uses cluster analysis, conical correlation, and mathematical formulae to "plot the orientation of the offender characteristic vector arrows."[78]

Crime action profiling is the newest approach to offender profiling. As such, few reviews and little research have been undertaken. Nevertheless, crime action profiling has contributed to the efforts to find a scientific basis to offender profiling.

Each of the approaches to offender profiling has strengths and weaknesses, and it is only when they come together as a team that offender profiling will muster a scientific basis, gain general recognition in the various disciplines, and easily pass a strict legal admissibility standard such as the *Daubert* standard. The greatest strength of the diagnostic evaluation approach lies in its ability to provide better explanations on the motivations underlying certain criminal actions. The FBI approach shows much strength in its various classification methods, grouping offenders as either organized or disorganized, and its classification of crime scenes and rapists have proved to be very useful. Investigative psychology's greatest strength is in its ability to apply psychological theories, and using statistical analysis, in trying to predict the residential location of serial offenders.

Expert Testimony: Conflicting Rules and Standards

The admissibility of any form of scientific evidence has always been problematic, full of controversy and inconsistencies. The introduction of scientific evidence into the courtroom can sway a case one way or the other. In fact, Peterson et al. noted that "about one quarter of the citizens who had served on juries which were presented with scientific evidence believed that had such evidence been absent, they would have changed their verdicts—from guilty to not guilty."[1] The courts are fully aware of this and therefore, special rules have been adopted to help courts to decide whether to admit or exclude any scientific evidence. New scientific techniques and fields of knowledge emerge and the court must be satisfied, not only that the witness is qualified, but whether such evidence should be given.[2] Scientific evidence is not well understood by a lot of people including judges, lawyers, and jurors.

FRYE V. UNITED STATES

In the United States, the decision in *Frye v. United States*[3] (also known as the General Acceptance Rule) was the main rule that governed the admissibility of scientific evidence for 70 years (1923–1993). *Frye* was decided in 1923 by the United States Court of Appeals for the District of Columbia in a case that involved the admissibility of opinion evidence derived from a systolic blood pressure deception test.

In this case, the defendant, James Alphonzo Frye, was convicted of the murder of Dr. Robert W. Brown, in the second degree. During the trial, the defendant sought to introduce testimony based on a systolic blood pressure deception test. This is the early form of the polygraph lie-detector test. The systolic blood pressure deception test is based on the theory that:

... truth is spontaneous, and comes without conscious effort, while the utterance of a falsehood requires a conscious effort, which is reflected in the blood pressure. The rise thus produced is easily detected and distinguished from the rise produced by mere fear of the examination itself. In the former instance, the pressure rises higher than in the latter, and is more pronounced as the examination proceeds, while in the latter case, if the subject is telling the truth, the pressure registers highest at the beginning of the examination, and gradually diminishes as the examination proceeds."[4]

It should be noted that before the trial, the defendant was subjected to this test and it showed that he was telling the truth when he denied that he committed the murder. He therefore, prayed upon the court to accept the testimony of Dr. William Moulton Martson (the inventor of the test), which supported his plea of innocence. The government counsel raised an objection which was sustained. The defense counsel further offered to have. Martson conduct a new test in the presence of the jury; the government counsel again raised an objection, which was also sustained. The trial court excluded the testimony. The defendant was convicted and he appealed. In their brief, Richard V. Mattingly and Foster Wood, counsel for the defendant, stated that:

The rule is that the opinions of experts or skilled witnesses are admissible in evidence in those cases in which the matter of inquiry is such that inexperienced persons are unlikely to prove capable of forming a correct judgment upon it, for the reason that the subject-matter so far partakes of a science, art, or trade as to require a previous habit or experience or study of it, in order to acquire a knowledge of it. When the question involved does not lie within the range of common experience or common knowledge, but requires special experience or common knowledge, then the opinions of witnesses skilled in that particular science, art, or trade to which the question relates are admissible in evidence.[5]

In its ruling, the United States Court of Appeals affirmed the trial court's decision to exclude the testimony and held that "the systolic blood pressure deception [test] has not yet gained such standing and scientific recognition among physiological and psychological authorities as would justify the courts in admitting expert testimony deduced from the discovery, development, and experiments thus far made."[6] Fundamentally, the court stated that scientific evidence is admissible if it is generally accepted that the methods and principles underlying it had achieved widespread acceptance in the relevant discipline. Justice Josiah A. Van Orsdel, delivering the opinion of the court, stated that:

Just when a scientific principle or discovery crosses the line between the experimental and demonstrable stages is difficult to define. Somewhere in this twilight zone the evidential force of the principle must be recognized, and while courts will go a long way in admitting expert testimony deduced from a well-recognized scientific principle or discovery, the thing from which the deduction is made must be sufficiently established to have gained general acceptance in the particular field in which it belongs.[7]

The court in *Frye* did not cite any authority in formulating the new rule. This decision thus raised several questions: What exactly was the "thing" that must be sufficiently established? What is the "relevant scientific community?" Who defines it? How do judges determine "general acceptance?" Does *Frye* require that general acceptance within the scientific community be established by disinterested scientists?[8]

The *Frye* test became the main rule governing the admissibility of scientific evidence but courts and scholars battled with answers to the above questions. *Frye* did not state what exactly was not generally accepted. "Was it the validity of the principle that deception is reflected in discernible changes in the blood pressure of the prevaricator? Or was it, rather, the validity of the systolic blood pressure test (the sphygmomanometer) to detect such alterations in blood pressure?"[9]

Identifying the relevant scientific community under which a technique would fall also proved very problematic, and courts battled to arrive at an acceptable way. The identification of the discipline to which the "thing" falls is a very determinative factor in any trial involving scientific evidence.

If the relevant scientific field requirement is construed broadly, the *Frye* test acts as a formidable barrier to admissibility. In *Cornet v. State*,[10] for example, the relevant scientific community for purposes of spectrograph (voiceprint) analysis was held to include engineers, linguists, and psychologists, as well as those who use voice spectrography for identification purposes. Because different disciplines do not share a common view of a particular scientific method, the burden of establishing general acceptance is undoubtedly onerous. Consequently, the broader the construction of the relevant scientific field, the less likely the party will be able to utilize the novel scientific evidence.[11]

Some courts found it difficult to determine the proper discipline within which some techniques belonged, especially in situations where the new technique encompasses elements of many disciplines; with no one discipline claiming ownership of the new novel process.[12] A typical example was sound spectrographic voice identification technique where there were arguments as to which field the technique should be generally accepted. Was it the field of radio communications, speech and audiology, fingerprint identification, or voice examination?[13]

As we mentioned earlier, the United States Court of Appeals in *Frye* did not cite any authority or give any justification for formulating the general acceptance rule. Other courts however, have defended the decision and offered some justifications. In fact, three major court rulings have justified *Frye* and stated the advantages of the rule.

First, in *United States v. Addison*,[14] the United States Court of Appeals, District of Columbia Circuit stated that the *Frye* test ensures that there exists a minimal reserve of experts who can examine the validity of any scientific evidence. The case involved two defendants, Roland Addison and Henry Raymond, who were both convicted in 1972 by the United States District Court for the District of Columbia on charges of assault with intent to kill while armed and assault on a member of the police force with a dangerous weapon. Raymond was also charged and convicted of carrying a dangerous weapon.

During the trial, the government counsel proffered evidence of voice-print analysis (spectrographic identification) that proved that the defendant, Raymond, made the telephone call to which a police officer, Sergeant Wilkins was responding when he was shot. Lieutenant Ernest Nash, a voice technician at the Michigan State Police Department, gave expert testimony that the voiceprint analysis showed that Raymond made the call that led the police officer to the scene where he was shot. It should be noted that Raymond raised an objection to the order requiring him to submit his voice sample for analysis. He argued that the order violated his Fourth Amendment right to privacy. He also contended that he was deprived of effective assistance of counsel because his counsel was denied adequate time to consider the new scientific technique and the associated novel issues.

In its ruling, the United States Court of Appeals held that the district court erred in admitting the voiceprint analysis evidence. The court also ruled, however, that the jury's judgment was not substantially swayed by the error and therefore affirmed the conviction. The court held that spectrographic identification technique was not sufficiently accepted by the scientific community as being a reliable method to be used by the jury in deciding the guilt or innocence of a defendant. The court of appeals ruled that spectrographic identification was inadmissible. The court of appeals further stated that even though the district court erred by admitting the evidence, the error was harmless and so the judgment could not be reversed. Above all, the court stated that there was overwhelming evidence of the defendant's guilt in this case.

Circuit Judge Carl E. McGowan, stated that the decision in *Frye v. United States* was the proper standard for resolving issues concerning new scientific techniques.[15] The court defended *Frye* and stated that:

The requirement of general acceptance in the scientific community assures that those most qualified to assess the general validity of a scientific method will have the determinative voice. Additionally, the *Frye* test protects prosecution and defense alike by assuring that a minimal reserve of experts exists who can critically examine the validity of a scientific determination in a particular case. Since scientific proof may in some instances assume a posture of mystic infallibility in the eyes of a jury of laymen, the ability to produce rebuttal experts, equally conversant with the mechanics and methods of a particular technique, may prove to be essential.[16]

In *People v. Kelly,*[17] another case that involved voiceprint analysis, the Supreme Court of California also justified the decision in *Frye*, stating that the *Frye* test ensures uniformity of judicial decisions. The case involved Robert Emmett Kelly who was convicted of extortion by the Superior Court of Orange County, California. The extortion arose from several anonymous and threatening telephone calls that the defendant made to Terry Waskin. The police, with Waskin's consent, tape-recorded two of the telephone calls. A police informant later identified the defendant as the person whose voice was on the tapes. The defendant's voice example and the two tape-recorded calls were sent to Lieutenant Ernest Nash, the voiceprint analysis technician at Michigan State Police Department for analysis. Lt. Nash concluded that the voices on the tapes were that of the defendant, and he was allowed to testify. The trial court ruled that voiceprint analysis has achieved sufficient scientific acceptance and therefore the expert's testimony was admissible. Kelly was convicted and he appealed.

The defendant argued that: 1) Lieutenant Nash, the voiceprint expert, failed to sufficiently establish that the technique has achieved general acceptance in the scientific community; 2) that Lt. Nash was not qualified as an expert; and 3) that the procedure was not carried out in a fair and impartial manner. In its ruling, the Supreme Court of California stated that voiceprint analysis had not achieved general scientific acceptance as a reliable technique and that the trial court erred in admitting the testimony. The court therefore, reversed the judgment of conviction.

The Supreme Court of California, in reversing the judgment, also stated that, "we have expressly adopted the foregoing *Frye* test and California courts, when faced with a novel method of proof, have required a preliminary showing of general acceptance of the new technique in the relevant scientific community.... we are satisfied that there is ample justification for the exercise of considerable judicial caution in the acceptance of evidence developed by new scientific techniques."[18] The court restated the United States Court of Appeals for the District of Columbia's decision in *United States v. Addison*[19] and added that, "moreover, a beneficial consequence of the *Frye* test is that it may well promote a degree of uniformity of decision. Individual judges whose particular conclusions may differ regarding the reliability of a particular scientific evidence, may discover substantial agreement and consensus in the scientific community."[20] The court reaffirmed its allegiance to *Frye* and its general acceptance requirement.[21]

The third major case where a court justified the decision in *Frye* was in *Reed v. State,*[22] where the Court of Appeals of Maryland stated that *Frye* ensures judicial economy, by avoiding the time-consuming examination and cross-examination of witnesses. In this case, the defendant, James Reed, was convicted of rape, unnatural and perverted sex acts, robbery, verbal threats, and unlawful use of telephone, by the Circuit Court, Montgomery County, Maryland. The facts of the case are that in September 1974, a woman was raped outside her home in Montgomery County, Maryland. She reported the rape to the police. The following day, she received a telephone call from a man saying that he was the person who raped her. She immediately called the police, and it was decided that her telephone calls should be tape-recorded in case the assailant called again. As the police predicted, the assailant called several times within three days. During one of the telephone calls, the assailant told the woman that he would like to have sexual inter-course with her again, but the woman said no, and offered to pay the assail-ant $1,000 dollars so that he would leave her alone. The assailant called again to accept the offer and instructed her to leave the money inside one of the lockers in the locker room of the Greyhound Bus Station in the District of Columbia. By this time, the police put the locker room under surveillance and when the assailant came to collect the money, he was arrested.

During the trial, the defendant was ordered to submit a voice exemplar that was then sent to the voice identification unit at Michigan State Police Department for analysis. The defendant's voice exemplar was compared to those recorded on the tapes, but the results were deemed inconclusive. The defendant was ordered to submit another voice exemplar and the second voiceprint analysis showed that there was a match. The voiceprint expert was allowed to testify in court identifying Reed as the person who made the calls. The jury could not reach a decision after two and half days of deliber-ation, and a mistrial was declared. There was a retrial in March 1976, how-ever, and Reed was convicted. The defendant appealed, arguing that the voiceprint analysis should not have been admitted because the technique is not generally accepted by the scientific community as being sufficiently reliable; and also that the second request for his voice exemplar is a viola-tion of the Best Evidence Rule.

The Court of Appeals of Maryland reversed the judgment of conviction and remanded it to the lower court with directions. It was held that voice-print analysis is not admissible in Maryland courts because it had not reached widespread acceptance in the scientific community.[23] The court went on to justify the *Frye* test and stated that:

Without the *Frye* test or something similar, the reliability of an experimental scien-tific technique is likely to become a central issue in each trial in which it is intro-duced, as long as there remains serious disagreement in the scientific community over its reliability. Again and again, the examination and cross-examination of expert witnesses will be as protracted and time-consuming as it was at the trial in the instant case, and proceedings may well degenerate into trials of the technique itself. The *Frye* test is designed to forestall this difficulty as well.[24]

While the *Frye* test standard has been adopted by many states, it should be noted that *Frye* has faced much criticism. *Frye* has been criticized because it did not "cite any policy justification for the general acceptance standard: The court merely mandated the standard as *ipse dixit*."[25]

Another criticism leveled against *Frye* relates to the difficulty in deciding when a scientific technique has achieved general acceptance. Faigman et al. contended that *Frye* did not state what percentage of the relevant community actually constitutes general acceptance.[26]

Moreover, the *Frye* test requires general acceptance in the particular field. But there are no standards defining which field to consult. Courts have had considerable difficulty assessing scientific information under this standard because it often extends into more than one academic or professional discipline. Furthermore, each field may contain subspecialties. This difficulty leads to paradoxical results. General acceptance, often criticized for being the most conservative test of admissibility, in practice can produce the most liberal standards of admission. The more narrowly a court defines the pertinent field, the more agreement it is likely to find. The general acceptance test thus degenerates into a process of deciding whose noses to count. The definition of the pertinent field can be overinclusive or underinclusive. Because the pertinent field can be so readily manipulated, the test by itself provides courts with little protection against shoddy science.[27]

Frye has also been criticized as being conservative. *Frye* appeared to exclude relevant and reliable expert evidence until it has been generally accepted by the relevant scientific community. "A literal reading of *Frye v. United States* would require that the courts always await the passing of a 'cultural lag' during which period the new method will have had sufficient time to diffuse through scientific discipline and create a requisite body of scientific opinion needed for acceptability."[28]

Furthermore, under *Frye,* valid scientific techniques must go through a waiting period before general legal acceptance can be achieved.[29] Thus, in *Coppolino v. State,*[30] the Court of Appeals of Florida rejected the *Frye* test and was critical of the general acceptance rule. The defendant, Carl, an anesthesiologist, was charged with the murder of his wife, Carmella Coppolino, by poisoning. From the beginning, there was evidence showing that Coppolino had bought some quantity of a substance called succinylcholine chloride about three months before the murder of his wife. During the trial, both the defense and prosecution offered medical and scientific witnesses regarding the cause of death. The expert witnesses for the state included Dr. Milton Helpern (a pathologist), Dr. Charles Joe Umberger (a toxicologist), Dr. Bert La Du, and Dr. Frank Cleveland. In his testimony, Helpern said his autopsy on the victim showed that she was in good health at the time of death. He also said that even though the autopsy was inconclusive as to the cause of death, he found a needle injection tract in the left buttock of the deceased. He therefore called Umberger to perform chemical analysis and tests on the body tissues.

At the time of the trial, there were no known medical or scientific methods for detecting the substance (succinic acid) in body tissues, but Umberger used various procedures and was able for the first time in medical history to detect succinic acid in the body tissue. Based on the results of some of the standard tests and procedures and on the results of his new "generally unknown" test, Umberger concluded that Carmela Coppolino received a toxic dose of succinylcholine chloride.[31]

It should be noted that when Helpern was recalled, he testified that based on the autopsy, and on Umberger's findings, he concluded that the victim died from an overdose of succinylcholine chloride. La Du also testified that he found a minute quantity of succinylcholine chloride at the needle injection tract on the victim's left buttocks, and therefore, was of the opinion that the victim died as a result of the succinylcholine chloride. Cleveland also testified that based on the negative findings in Helpern's autopsy report and the positive findings of Umberger, he was of the opinion that the victim died as a result of an overdose of succinylcholine chloride.

It should also be noted that the state called Marjorie Farber to testify. She was Dr. Coppolino's lover between 1962 and 1964 during which time the defendant was married to the victim. She testified that the defendant made certain incriminating statements regarding the death of his wife during the time of their affair. The defense raised an objection but it was denied, and the testimony was admitted. The defendant called several expert witnesses who testified that it was not possible for medical scientists to detect the presence of succinylcholine chloride or its component parts in humans at the time of the trial. The defendant was however, convicted and he appealed. The defendant argued among other things that:

1. The scientific tests that Umberger performed were unreliable and scientifically unacceptable, that their admission into evidence was error;
2. The trial court committed reversible error by instructing the jury on second- and third-degree murder and manslaughter; and
3. The trial judge erred by admitting into evidence the testimony given by Marjorie Farber.

In its ruling, the Florida Court of Appeals, Second District, affirmed the trial court's judgment and held that the defendant had failed to show that the trial judge abused his discretion. It was also held that the trial court's instruction of the jury on the second- and third-degree murder and manslaughter was not an error because under the authority of Florida Statute Ch. 919.14, the jury was permitted to find defendant guilty of the degree charged or lesser degree. The court of appeals, however, held that the trial court erred by admitting the testimony given by Marjorie Farber. The court stated that Farber's testimony was irrelevant and was only introduced to attack the defendant's character. The court stated that even though the admission of the testimony was in error that it did not harmfully prejudice the case and so does not require a reversal.[32] The court of appeal further stated that, "the tests by which the medical examiner sought to determine whether death was caused by succinylcholine chloride were novel and devised specifically for this case. This does not render the evidence inadmissible. Society need not tolerate homicide until there develops a body of medical literature about some particular lethal agent. The expert witnesses were examined and cross-examined at great length and the jury could either believe or doubt the prosecution's testimony as it chose."[33]

The *Frye* test has also been criticized for leading to inconsistencies. It has been argued that *Frye* has different meanings for different people. Forensic scientists and prosecutors see *Frye* as an obstacle that often excludes novel scientific evidence; defense attorneys and some forensic scientists working for the defense see the *Frye* rule as an ineffective barrier to the admission of unreliable evidence being proffered by the prosecution, and many judges do not see *Frye* as a significant issue.[34]

Another criticism leveled against the *Frye* test is its inflexibility, confusion of issues, and superfluity.[35] Furthermore, it has been argued that by focusing particularly on general acceptance, *Frye* obscures other critical problems in the use of a particular technique.[36] Giannelli gave the admissibility of neutron activation analysis (NAA) as an example, arguing that "under the *Frye,* courts have concentrated primarily on the general acceptance of NAA" and that "this approach tends to conceal the most critical aspects of NAA—whether, as interpreted, the results of the test are relevant to the issues in dispute."[37]

Following the criticisms of the *Frye* test, some scholars have suggested alternative rules for admitting scientific evidence. Professor Charles McCormick for instance, argued that the "relevancy test" is the appropriate standard. He maintained that "any relevant conclusions which are supported by a qualified expert witness should be received unless there are other reasons for exclusion. Particularly, its probative value may be overborne by the familiar dangers of prejudicing or misleading the jury, unfair surprise and undue consumption of time."[38] Fundamentally, McCormick argued that any scientific evidence should be admitted if it is relevant to the facts of the case and if an expert testifies to its validity. Many scholars and courts were very critical of this suggestion. In fact, the Court of Appeals of Maryland in *Reed v. State*[39] addressed this suggestion from

McCormick. The Maryland court stated that judges and jurors are not equipped to assess the reliability of scientific techniques when scientists disagree on the issue. The court stated that:

This view seems to us unacceptable. It fails to recognize that laymen should not on a case-by-case basis resolve a dispute in the scientific community concerning the validity of a new scientific technique. When the positions of the contending factions are fixed in the scientific community, it is evident that controversies will be resolved only by further scientific analysis, studies, and experiments. Juries and judges, however, cannot experiment. If a judge or jurors have no foundation, either in their experience or in the accepted principles of scientists, on which they might base an informed judgment, they will be left to follow their fancy. Thus, courts should be properly reluctant to resolve the disputes of science. "It is not for the law to experiment but for science to do so," *State v. Cary*, supra, 99 N. J. Super. at 332, 239 A. 2d at 684.[40]

Professor James Richardson also called for the substitution of "general acceptance" by "substantial acceptance." "Is the basis of admissibility to be universal acceptance by scientific thought? Is it to be general acceptance by science? Or is it to be substantial acceptance which gives a reliable degree of credibility?"[41] Many scholars are not in support of substituting "substantial acceptance" for "general acceptance." Hence, it has been argued that substantial acceptance is not any less amorphous or difficult to define as general acceptance.[42]

The establishment of a "science court" has also been suggested by Arthur Kantrowitz, an American scientist. He called for the establishment of a "science court" to screen any new scientific technique before it is introduced into the courtroom.[43] The reasons for creating a science court are the "need for accurate information to serve as a basis for deciding basic policy questions"[44] and the need for an institution that will "limit to the power exercised by scientists."[45] Giannelli maintained that the advantages of such a panel of experts and tribunals are that the screening would be done by a group of scientists and that their evaluations would be carried out by a group of scientists who have no financial or professional interests in the technique, thereby solving the problem of partiality.[46]

The creation of a science court has been described as time consuming and inconclusive, however.[47] Justice David Bazelon supports the goals of a science court but finds some of the court's features worrying. He argued that a science court will be time consuming. "A lengthy adversary proceeding, limited solely to factual issues, might well exaggerate the importance of those issues, and might tend to diminish the importance of the underlying value choices. A factual decision by a science court, surrounded by all the mystique of both science and the law, might well have enormous, and unwarranted, political impact."[48]

In the final analysis, it should be noted that none of these suggested alternatives to *Frye* was adopted. It seems that the *Frye* test has come to stay. In fact, *Frye* remained the main rule governing the admissibility of scientific evidence even after the enactment of the Federal Rules of Evidence in 1975. As of today *Frye* is still the main admissibility rule in many states. It is also noteworthy to point out that *Frye* has been adopted by arguably all the highly litigious states such as California, Florida, and New York.[49]

FEDERAL RULES OF EVIDENCE

The Federal Rules of Evidence date back as far as 1961 when U. S. Supreme Court Chief Justice Earl Warren appointed a Special Committee on Evidence, charged with the responsibility of determining how feasible and desirable a uniform code of evidence would be for federal courts. In 1962, the special committee recommended the adoption of federal rules of evidence. Chief Justice Warren, therefore, appointed an advisory committee in 1965 to draft the rules of evidence. In 1969, the first draft was published followed by a revised draft in 1971. In 1972, the United States Supreme Court promulgated the Federal Rules of Evidence. It should be noted that congressional hearings on the rules were held between 1973 and 1974. The U. S. House of Representatives completed its hearings in February 1974 and the U. S. Senate did so in November 1974. The legislation was then sent to President Gerald Ford who signed the rules into law on January 2, 1975. The Federal Rules of Evidence took effect on July 1, 1975 as Public Law 93-595 and have been periodically amended through Acts of Congress and by the U. S. Supreme Court. They were last amended on December 1, 2006 by the Judiciary Committee of the U. S. House of Representatives. Most of the comments on the amendment were positive.

Rule 702 of the Federal Rules of Evidence governs the admissibility of expert testimony. Rule 702 states that, "If scientific, technical, or other specialized knowledge will assist the trier of fact to understand the evidence or to determine a fact in issue, a witness qualified as an expert by knowledge, skill, experience, training, or education may testify thereto in the form of an opinion or otherwise . . ."[50]

Rules 401, 402, 403, 703, 704 and 705 also affect the admissibility of expert scientific testimony. It is therefore, very important to cite them at length. These rules are also pertinent to our subsequent discussions.

Rule 401. *Definition of "Relevant Evidence."* "Relevant evidence" means evidence having any tendency to make the existence of any fact that is of consequence to the determination of the action more probable or less probable than it would be without the evidence.[51]

Rule 402. Relevant Evidence Generally Admissible; Irrelevant Evidence Inadmissible. All relevant evidence is admissible, except as otherwise provided by the Constitution of the United States, by Act of Congress, by these rules, or by other rules prescribed by the Supreme Court pursuant to statutory authority. Evidence which is not relevant is not admissible.[52]

Rule 403. Exclusion of Relevant Evidence on Grounds of Prejudice, Confusion, or Waste of Time. Although relevant, evidence may be excluded if its probative value is substantially outweighed by the danger of unfair prejudice, confusion of the issues, misleading the jury, or by consideration of undue delay, waste of time, needless presentation of cumulative evidence.[53]

Rule 703. Bases of Opinion Testimony by Experts. The facts or data in the particular case upon which an expert bases an opinion or inference may be those perceived by or made known to the expert at or before the hearing. If of a type reasonably relied upon by experts in the particular field in forming opinions or inferences, upon the subject, the facts or data need not be admissible in evidence in order for the opinion or inference to be admitted. Facts or data that are otherwise inadmissible shall not be disclosed to the jury by the proponent of the opinion or inference unless the court determines that their probative value in assisting the jury to evaluate the expert's opinion substantially outweighs their prejudicial effect.[54]

Rule 704. Opinion on Ultimate Issue. (a) Except as provided in subdivision (b), testimony in the form of an opinion or inference otherwise admissible is not objectionable because it embraces an ultimate issue to be decided by the trier of fact.

(b) No expert witness testifying with respect to the mental state or condition of a defendant in a criminal case may state an opinion or inference as to whether the defendant did or did not have the mental state or condition constituting an element of the crime charged or of a defense thereto. Such ultimate issues are matters for the trier of fact alone.[55]

Rule 705. Disclosure of Facts or Data Underlying Expert Opinion. The expert may testify in terms of opinion or inference and give reasons therefor without first testifying to the underlying facts or data, unless the court requires otherwise. The expert may in any event be required to disclose the underlying facts or data on cross-examination.[56]

The adoption of the Federal Rules of Evidence in 1975 raised one key question: Did the Federal Rules supersede the *Frye* test? This question was not addressed either in the advisory committee notes, the Congressional hearing committee reports or during the Congressional hearings. Trial courts were left to decide for themselves. Many courts continued with *Frye*, some adopted the new Federal Rules of Evidence, and some combined the two rules.

In *United States v. Smith,*[57] for instance, the court continued with the *Frye* test while at the same time recognized the authority of the Federal

Rules of Evidence. Delivering the opinion of the United States Court of Appeals, Seventh Circuit, Circuit Judge Michael S. Kanne, said: "although the validity of the judge-made rule in *Frye* has been criticized by some courts and commentators for numerous reasons, this circuit has continued to affirm (and to apply) the *Frye* standard."[58]

In *United States v. Downing,*[59] the United States Court of Apeals, Third Circuit, rejected *Frye* and adopted the new Federal Rules of Evidence. The Third Circuit Court stated that *Frye* was inconsistent with the Federal Rules of Evidence based upon the Rules' broad scope of relevance. In this case, Circuit Judge Edward R. Becker, said: "We conclude that the status of the *Frye* test under Rule 702 is somewhat uncertain, but reject that test for reasons of policy. In section IV, we set forth an alternative standard for evaluating novel scientific evidence that we believe comports with the language and policy of Rule 702."[60] The court rejected the *Frye* test[61] and stated that:

In sum, the *Frye* test suffers from serious flaws. The test has proved to be too malleable to provide the method for orderly and uniform decisionmaking envisioned by some of its proponents. Moreover, in its pristine form the general acceptance standard reflects a conservative approach to the admissibility of scientific evidence that is at odds with the spirit, if not the precise language, of the Federal Rules of Evidence. For these reasons, we conclude that "general acceptance in the particular field to which [a scientific technique] belong[s]," should be rejected as an independent controlling standard of admissibility. Accordingly, we hold that a particular degree of acceptance of a scientific technique within the scientific community is neither a necessary nor a sufficient condition for admissibility; it is, however, one factor that a district court normally should consider in deciding whether to admit evidence based upon the technique.[62]

In *State v. Kersting,*[63] it was held that "scientific evidence which is not generally accepted may nevertheless be admitted if there is credible evidence on which the trial judge can rely in making the initial determination that the technique is reasonably reliable."[64] The case involved Dennis Dean Kersting, who was convicted of murder by the Circuit Court, Multnomah County, Oregon, a conviction that he appealed. At the trial, the state presented an expert who testified that certain hairs obtained from the defendant were indistinguishable from or similar to hairs found on the victim. The defendant argued that that this was irrelevant to the case.

At the Court of Appeals of Oregon, the defendant argued that the scientific techniques used by the state's expert were not generally accepted in the scientific community as being reasonably reliable, therefore, the trial court erred by admitting the expert's testimony. In its ruling, the Court of Appeals of Oregon stated that "where judicial notice may not be taken properly because relatively new scientific techniques are involved, some foundation is required as a prerequisite to admission of such evidence; however, only foundation required is that there be credible evidence on which the trial judge may make the initial determination that the technique is reasonably reliable and, if so, the evidence may be admitted and the weight to be given it is for the jury, who may consider evidence as to its reliability."[65] The Court of Appeals affirmed the trial court's decision. The case reached the Supreme Court of Oregon, *En banc*, which affirmed the Court of Appeals' decision.

The above case sits in contrast to *Christophersen v. Allied-Signal Corp.*,[66] where both the *Frye* test and Federal Rules of Evidence were combined. The case involved Rosemarie Christophersen (the surviving spouse of Albert Roy Christophersen, deceased), and Steven Roy Christophersen, who sued Allied-Signal Corporation, alleging that exposure to fumes that contained particles of nickel and cadmium resulted in the development of small-cell cancer that led to Albert Christophersen's death in 1986. Albert Christophersen worked for 14 consecutive years prior to his death for Allied-Signal at its plant based in Waco, Texas, where nickel and cadmium batteries were produced.

During the trial, the plaintiffs proffered expert testimony that exposure to cadmium and nickel fumes caused Albert's death. The defendants argued that the plaintiffs' expert testimony did not meet the *Frye* test, because the expert did not follow the generally accepted methods in reaching his conclusion, and that the basis for the expert's opinion was insufficiently reliable. The United States District Court for the Western District of Texas excluded the expert testimony. The district court stated that the plaintiffs' expert testimony did not meet the *Frye* criteria and granted summary judgment in favor of the defendants. There was an appeal. The issue centered on the appropriate criteria for admitting expert testimony.

The United States Court of Appeals, Fifth Circuit, affirmed the trial court's summary judgment. The court of appeals in its ruling combined the *Frye* test and the Federal Rules of Evidence. The court, through Justice Clark, stated that:

The Federal Rules of Evidence, combined with *Frye v. United States, 293 F. 1013 (D.C Cir. 1923)*, provide a framework for trial judges struggling with proffered expert testimony. The signals are not neatly cabined categories, and we disentangle them only to accent the independent significance of each:

1. Whether the witness is qualified to express an expert opinion, Fed. R. Evid. 702;
2. Whether the facts upon which the expert relies are the same type as are relied upon by other experts in the field, Fed. R. Evid. 703;
3. Whether in reaching his conclusion the expert used a well-founded methodology, *Frye*; and

4. Assuming the expert's testimony has passed Rules 702 and 703, and the *Frye* test, whether under Fed. R. Evid. 403 the testimony's potential for unfair prejudice substantially outweighs its probative value.

These four signals or inquiries introduce no new concepts to our jurisprudence. They are only guideposts drawn from the Federal Rules of Evidence and our cases. We list these inquiries, but in doing so we do not intend that they be applied mechanically. At the same time, they often will naturally lend themselves to sequential application. The reality is that trials are too varied for fixed mold; we construct none today.[67]

The Federal Rules of Evidence were criticized. As we stated earlier on, the Rules did not mention the *Frye* general acceptance criteria. They did not state whether expert evidence must be generally accepted in the relevant scientific community. The Federal Rules of Evidence are also too loose, too liberal, and less stringent than *Frye*. Rule 702, for instance, states that an expert can be qualified by knowledge, skill, experience, training or education. This in effect means that almost anybody can qualify as an expert witness.

Many scholars were also concerned about the appropriate interpretation of the Federal Rules of Evidence. Should the Rules be interpreted as a statute? Glen Weissenberger, for instance, argued that the Federal Rules of Evidence are not a statute. He maintained that the Federal Rules of Evidence was developed through a multibranch process which is not usually the case with a typical statute. He contended that Congress's role in the Federal Rules of Evidence was mainly that of reviewing and ratifying the rule. He noted however, that Congress did modify the Federal Rules of Evidence "only in isolated instances."[68] Fundamentally, Weissenberger argued that the Federal Rules of Evidence "should not be interpreted as a typical statute, but should rather be subject to a unique set of hermeneutics that reflects the Rules' identity as a codification of the common law."[69] On the other hand, Edward Imwinkelried argued that the Federal Rules of Evidence are a statute and should be interpreted according to moderate textual principles of statutory construction.[70]

This argument among scholars as to the proper interpretation of the Federal Rules of Evidence and whether the Federal Rules of Evidence superseded the *Frye* test continued until the United States Supreme Court addressed the issue in *Daubert v. Merrell Dow Pharmaceuticals, Inc.*[71] In *Daubert,* the Supreme Court, through Justice Harry A. Blackmun, stated that the legislatively enacted Federal Rules of Evidence are a statute.[72] The Supreme Court also stated that the *Frye* test was superseded by the Federal Rules of Evidence.[73]

It should be noted that on April 17, 2000, United States Chief Justice William H. Rehnquist wrote to the speaker of the United States House of

Representatives proposing an amendment to Rule 702. Thus, on December 1, 2000, Rule 702 was amended and three crucial requirements were added:

If scientific, technical, or other specialized knowledge will assist the trier of fact to understand the evidence or to determine a fact in issue, a witness qualified as an expert by knowledge, skill, experience, training, or education may testify thereto in the form of an opinion or otherwise, if *a) the testimony is based upon sufficient facts or data, b) the testimony is the product of reliable principles and methods, and c) the witness has applied the principles and methods reliably to the facts of the case.*[74]

DAUBERT V. MERRELL DOW PHARMACEUTICALS, INC.

Following the criticisms of *Frye* and the confusion on whether the Federal Rules of Evidence replaced *Frye*, the United States Supreme Court in *Daubert v. Merrell Dow Pharmaceuticals Inc.*,[75] overturned the *Frye* test and stated that it had been superseded by the Federal Rules of Evidence. The facts of the case are that the petitioners, two minor children, Jason Daubert and Eric Schuller, were born with severe birth defects, and their parents sued Merrell Dow Pharmaceuticals Company, alleging that the birth defects were caused by the mothers' use of Bendectin, an antinausea drug that the company marketed. At the trial, the respondents offered expert testimony to prove that the use of Bendectin during pregnancy does not cause birth defects in humans. They called Dr. Steven H. Lamm, a physician and epidemiologist, who testified that his review of all literature on Bendectin and human defects and more than 30 published studies that involved 130,000 patients, did not find any causal link between Bendectin and malformations in fetuses.[76] Lamm concluded, therefore, that based on these studies, the mothers' use of Bendectin during the first trimester of the pregnancy did not cause the birth defects.

The petitioners on the other hand, called eight experts who testified and concluded that Bendectin can cause birth defects. Their experts included Dr. Shanna Helen Swan and Dr. Stuart A. Newman. The experts drew their conclusions from: 1) "in vitro" (test tube), and "in vivo" (live) animal studies that found a link between Bendectin and malformations, 2) pharmacological studies of the chemical structure of Bendectin, which found similarities between the chemical structure of Bendectin and other substances that cause birth defects, and 3) "reanalysis" of previously published epidemiological (human statistical) studies, which also found a link between Bendectin and birth defects.

The United States District Court for the Southern District of California, in its ruling, granted the company's motion for summary judgment. The district court stated that scientific evidence is admissible only if the principle upon which it is based is "sufficiently established to have general acceptance in the field to which it belongs."[77] The court held that the testimony given by the petitioners' expert witnesses did not meet the applicable "general acceptance" standard for the admission of expert testimony. It was also held that expert opinion not based on epidemiological (human statistical) studies are not admissible to establish causation.[78] "Thus, the animal-cell studies, live animal studies, and chemical-structure analyses on which petitioners had relied could not raise by themselves a reasonably disputable jury issue regarding causation. Petitioners' epidemiological analyses, based as they were on recalculations of data in previously published studies that had found no causal link between the drug and birth defects, were ruled to be inadmissible because they had not been published or subjected to peer review."[79] The district court therefore, granted the company's motion for summary judgment and the petitioners appealed.

The United States Court of Appeals for the Ninth Circuit affirmed the district court's decision and stated that expert testimony based on a scientific technique is not admissible unless the technique is "generally accepted" as being reliable by the relevant scientific community.[80] The court of appeals also stated that expert opinion based on a methodology that diverges "significantly from the procedures accepted by recognized authorities in the field cannot be shown to be 'generally accepted as a reliable technique'."[81]

The court of appeals rejected the "reanalysis" of the epidemiological studies presented by the petitioners' experts and stated that reanalysis is generally accepted by the scientific community only when it has been verified and scrutinized by other experts in that particular field.[82] In affirming the district court's decision, the court of appeals further stated that the reanalyses presented in this case was not published and peer-reviewed. The court of appeals stated that the reanalysis of the epidemiological studies was generated solely for use in litigation[83] and that the petitioners' experts provided insufficient foundation to prove that Bendectin caused the birth defects.

The case reached the United States Supreme Court. Michael H. Gottesman, counsel for the petitioners, argued that *Frye's* "general acceptance" criteria has been superseded by the Federal Rules of Evidence. The Supreme Court in its ruling agreed with the petitioners and stated that the Federal Rules of Evidence, not *Frye* provide the standard for admitting expert scientific testimony in a federal trial.[84] The Supreme Court stated that *Frye's* "general acceptance" test was superseded by the adoption of the Federal Rules of Evidence. It was held that "nothing in the Rules as a whole or in the text and drafting history of Rule 702, which specifically governs expert testimony, gives any indication that "general acceptance" is a necessary precondition to the admissibility of scientific evidence.

Moreover, such a rigid standard would be at odds with the Rules' liberal thrust and their general approach of relaxing the traditional barriers to "opinion testimony."[85] The Supreme Court further stated that:

Faced with a proffer of expert scientific testimony under Rule 702, the trial judge, pursuant to Rule 104(a), must make a preliminary assessment of whether the testimony's underlying reasoning or methodology is scientifically valid and properly can be applied to the facts at issue. Many considerations will bear on the inquiry, including whether the theory or technique in question can be (and has been) tested, whether it has been subjected to peer review and publication, its known or potential error rate and the existence and maintenance of standards controlling its operation, and whether it has attracted widespread acceptance within a relevant scientific community. The inquiry is a flexible one, and its focus must be solely on principles and methodology, not on conclusions that they generate. Throughout, the judge should also be mindful of other applicable Rules.[86]

Justice Blackmun stated that trial judges function as "gatekeepers" and determine whether the testimony being presented is reliable and scientifically valid. The Supreme Court stated that Rule 402 provides the guideline: "All relevant evidence is admissible, except as otherwise provided by the Constitution of the United States, by Act of Congress, by these rules, or by other rules prescribed by the Supreme Court pursuant to statutory authority. Evidence which is not relevant is not admissible."[87]

The Supreme Court went on to say that "given the Rules' permissive backdrop and their inclusion of a specific rule on expert testimony that does not mention "general acceptance," the assertion that the Rules somehow assimilated *Frye* is unconvincing. *Frye* made "general acceptance" the exclusive test for admitting expert scientific testimony. That austere standard, absent from, and incompatible with, the Federal Rules of Evidence, should not be applied in federal trials."[88] The United States Supreme Court vacated the decision of the United States Court of Appeals for the Ninth Circuit and remanded the case for further proceedings.

The Supreme Court's decision in *Daubert* has been criticized extensively. The opinion in *Daubert* created difficult burdens for trial judges; the opinion is still ambiguous; it did not address crucial questions; and it did not provide specific guidelines to trial courts. Above all, it did not state whether the *Daubert* criteria also applied to nonscientific evidence. Under *Daubert*, trial judges became "gatekeepers" who have to decide what is a reliable or an unreliable scientific technique. In fact it has been pointed out that "judges are trained lawyers and only rarely trained scientists, which explains their failure to provide coherent guidelines on how to accomplish this task."[89] Indeed, one of the main problems for trial judges is how to separate reliable and accurate expert testimony from unreliable and inaccurate testimony.[90] Furthermore, *Daubert* is unclear, a disappointment, and confusing.[91]

At best, *Daubert* offers an awkward analytical model. The Court failed to provide trial judges with a well-defined standard for separating unreliable scientific evidence from reliable scientific evidence. Perhaps none exists. *Daubert* specifically ruled out the general acceptance standard as a precondition of admissibility, but offered only "general observations" in return. The Court failed to clarify whether *Daubert* expands or contracts the role of the trial judge in considering the admissibility of scientific evidence. After all, we all already knew that we are the "gatekeepers." Moreover, the Court sent conflicting signals to trial courts by abandoning *Frye's* general acceptance test, only to resurrect it as one consideration under the new standard.[92]

In a similar vein, it has been argued that *Daubert* requires trial judges who are not scientists to evaluate science in a way that may exceed their scientific abilities and also that *Daubert* did not state clearly the degree or the level of reliability that should be accepted by trial judges.[93]

The *Daubert* decision has also been described as being unclear and based on unarticulated assumptions.[94] *Daubert* failed to address crucial questions. For instance, what happens if the error rate is known? "If the error rate is less than fifty percent does it satisfy a preponderance of the evidence notion of reliability? Or does the error rate have to be small enough to conform to 'scientific' notions of confidence? Is there a connection between error rates and the statistical tests that normally require scientists to reach a ninety-five percent confidence level?"[95] These questions and many more were left unanswered by the Supreme Court in *Daubert*.

In fact, courts have been cautioned not to reach a conclusion on a scientific method or technique based simply on peer review and publication because "peer review is hardly a perfect system—it is often less than demanding because scientists are busy or because of conflicts of interest."[96] The fact that something is published does not mean that it went through strict scrutiny.[97]

Daubert has also been described as being ambiguous and full of confusing contradictions rather than clarity and could lead to inconsistencies in judicial interpretations.[98] "The Supreme Court in *Daubert* did not see fit to create distinctions between proof in criminal versus civil cases, as far as reliability is concerned, even though literature and case law frequently cautioned that in criminal cases, where a person's freedom is at stake, courts ought to be more reluctant to admit evidence based on new, as yet unproven, techniques when such evidence is being offered by the prosecution."[99]

Therefore, extra judicial caution has been suggested for the following reasons:

- Most witnesses are not truly scientists but are technicians;
- Pro-prosecution bias may impair scientific impartiality;
- Experts tend to testify beyond their expertise;
- Experts prevaricate on their credentials;
- There are doubts as to the proficiency of crime laboratories; and
- Humans commit errors, which can result in reaching wrong conclusions, among other reasons.[100]

Some states rejected *Daubert* and continued with *Frye*. In *People v. Leahy*,[101] for instance, the Supreme Court of California rejected *Daubert* and stated that *Kelly/Frye* remained the standard for the admissibility of new scientific evidence. The case involved William Michael Leahy who was convicted by the Municipal Court, West Orange County Judicial District, of driving under the influence of alcohol and driving with blood alcohol level in excess of 0.08 percent. On the day he was arrested, the police officer gave the defendant some field sobriety tests, including the HGN (horizontal gaze nystagmus) test. "An inability of the eyes to maintain visual fixation as they turned from side to side (in other words, jerking or bouncing) is known as horizontal gaze nystagmus, or HGN."[102] At the trial, the court admitted the HGN test without a *Kelly/Frye* hearing. The defendant was convicted and he appealed, arguing that the HGN test should not have been admitted without a *Kelly/Frye* hearing.

At the Court of Appeals of California, the issue centered on whether HGN tests are admissible without a *Kelly/Frye* hearing. In its ruling, the court of appeals reversed the trial court's judgment of conviction because the court failed to apply the *Kelly/Frye* standard. The Supreme Court of California granted review to decide whether the *Kelly/Frye* standard should be modified in view of the United States Supreme Court decision in *Daubert*.

Delivering the opinion of the Supreme Court of California, Chief Justice Malcolm Lucas stated that the *Kelly/Frye* formulation remained the prerequisite for the admissibility of expert testimony on new scientific techniques and methods in California. The Supreme Court of California agreed with the Court of Appeal's ruling that the HGN test is a new scientific technique. Therefore, the Supreme Court of California ruled that the trial court erred by admitting the expert testimony on HGN test without a *Kelly* hearing.[103] Chief Justice Lucas also stated that "*Daubert* affords no compelling reason for abandoning *Kelly* in favor of the more 'flexible' approach outlined in *Daubert*."[104] Chief Justice Lucas said:

In sum, *Kelly* sets forth the various reasons why the more 'conservative' *Frye* approach to determining the reliability of expert testimony regarding scientific techniques represents an appropriate one. *Daubert*, which avoided the issue of *Frye*'s 'merits,' presents no justification for reconsidering that aspect of our holding in

Kelly. Thus, we conclude that the *Kelly* formulation survived *Daubert* in this state, and that none of the above described authorities critical of that formulation persuades us to reconsider or modify it at this time.[105]

Therefore, *Kelly* survived *Daubert* and remained the standard to be used when deciding whether to admit or exclude any new scientific technique. Chief Justice Lucas also stated that "general acceptance" under *Kelly* means a consensus drawn from a typical cross-section of the relevant, qualified scientific community.[106]

GENERAL ELECTRIC CO. V. JOINER

In *General Electric v. Joiner*,[107] the United States Supreme Court restated the function of the trial judge to determine when to admit or exclude scientific evidence. It was held that the abuse-of-discretion is the proper standard for appellate review regarding trial court decisions on the admissibility of evidence. Robert Joiner, an electrician, and his wife, sued General Electric and Westinghouse Electric, where Joiner worked, alleging that his lung cancer was "promoted" by his exposure to polychlorinated biphenyls (PCBs) and their derivatives—furans and dioxins. PCBs are hazardous substances that were banned by Congress in 1978, with limited exceptions.

Joiner called expert witnesses (Dr. Arnold Schecter and Dr. Daniel Teitelbaum), who testified that PCBs, furans, and dioxins can "promote" lung cancer and therefore, concluded that Joiner's lung cancer was likely to have been caused by his exposure to PCBs at his workplace. The experts based their conclusions on the following:

1. Studies showing that infant mice developed cancer after being injected with massive doses of PCBs;
2. An epidemiological study that involved workers who were exposed to PCBs at an Italian electrical plant. The study by Bertazzi, Riboldi, Pesatori, Radice, and Zocchetti (1987), found that lung cancer deaths among the ex-workers at the Italian plant were higher than expected. It should be noted however, that these authors were unwilling to state that PCBs had caused the lung cancer in the ex-workers;
3. An epidemiological study that involved ex-employees at Monsanto's PCB production plant in Sauget, Illinois. The authors of the study (J. Zack and D. Musch 1979) also found that lung cancer deaths among the ex-employees were higher than expected. The authors noted however that their finding was not statistically significant and so could not suggest a link between the increase in lung cancer deaths and exposure to PCB;.

4. An epidemiological study involving workers at a Norwegian Cable manufacturing company, who were exposed to mineral oil. The authors of the study (Ronneberg, Andersen, and Skyberg 1988) found a statistically significant increase in lung cancer in the workers, but the study did not mention PCBs; and

5. An epidemiological study involving workers exposed to PCBs in Japan. The authors (Kuratsune, Nakamura, Ikeda, and Hirohata 1987) found a statistically significant increase in lung cancer among the workers, but the workers were exposed to numerous potential carcinogens. The workers were also exposed to toxic rice oil.[108]

Based on the above studies, Joiner's expert witness, Schecter, testified that it is more likely that the defendant's lung cancer was caused by cigarette smoking and PCB exposure.[109] Teitelbaum also testified that Joiner's lung cancer was caused by or contributed to in a significant degree by his exposure to the substances at the plant where he worked. The petitioners on the other hand argued that the experts' conclusions were mere speculation, not supported by appropriate epidemiological studies, and were based on studies with laboratory animals.

In its ruling, the United States District Court for the Northern District of Georgia excluded the experts' testimony and stated that the animal studies that the experts relied on did not support Joiner's contention that the PCBs promoted his small cell cancer.[110] The district court stated that the study involving infant mice that were injected with highly concentrated and massive doses of PCBs was different from the case of Robert Joiner, who is an adult human, and who was only exposed to PCBs on a small scale. The court also rejected the four epidemiological studies presented by Joiner's experts. It was held that the studies did not provide a sufficient basis for an expert's opinion, since the authors of the studies were unwilling to suggest a link between increases in lung cancer and exposure to PCBs. The court stated that the third epidemiological study that involved workers who were exposed to mineral oil was not relevant to the case. Similarly, the district court also rejected the fourth study that involved workers exposed to many carcinogens, plus PCBs. The study was not specific to PCBs. The court therefore, granted summary judgment to the petitioners and stated that experts' testimony had failed to show that there was a causal link between exposure to PCBs and small-cell lung cancer. Therefore, the expert testimony was ruled inadmissible because it did not rise above "subjective belief or unsupported speculation."[111]

There was an appeal to the Eleventh Circuit Court of Appeals, which reversed the judgment and ruled that the district court erred in excluding the testimony of the respondent's expert witnesses.[112] The case reached the United States Supreme Court. The Supreme Court granted *certiorari* to determine the appropriate standard for appellate review in a case where a trial court based its decision on the *Daubert* criteria.[113] The Supreme Court reversed the judgment of the court of appeals. Delivering the judgment, Chief Justice William Rehnquist stated that abuse-of-discretion is the appropriate standard and that the district court did not abuse its discretion by excluding the expert testimony. Chief Justice Rehnquist further stated that "the court of appeals erred in its review of the exclusion of Joiner's experts' testimony. In applying an overly 'stringent' review to that ruling, it failed to give the trial court the deference that is the hallmark of abuse-of-discretion review."[114]

Chief Justice Rehnquist said:

Respondent points to *Daubert's* language that the "focus, of course, must be solely on principles and methodology, not on the conclusions that they generate." ... He claims that because the District Court's disagreement was with the conclusion that the experts drew from the studies, the district court committed legal error and was properly reversed by the court of appeals. But conclusions and methodology are not entirely distinct from one another. Trained experts commonly extrapolate from existing data. But nothing in either *Daubert* or the Federal Rules of Evidence requires a district court to admit opinion evidence that is connected to existing data only by the *ipse dixit* of the expert. A court may conclude that there is simply too great an analytical gap between the data and the opinion proffered ... That is what the District Court did here, and we hold that it did not abuse its discretion in so doing.[115]

In reversing the judgment, the Supreme Court stated that abuse-of-discretion is the proper standard to be used in reviewing a district court's decision to admit or exclude any scientific evidence. The Supreme Court reversed the judgment of the court of appeals and remanded the case for further proceedings. The Supreme Court's decision in this case has been criticized on the argument that the decision "seems to support the theme of liberal admissibility."[116] The Supreme Court ruled that abuse-of-discretion was the proper standard for appellate review without given consideration to *de novo* review, which is the alternative.[117]

KUMHO TIRE CO. V. CARMICHAEL

As mentioned earlier, the *Daubert* decision was criticized on the basis of several issues. One of these was the unresolved issue of whether the *Daubert* criteria also applied to nonscientific testimony. Thus, on March 23, 1999, the United States Supreme Court in the case of *Kumho Tire Co. v. Carmichael*,[118] stated that the function of trial judges to act as "gatekeepers," requiring an inquiry into both the relevance and reliability of expert testimony, applied to all expert testimony, both scientific and nonscientific.[119]

On July 6, 1993, Patrick Carmichael was driving his minivan when the right rear tire on the van blew out and the van overturned. One passenger died while others sustained serious injuries. Carmichael and the others sued the tire manufacturer and distributor (collectively called *Kumho Tire Co.*), for the death and the injuries. They claimed the tire failed because it was defective. They called a tire failure analyst, Dennis Carlson, Jr., who testified that he had examined the failed tire, and was of the opinion that a defect in the tire's manufacture or the design caused the tire to blow out. His analysis of the failed tire showed that the tread of the tire separated from the steel-belted carcass, which means that the separation was caused by either a defect or from over-deflection, which is a type of tire abuse. Carlson based his conclusions on: 1) a visual and tactile inspection of the failed tire, and 2) on his own theory that if at least two of the four specific physical symptoms were absent, then the tire failure, such as the one that occurred in this case, resulted from a defect in the tire's manufacture.[120] According to Carlson, the symptoms include the following:

1. Tread wear on the tire's shoulder that is greater than the tread wear along the tire's center;
2. Signs of a "bead groove," where the beads have been pushed too hard against the bead seat on the inside of the tire's rim;
3. Sidewalls of the tire with physical signs of deterioration, such as discoloration; and
4. Marks on the tire's rim flange.[121]

During his testimony, Carlson noted that: 1) the failed tire was made in 1988 and was installed before Carmichael bought the van in March 1993, 2) the Carmichaels had driven the van approximately 7,000 additional miles in the two months that he owned the van, and 3) the tire tread had at least two punctures that had been repaired inadequately.[122]

Counsel for *Kumho Tire Co.* argued that the expert's testimony should be excluded because the methodology used by the expert in reaching his conclusion was unreliable. *Kumho Tire Co.* also argued that the methodology did not satisfy the Federal Rule of Evidence 702, which requires expert testimony to be both relevant and reliable. They also argued that the methodology did not satisfy the *Daubert* criteria.

The United States District Court for the Southern District of Alabama excluded the expert's testimony and granted summary judgment for defendants.[123] In excluding the testimony, the district court stated that the Federal Rule of Evidence 702 requires the trial judge to ensure that scientific testimony is relevant and also reliable. The district court also recognized the fact that *Daubert* required trial judges to act as "gatekeepers" and consider four factors when deciding whether to admit or exclude expert testimony. In the court's view, Carlson's testimony did not satisfy *Daubert*'s four factors: testability, peer review and publication, error rate, and general acceptance.

The plaintiffs then filed a motion for reconsideration, stating that the *Daubert* factors should be applied flexibly. The district court granted their motion for reconsideration and agreed that "*Daubert* should be applied flexibly, that its four factors were simply illustrative, and that other factors could argue in favor of admissibility."[124] The district court however, affirmed its earlier decision, stating that the methods used by the expert had not been shown to be sufficiently reliable. The plaintiffs appealed.

The Court of Appeals for the Eleventh Circuit reversed the judgment and remanded the case for further proceedings. The court of appeals held that the district court erred as a matter of law in applying the *Daubert* standard. Following a *de novo review* of the district court's decision to apply the *Daubert* criteria, the court of appeals stated that *Daubert* only applied to "scientific" testimony, and that Carlson's testimony was not scientific and therefore falls outside the scope of *Daubert*.[125]

The case reached the United States Supreme Court, which granted *certiorari* and reversed the court of appeals decision. The issue centered on whether the *Daubert* factors also applied to nonscientific expert testimony. The Supreme Court held that the district court's decision to exclude Carlson's testimony was within its discretion and was lawful. The Supreme Court also noted that there was no reference to any articles or papers that validates Carlson's methodology. The Supreme Court stated that:

> The *Daubert* "gatekeeping" obligation applies not only to "scientific" testimony, but to all expert testimony. Rule 702 does not distinguish between "scientific" knowledge and "technical" or "other specialized" knowledge, but makes clear that any such knowledge might become the subject of expert testimony. It is the Rule's word "knowledge," not the words (like "scientific") that modify that word, ... [which] establishes a standard of evidentiary reliability. *Daubert* referred only to "scientific" knowledge because that was the nature of the expertise there at issue. Neither is the evidentiary rationale underlying *Daubert's* "gatekeeping" determination limited to "scientific" knowledge. Rules 702 and 703 grant all expert witnesses, not just "scientific" ones, testimonial latitude unavailable to other witnesses on the assumption that the expert's opinion will have a reliable basis in the knowledge and experience of his discipline. Finally, it would prove difficult, if not impossible, for judges to administer evidentiary rules under which a "gatekeeping" obligation depended upon a distinction between "scientific" knowledge and "technical" or "other specialized" knowledge, since there is no clear line dividing the one from the others and no convincing need to make such distinctions.[126]

The Supreme Court further stated that a trial judge may consider one or more of the *Daubert* factors when deciding whether to admit or exclude expert testimony. The Supreme Court therefore, held that "the Court of Appeals erred insofar as it ruled those factors out in such cases. In determining whether particular expert testimony is reliable, the trial court should consider the specific *Daubert* factors where they are reasonable measures of reliability."[127] Justice Stephen Breyer, delivering the opinion of the Supreme Court, also stated that a court of appeals must apply an abuse-of-discretion standard when reviewing a trial court's decision on expert testimony. Justice Breyer further stated that:

We must therefore disagree with the Eleventh Circuit's holding that a trial judge may ask questions of the sort *Daubert* mentioned only where an expert "relies on the application of scientific principles," but not where an expert relies "on skill or experience-based observation." We do not believe that Rule 702 creates a schematism that segregates expertise by type while mapping certain kinds of questions to certain kinds of experts. Life and the legal cases that it generates are too complex to warrant so definitive a match.[128]

In a nutshell, the Supreme Court recognized the fact that not all the *Daubert* factors applied to all forms of expert testimony; and that the *Daubert* factors did not constitute mandates but are flexible guidelines, and that trial judges must look at other factors bearing in mind the circumstances of each case. The Supreme Court's decision in this case has faced some criticisms.[129]

In summary, this chapter has revealed the confusion, controversy, and inconsistencies surrounding the admissibility of expert testimony. We have discussed the three main rules guiding the admissibility of expert testimony, bringing out their various strengths and weaknesses. The *Frye* test emphasizes general acceptance of a technique in the relevant discipline. The Federal Rule of Evidence 702 emphasizes relevance and reliability of a technique. This rule also stresses that a method or technique can be scientific, technical, or other specialized field of knowledge. Rule 702 further stresses that if a method or technique can assist judges and jurors, then an expert qualified by knowledge, skill, experience, or training should be allowed to give expert testimony. *Daubert* emphasizes relevance, reliability, and validity. *Daubert* stresses that trial judges have the function to act as "gatekeepers." Above all, *Daubert* also emphasizes that there are four factors that trial judges should be considering when deciding to admit or exclude expert testimony (testability, peer review, error rate, and general acceptance).

Offender Profiling in the Courtroom

Offender profiling is a crime investigation technique based on probabilities, stereotypes, suspicion, and assumptions. It does not point to a specific offender as being responsible for a specific offense. Offender profiling only generalizes. As such it is not a method sufficiently reliable to prove the guilt or innocence of an accused. There are no questions as to its usefulness in crime investigations. Questions and problems arise, however, when it is being introduced into the courtroom as evidence. The reliability and validity of offender profiling cannot be ascertained at the moment by any objective method.

The nature of offender profiling does not lend this technique to any form of reliable testing. There is the problem of replicating a crime scene. No one can state with certainty that one offender will commit all crimes in the same manner or exhibit the same characteristics at subsequent crimes. Offenders, especially serial offenders, will learn from experiences, media, and from victim responses and then may change their method of operation. They may also develop new fantasies; hence the signature aspects of their crime may change.

The current position in United States courts is that offender profiling and its derivatives have been admitted in many cases and also have been excluded in many others. There have been many inconsistencies. This chapter, hence, will discuss the central problems of offender profiling evidence. In some cases where offender profiling or its derivatives were admitted, it is surprising that the reliability of this technique was never questioned. Some courts appeared to have been taken in by the credentials of the profilers at the expense of assessing the reliability and validity of this technique. The fact that a technique is useful in crime investigation does not render it a reliable tool for courtroom use. Utility does not equal/amount to reliability.

IS OFFENDER PROFILING IMPERMISSIBLE CHARACTER EVIDENCE?

There are many problems with the introduction of offender profiling in the courtroom. The first relates to whether offender profiling constitutes impermissible character evidence. There is general disagreement among scholars and courts on this question. The Federal Rules of Evidence, Rule 404, deals with character evidence and provides the guideline. Rules 405 and 406 also affect character evidence. It is therefore, important to cite these rules at length.

Rule 404. Character Evidence Not Admissible to Prove Conduct; Exceptions; Other Crimes

(a) Character evidence generally—Evidence of a person's character or trait of character is not admissible for the purpose of proving action in conformity therewith on a particular occasion, except:

 (1) Character of accused—In a criminal case, evidence of a pertinent trait of character offered by an accused, or by the prosecution to rebut the same, or if evidence of a trait of character of the alleged victim of the crime is offered by an accused and admitted under Rule 404(a)(2), evidence of the same trait of character of the accused offered by the prosecution;

 (2) Character of alleged victim.—In a criminal case, and subject to the limitations imposed by Rule 412, evidence of a pertinent trait of character of the alleged victim of the crime offered by an accused, or by the prosecution to rebut the same, or evidence of a character trait of peacefulness of the alleged victim offered by the prosecution in a homicide case to rebut evidence that the alleged victim was the first aggressor;

 (3) Character of witness.—Evidence of the character of a witness, as provided in Rules 607, 608, and 609.

(b) Other crimes, wrongs, or acts. Evidence of other crimes, wrongs, or acts is not admissible to prove the character of a person in order to show action in conformity therewith. It may, however, be admissible for other purposes, such as proof of motive, opportunity, intent, preparation, plan, knowledge, identity, or absence of mistake or accident, provided that upon request by the accused, the prosecution in a criminal case shall provide reasonable notice in advance of trial, or during trial if the court excuses pretrial notice on good cause shown, of the general nature of any such evidence it intends to introduce at trial.[1]

Rule 405. Methods of Proving Character

(a) Reputation or opinion. In all cases in which evidence of character or a trait of character of a person is admissible, proof may be made by testimony as to reputation or by testimony in the form of an opinion. On cross-examination, inquiry is allowable into relevant specific instances of conduct.

(b) Specific instances of conduct. In cases in which character or trait of character of a person is an essential element of a charge, claim, or defense, proof may also be made of specific instances of that person's conduct.[2]

Rule 406. Habit; Routine Practice

Evidence of the habit of a person or of the routine practice of an organization, whether corroborated or not and regardless of the presence of eyewitnesses, is relevant to prove that the conduct of the person or organization on a particular occasion was in conformity with the habit or routine practice.[3]

In general terms, offender profiling deals with the character traits of individuals. As such it is character evidence. Whether it will be seen as permissible or impermissible character evidence largely depends on two things, however. First, for it to be admissible the defendant must first put his or her character at issue. If the prosecution offers character evidence before the defendant, it will be ruled inadmissible. Second, whether it will be ruled admissible or inadmissible also depends on the purpose of its introduction. By purpose, we mean, Is it being introduced to show criminal intent, criminal propensity, or is it simply to assist the fact-finders? It is generally permissible when it is being used to show criminal intent as opposed to when it is being offered to show criminal propensity.

In *State v. Haynes*,[4] the expert testimony of a criminal profiler was seen as impermissible character evidence, and therefore inadmissible. Richard Haynes was charged with murder and grand theft of a motor vehicle and was convicted by the Common Pleas Court, County of Lorain, Ohio. Richard Haynes claimed that on October 20, 1986, he went to Douglas Fauver's home to fill out a job application form and was offered some drinks and some pills (speed). He claimed that at 11:30 pm he woke up from sleep and found out that he was still at Fauver's home and that Fauver was sitting across from him, completely naked. Fauver then told him that he had sexual intercourse with him and wanted to know if he enjoyed it. Haynes said that he then went to the bathroom to clean up. Fauver then came at him with a small knife and they engaged in a fight. Haynes also stated that he stabbed Fauver twice in the chest and once in the back, after Fauver had cut his (Haynes) wrist. Haynes claimed that he then waited for two hours for the police to arrive, but they did not. He said that he thought the neighbors had called the police when they heard the noise during the fight. Haynes later used a stolen car to get away and was arrested in Arizona for another crime. It should be noted that Fauver died in his home and his body was discovered the next day.

At the trial, the state called Robert Walter, a psychologist and criminal profiler, to testify in support of the state's argument that the murder was anger-retaliatory and "not a homophobic murder done out of panic after an unsolicited homosexual encounter."[5] The state believed and argued that the timing of the events, along with other factors, implied that Fauver's murder was anger-retaliatory. Walter testified that there is what he called homophobic murder and anger-retaliatory murder and that each type has distinctive patterns. He stated that his analysis of the crime scene characteristics and reports revealed patterns consistent with anger-retaliatory murders. Therefore, he was of the opinion that the murder was not committed as a result of panic. Haynes claimed that he acted in self-defense and that the state "set up the theory of homophobic murder as a strawman argument and then set out to attack it."[6] The expert's testimony was admitted, however.

Haynes was convicted and sentenced to a term of 15 years to life for the murder and a consecutive term of 2 years for the theft. He appealed his conviction. The defendant argued that Walter's theory was not generally accepted, not scientifically reliable, and should not have been admitted. The defense also argued that the prejudicial effect of the expert testimony far outweighed its probative value. Furthermore, the defendant argued that "the state has overlooked the principle that unless scientific evidence and/ or theory can be considered reliable, it cannot be of assistance to the trier of fact."[7]

The Court of Appeals of Ohio, Ninth District., Lorain County, ruled that the expert's testimony violated other evidence rules and therefore, its admission was in error. The court did not see offender profiling as being reliable and stated that even though the expert's testimony may indicate that offender profiles may be a reliable technique of crime investigation, there is still little available evidence in the record to show that it is a reliable tool to be used in the courtroom.

On the issue of whether the criminal profiling testimony assisted the trier of fact, the court of appeals stated that the expert testimony was within the understanding of an average juror. Therefore, testimony that does not assist the jury is generally inadmissible. Delivering the judgment, Justice Mary Cacioppo, stated that the expert testimony was more prejudicial than probative, and ruled that:

The issues of timing and sudden panic are directly related to the distinction between voluntary manslaughter and murder. From the defendant's confession, a jury could decide for themselves that he did not kill Fauver immediately after discovering that he had been assaulted, but that a period of time had elapsed in which he could have "cooled off." The use of expert testimony for this purpose was improper; the prejudicial impact outweighed probative value, as it tended to "sensationalize" the facts and issues.[8]

Furthermore, the court of appeals held that the testimony relating to timing and sudden panic fell within the ultimate issue to be decided by the jury. It was also held that the expert's testimony confused the issues and/or misled the jury, by setting up the strawman argument.[9]

Interestingly, the court of appeals also ruled that the admission of the expert testimony violated Evidence Rule 404(A)(1), regarding character evidence. Justice Cacioppo stated that in this case, "Walter testified that the appellant's version of the killing and his subsequent actions were classically typical of an anger-retaliatory murder. In fact, Walter testified at great length and in great detail as to the traits and characteristics of such a type of murderer, and found that the appellant's actions and motivations matched that profile."[10] The possibility of stereotyping the defendant also led to the possibility that the admission of the testimony violated Evidence Rule 404(A)(1).[11]

The court of appeals further stated that since the defendant did not testify, he did not put his character in issue.[12] The court also stated that the expert's testimony on the anger-retaliatory profile contained many references to personality and character traits of the defendant that matched the profile of a deliberate killer. Therefore, the testimony was inadmissible based on Evidence Rule 404(A)(1).[13] The court also held that the expert testimony was inadmissible based on the hearsay rule. It should be noted that during cross-examination, Walter stated that he based his opinion on the police reports, autopsy reports, and conversations with the police and the prosecutor. The conversations with the police and prosecutor were not admitted into evidence, and so constitute inadmissible hearsay based on Evidence Rule 703.[14] The autopsy report was admitted.

The court of appeals therefore concluded that there was a reasonable possibility that the admission of the expert testimony contributed to the conviction and that its admission was harmful error. Haynes's conviction was therefore reversed and remanded for a new trial.

In *State v. Roquemore*,[15] the opinion testimony of an offender profiler was ruled inadmissible. It was seen to be impermissible character evidence. The court stated that such testimony that stereotypes the defendant violates the Federal Rule of Evidence 404(A)(1).[16] The defendant, Dennis Roquemore, was convicted of two counts of rape and one count of involuntary manslaughter by the Franklin County Court of Common Pleas, Ohio. The defendant knew the victim, Yvonne Mathis, for 10 years and they lived together for 1 year in 1990. Roquemore claimed that on September 1, 1990, they both went to a friend's house where they drank and socialized with other people and that on their way back to their home, Mathis was angry because of certain jokes at the friend's house. Roquemore claimed that later on he "wrestled" with Mathis and they had "rough"' sexual intercourse, and that afterwards he noticed that Mathis was unconscious.[17] He also claimed that he tried to resuscitate her, carried her into the bathroom, and ran water over her to see if she would regain consciousness. He said he panicked and left the house.[18] Roquemore further claimed that he then went to an ex-girlfriend's house but there was no answer. He therefore telephoned her and told her what happened and she called the police. Roquemore said that the police went to the wrong house and he went to Alum Creek Reservoir to kill himself but he could not, and then he went back to the house and called the police.

At the trial, the state argued that Roquemore raped Mathis and that Mathis died as a result of rape trauma. The state called a criminal profiler, Richard Walter, who testified that his review of the crime scene, the crime scene photographs, police reports, and pathological reports showed that rape occurred. The main reason the state called the profiler was to give testimony on the crime scene assessment, in order to bolster their argument that the defendant raped the victim and that the victim died as a result of heart stoppage from the rape trauma. Walter testified that the crime scene showed patterns of violent rape behavior. In his testimony, Walter stated that the crime scene fell into patterns of known violent behavior that he had studied in the past. It should be noted that during cross-examination, Walter was asked if he was going to give an opinion on whether rape occurred and he answered in the affirmative.[19]

The defense argued that the expert's testimony should be excluded. The defendant acknowledged that they had rough sex that night and that they had had rough sex in the past, and that he did not rape Mathis. The state argued that Walter's testimony should be admitted because he was testifying about the patterns of violent behavior that occurred, and not to the conduct of the defendant. The state further presented the medical examiner, who testified that Mathis's death was "related to the rectal and vaginal trauma that she had suffered and subsequent, due to pain, emotional disability from this abnormality, that she had sudden cardiac stoppage on the basis of a neurogenic response to the trauma that she suffered and this caused her heart to stop beating and she subsequently expired because it did not start beating again."[20] The medical examiner further stated that the injuries Mathis received would not have led to her death if the nerve response had not occurred.

The expert's testimony was admitted. The defendant was convicted and he appealed. Among other issues, the defendant argued that the trial court erred by admitting the profile testimony. He argued that the testimony was inadmissible because it violated Evidence Rules 402, 403, and 703; hence, he was denied due process of law. The defendant also argued that the profile testimony was irrelevant and unfairly prejudicial.

In its ruling, the Court of Appeals of Ohio, Tenth District, held that even though the expert's testimony was relevant, it ought to have been excluded because it violated other evidence rules. Delivering the opinion of the appeals court, Justice Alba Whiteside said that the expert testimony was relevant to the case because it indicated a pattern of violence. That the testimony made the issue of whether the victim was raped more probable than without the expert testimony. Justice Whiteside however, stated that the fact that the expert evidence was relevant to the facts of the case did not on that basis alone make it admissible evidence. Relevant evidence is inadmissible if it conflicts with other evidentiary rules.[21]

Justice Whiteside went on to say that under the Federal Rule of Evidence 702, expert testimony is admissible only if it will assist the trier of fact and that the expert evidence must have sufficient indicia of reliability.[22] In this case, the expert witness testified that the methodology he used was based on probability, that he did not keep the files or statistics of all the cases he had reviewed. In fact, the expert stated that he used statistics from the FBI and from other sources. Justice Whiteside therefore, ruled that the expert witness in this case failed to give an indication as to how he drew his conclusions.

Hence, the court of appeals held that there was a distinct possibility of stereotyping the defendant in this case. "The witness testified only concerning the 'typical' crime scene pattern and the 'typical' violence associated with such a crime scene. The witness did not interview or evaluate the defendant or 'profile' a specific person. He profiles for a type of person who would do a particular crime that has been assessed as a member of that group. This stereotyping of the defendant has several problems. First, the stereotyping can prejudice the jury."[23] The court therefore, ruled that assuming that a testimony satisfied the relevancy requirement, it must still be excluded if its prejudicial effect substantially outweighed its probative value. The court concluded that these generalities and typical facts are not specific facts and generally tend to stereotype the defendant.[24]

The court of appeals held that profile testimony, which stereotypes a defendant violates Evidence Rule 404 (a)(1) on character evidence. The court of appeals restated the fact that the rule does not allow the prosecution to procure testimony about character traits of the defendant unless the defendant first puts his character in issue. The testimony in this case was seen by the court as character evidence, which is generally inadmissible unless the defendant first puts his character at issue. In classifying the case, Walter talked about anger, revenge, hostility, and problems with women.[25] All these constitute individual character traits. Therefore, the court was right in its decision that Walter's testimony violated Evidence Rule 404(A)(1).

Justice Whiteside further stated that the profile testimony had to be excluded as it conflicted with Evidence Rule 703, which provides that "the facts or data in the particular case upon which an expert bases an opinion or inference may be those perceived by him or admitted in evidence at the hearing."[26] Justice Whiteside said:

In this case, the witness based his opinions on the crime scene photos, the police reports, and the pathological report. When a direct opinion based solely on the police report was about to be given, the court instructed the jury not to accept or consider the opinion of this witness based on the police report in this case. This instruction is a curative one and we assume the jury followed the instruction. However, to the extent any other opinions of this witness, such as how he determined in which classification these events belonged, were based on the police report, these opinions are inadmissible based upon Evid[ence] R. 703, since the police reports were not admissible into evidence.[27]

It was also held that "since the witness purported to base his opinion on his own 'studies' rather than upon an accepted scientific basis, the opinion testimony is not admissible."[28] In the court's view, the expert testimony was prejudicial to the defendant and that there was a reasonable possibility that the expert testimony contributed to the defendant's conviction. The error in admitting the expert testimony was seen to be substantially harmful. The court of appeals therefore, reversed the trial court's judgment and remanded the case for further proceedings.

Offender profile evidence was also ruled to be impermissible character evidence in *State v. Parkinson*,[29] where sex offender profile testimony by a psychologist and by a former FBI agent was ruled inadmissible. The experts offered opinion that the defendant did not fit the profile of a sex offender. Kelly Parkinson was charged and convicted of sexual abuse of a child under the age of 16. On March 28, 1992, Parkinson's niece, E.F. (13 years) and her brother, B.F. (12 years), visited Parkinson and spent the night at his house. The two children and their cousin slept in one of the bedrooms; E.F. slept in the bed, while her brother and her cousin slept on the floor. It was reported that Parkinson went into the bedroom where the three children were sleeping three times that night and each time he sexually abused E.F. E.F. said that first, she woke up and found Parkinson rubbing her buttocks.[30] About two hours later, Parkinson came back and was "rubbing her breast and pulling at her nightgown."[31] Then Parkinson came back around 6:30 A.M. and again came to the bed and began rubbing E.F's buttocks. E.F said that her brother B.F. was awaken and was stirring at what was happening and Parkinson then left the bedroom. E.F. then started crying and told her brother what happened that night. On March 31, 1992, they told their mother what happened and she called the police.

At the trial, Parkinson called two expert witnesses, Dr. Marcel Chappuis, a psychologist, and Peter M. Welch, a former FBI agent. The defendant sought to introduce the experts to testify that he did not fit the psychological profile of a sex offender, and therefore, would not have committed the crime.

The trial judge denied the motion to introduce the testimony by the two experts. The trial court stated that: 1) the profile evidence was offered to bolster Parkinson's credibility and was thus impermissible because veracity is not a "fact in issue" subject to expert opinion; 2) the evidence at issue would not assist the trier of fact to understand the evidence; and 3) the expert opinion evidence would constitute a direct comment on the guilt or innocence of Parkinson and replace, rather than aid, the jury's function.[32] The trial court also stated that an adequate foundation had not been made for the admission of the testimony.

Parkinson was convicted by the District Court of the Seventh Judicial District, Madison County, Idaho. He appealed. Among many issues, the defendant argued that the trial court erred by excluding Chappuis's and Welch's testimony. In its ruling, the Court of Appeals of Idaho stated that there was no error in the exclusion of the testimony by the two expert witnesses. Delivering the opinion of the court, Justice Karen L. Lansing stated that the trial court did not err by excluding expert testimony on a scientific theory whose foundation had not been adequately established. The court of appeals held there was no showing of the reliability of Chappuis's assessment technique sufficient to meet the standards for admission of the testimony under Rule 702.[33] It should be noted that Chappuis did not explain the personality characteristics that made up the profile; did not state the error rate associated with his methodology; did not state whether the methodology has been tested; and whether the methodology was generally accepted by the psychological community as being sufficiently reliable.[34] On Welch's testimony, Justice Lansing also stated that:

Mr. Welch's proffered testimony suffers from similar defects in foundation. Mr. Welch acknowledged that the F.B.I. sex offender profile, which he utilized, was developed for use by law enforcement officials and that its application was more of an art than science. He did not identify the components of the profile or explain how it was developed, other than noting that its development involved interviews with convicted sex offenders. Mr. Welch did not state whether or how the resulting profile had been tested for accuracy or identify the technique's error rate. Although Mr. Welch testified that the profile is widely used in the law enforcement community, it is not apparent whether that use is primarily for devising profiles of perpetrators of unsolved crimes or for the purpose for which it was offered in the present case—to determine whether an accused identified by the alleged victim did in fact commit the crime. In short, Mr. Welch's testimony did not provide information from which it could reasonably be ascertained that the profile technique was trustworthy, that it was based upon valid scientific principles, or that it could properly be applied in the manner advocated by Parkinson. Therefore, the trial court did not abuse its discretion by excluding Mr. Welch's testimony.[35]

The court of appeals affirmed the trial court's decision.

In *Penson v. State*,[36] offender profiling testimony was also ruled to be impermissible character evidence. Allen Wayne Penson was charged with burglary and two counts of arson for entering and setting fire to the Walker County Rescue Building and to a vehicle. The prosecution stated that a person carrying a sandy-colored bag and fitting the description of the defendant was seen loitering near the building before the fire outbreak. When the police went to search Penson's house, which was about 500 feet from the scene of the arson, they found a sheet of notebook paper (which belonged to one of the members of the rescue building). This member identified the sheet and stated that Penson must have taken it at the time of the arson. A sandy-colored bag was also found at Penson's house and Penson had cuts and bruises on his arm.

At the trial, the state introduced a state fire investigator, Ken Palmer, who testified as an expert on arson. Palmer based his testimony on an FBI serial arsonist profile, titled "Record on Essential Findings of the Study of Serial Arsonists."[37] In his testimony, Palmer stated that serial arsonists have the following characteristics:

1. White males
2. Ages 18–27
3. Loners
4. Educational failures
5. Homosexuals or bisexuals
6. History of criminal activity
7. Medical or mental problems
8. Poor employment records
9. Alcohol and drug abuse
10. Dysfunctional family backgrounds
11. Mainly walkers who set fires within two miles of their home, and
12. Tendency to act on the spur of the moment, mainly for revenge.[38]

The defense raised an objection to this testimony with the defendant arguing that the prejudicial effect of the testimony far outweighed its probative value. The defendant also contended that the testimony should be excluded because he was not charged as a serial arsonist and that the profile was not used during the investigation. The motion to exclude Palmer's testimony was denied. The trial judge however, instructed the state not to apply the profile to the defendant, and also instructed that the expert should not give an opinion that the defendant was a serial arsonist.

Penson called two witnesses. Daphne Young testified that Penson was at her birthday party on the night of the arson. Jeffrey Cameron also testified that Penson was at his house after the party and was there when they heard the fire alarm.

At the Walker Superior Court, Georgia, Penson was convicted of burglary and two counts of arson, which he appealed. The defendant argued that the trial judge erred by admitting the FBI serial arsonist profile. The Court of Appeals of Georgia ruled that the admission of the serial arsonist profile by the trial court was in error. In the opinion delivered by Justice Harold R. Banke, it was held that the profile evidence was impermissible character evidence. Citing the decision in *Sanders v. State*,[39] Justice Banke stated that:

Unless a defendant has placed his character in issue or has raised some defense which the profile is relevant to rebut, the state may not introduce character evidence showing a defendant's personality traits and personal history as its foundation for demonstrating the defendant has the characteristics of a typical arsonist ... In this case, the profile did not rebut Penson's alibi defense that he was attending a birthday party at the time the fire originated or aid the jury in determining whether Penson was at the birthday on the night of the fire. Nor had Penson placed his character in issue.[40]

Justice Banke further stated that the trial judge's instruction to the state not to apply the serial arsonist profile to the defendant was meaningless because of the state's prior and extensive inquiry into the defendant's personal history and personality traits, and the attempts by the state to place the defendant into a serial arsonist profile.[41] Justice Banke therefore ruled that the trial court erred by admitting the serial arsonist profile. The court of appeals reversed the judgment and remanded for a new trial. Justice Banke stated that they were "unable to conclude that it is highly probable that the profile evidence did not contribute to the verdict."[42] One aspect of this case was that the prosecution did not have overwhelming evidence to prove the case beyond a reasonable doubt. Thus, the decision to reverse the trial court's judgment was justified.

Finally, it should be noted that many states have statutes that provide additional guidelines on the use of character evidence in cases involving sexual offenses. For instance, the California Evidence Code provides that:

(a) Except as provided in this section and in sections 1102 and 1103, evidence of a person's character or a trait of his or her character (whether in the form of an opinion, evidence of reputation, or evidence of specific instances of his of her conduct) is inadmissible when offered to prove his or her conduct on a specified occasion.

(b) Nothing in this section prohibits the admission of evidence that a person committed a crime, civil wrong, or other act when relevant to prove some fact (such as motive, opportunity, intent, preparation, plan, knowledge, identity, absence of mistake, or accident, or whether a defendant in a prosecution for an unlawful sexual act or attempted unlawful sexual act did not reasonably and in good faith believe that the victim consented) other than his or her disposition to commit such an act.

(c) Nothing in this section affects the admissibility of evidence offered to support or attack the credibility of a witness.[43]

WHO IS QUALIFIED TO GIVE EXPERT OFFENDER PROFILING TESTIMONY?

As discussed in Chapter 2, offender profiling is a multidisciplinary practice. Profilers come from different backgrounds, different academic areas, and with varying degrees of experience and knowledge. There is general disagreement among scholars as to who is qualified to give offender profiling testimony, however, it is ultimately the judge who decides who is qualified to give evidence. In the United States, the Federal Rule of Evidence 702 provides the guideline for the trial judges. Rule 702 states that:

If scientific, technical, or other specialized knowledge will assist the trier of fact to understand the evidence or to determine a fact in issue, a witness qualified as an expert by knowledge, skill, experience, training, or education, may testify thereto in the form of an opinion or otherwise, if (1) the testimony is based upon sufficient facts or data, (2) the testimony is the product of reliable principles and methods, and (3) the witness has applied the principles and method reliably to the facts of the case.[44]

The problems with this rule have been discussed in the previous chapter. The main problem is that the rule is so loosely defined that almost anyone can qualify as an expert, either by knowledge, skill, experience, training, or education. There is no acceptable professional body for profilers, resulting from an uneasy relationship among those who specialize in profiling. Each group thinks its offender profiling approach is an exclusive discipline, making it difficult to come together as one and move the field forward. Hence, the difficulty with establishing a professional body that will be acceptable by all the different practitioners.

There are two issues to bear in mind when discussing the question of who is qualified to give expert profiling testimony. The first is the fact that offender profiling is a multidisciplinary practice that cuts across many fields and professions. The second is the fact that the Federal Rule of Evidence 702 has created a huge dilemma for trial judges. They have been given the ultimate responsibility to decide who is qualified to give expert testimony; so we need to assist them in making that difficult decision. Allowing an unqualified expert to give testimony will or may result in a reversal, plus other dangers associated with that. Therefore, it is important to get it right from the beginning.

Brunson v. State[45] is one of the cases that highlight the problem with admitting expert testimony by an unqualified expert. This case also highlights the need to assist trial judges in this regard. Furthermore, this case clearly reveals and supports my argument that the Federal Rule of Evidence 702 is too loose and too liberal. In this case, the defendant, Larry Darnell Brunson, was charged with two counts of first-degree murder of his wife, Gloria Brunson, and her lover, Frankie Shaw in 1999. The state presented several witnesses including Gloria's children, law enforcement officers, Gloria's friends, and her co-workers. The state also presented Barbara Ann Neiss, who was qualified by the trial court as an expert on predictability that a batterer would become a murderer. During her testimony, Neiss stated that she was an expert on profiling batterers and could determine when they are likely to turn into murderers. She testified that there are 10 risk factors/ characteristics of these sorts of individuals. Neiss testified that these factors came from the work of Anne O'Dell, a police officer, who studied 70,000 cases and came up with what she called the "10 warning signs" that a domestic-violence offender will become a murderer.[46] O'Dell's article was titled, "Assessing Whether Batterers Will Kill." Neiss used a three-page summary of this article prepared by an attorney, Barbara Hart, and obtained from an Internet source and used it in her testimony.[47] Neiss testified that if more than three of the factors are met, then there is an "incredible duty" to warn a woman of the threat to her safety.[48] According to Neiss, the 10 risk factors are as follows:

1. Threats of homicide against his spouse or children or threats of suicide,
2. Fantasies of homicide or suicide,
3. Depression,
4. Access to weapons,
5. Obsessive behavior about his wife or family,
6. Centrality of the battered woman to the batterer's life,
7. Rage against the battered woman,
8. Drug or alcohol consumption,
9. Abuse of the battered woman's pet animal, and
10. Access to the battered woman.[49]

Neiss gave her qualifications as a bachelor's degree in political science and journalism, a master's degree in public administration, and current courses toward a second master's degree in social work. She also had attended several seminars on domestic violence; had worked for one year with the Arkansas Commission on Child Abuse, Rape and Domestic Violence; had been employed nearly three years as an executive director for Advocates for Battered Women; had volunteered for 10 years with the battered women's shelter; and worked at a mediation center for battered women and their husbands. She also had other work experiences in the domestic violence center and had once testified in a circuit court, and several times in a chancery court in support of protective orders, but not as an expert.[50]

Neiss testified that her analysis showed that the defendant met 8 of these 10 risk factors. The defendant raised an objection to the admission of this testimony, arguing that: 1) Neiss was not qualified to render an opinion that he has the characteristics of batterers who may eventually kill, 2) the testimony embraced the ultimate issue, and 3) the testimony was unduly prejudicial.

In his ruling, Justice Berlin C. Jones, for the Circuit Court, Jefferson County, Arkansas, stated that based on Arkansas Rule of Evidence 702, Neiss was qualified as an expert because she possessed specialized knowledge that would assist the jury.[51] Neiss's testimony was admitted. The defendant was convicted for the murders and sentenced to two terms of life imprisonment.

The case reached the Supreme Court of Arkansas, where the defendant argued that the trial court abused its discretion by qualifying Neiss as an expert, that the testimony placed him within the characteristics of batterers who kill, and therefore it was unduly prejudicial. The defendant also argued that the testimony fell into the ultimate issue. Delivering the opinion of the Supreme Court of Arkansas, Justice Robert L. Brown agreed with the defendant that Neiss was not qualified to render an expert opinion on the predictability that a batterer will become a murderer. Justice Brown said:

The state responds that Ms. Neiss's testimony was helpful to the jury and thus, it qualifies as expert testimony. Yet, in doing so the state only addresses one facet of Rule 702 and never squarely addresses the other facet of whether Ms. Neiss was qualified by knowledge, skill, experience, training, or education to give an opinion that was helpful to the jury. The problem we see with the state's argument is that testimony may be helpful to a jury but still may be properly excluded if that testimony is offered by a person who is not qualified to render the opinion. The trial court, in its ruling, appears to have similarly conflated the issue of a person's qualifications and the "helpfulness of the testimony."[52]

The Arkansas supreme court, citing its prior decision in *Dillion v. State*,[53] reiterated the fact that "while a proffered expert's experience might have been beyond that of persons who had no experience at all in the general area to which he would testify, it was not error to refuse to qualify him as an expert when his knowledge was below the standards of most recognized experts in the subject field."[54] The supreme court also stated that:

We have no doubt that predicting human behavior, and specifically whether a person has a proclivity to murder based on certain risk factors, requires a highly specialized psychological expertise ... Neiss, while a bona fide expert on domestic abuse, exceeded her expertise by profiling batterers who kill and by conveying to the jury that Brunson fell within that profile. A case in point of ... Neiss testifying far beyond her range of expertise was her conclusion that Brunson suffered from depression, one of the ten risk factors ... Neiss did not possess the necessary psychiatric background to render such a diagnosis. The trial court abused its discretion in qualifying her to so testify.[55]

The supreme court further ruled that Neiss's testimony violated Rule 403 of the Arkansas Rules of Evidence because its prejudicial effect far outweighed its probative value, and also fell on the ultimate issue. In reversing the judgment, the Supreme Court of Arkansas concluded that the expert testimony in this case placed the defendant within the category of batterers who would commit murder; and that the testimony was unduly prejudicial and therefore violated Rule 403. Justice Brown stated that the expert testimony indicated to the jury that the defendant committed the crime.

The above case has highlighted the problem that arises when profilers testify beyond their expertise. This is because offender profiling is not well understood by many people including judges. It also is compounded by the fact that many criminal profilers have what has been described as "intimidating credentials."[56] Judges and jurors seem to be seduced by impressive qualifications. The reliability of such testimony is thereby overlooked. Judges therefore, need assistance and further guidelines when deciding to qualify a criminal profiler as an expert.

It has been suggested that a profiler with intimidating credentials should "not be allowed to reveal his 'profiler credentials' to the jury beyond saying that he had worked for many years for the FBI (or other organization) as a specialist in the investigation of sexually driven crimes like rape and sexual homicide, and that in the course of his career, both through research and through involvement in actual cases, he or she had seen the details of many cases."[57] Therefore, such expert witnesses should only testify on the characteristics of the crime ... [that] they believe are rare in typical crimes.[58]

In deciding whether an expert is qualified to give offender profiling testimony, it is submitted that trial judges should first examine closely the purpose for which the expert is being called. From there the judge will have a better idea about whether such an expert is qualified in the area, assuming the testimony is relevant, and will assist the trier of fact. For example, if an expert is needed on crime scene characteristics, or on modus operandi, then a profiler with law enforcement background will be the best qualified person in this area. If expert testimony is needed to show elements of motives and fantasies, especially in sexual offenses, a forensic psychologist or a clinical psychiatrist will be better placed to give testimony in this area. A forensic psychiatrist, forensic psychologist or a criminologist is also better qualified to give expert testimony on victimology. Similarly, a profiler with forensic science background will be better placed to testify in cases where there were physical traces and inferences can be drawn from them. However, as we suggested in chapter two, a profiling team made up of the different segments provides the best alternative. In fact this was the case in the early days when DNA profiling was being introduced into the courtroom. Many experts, including geneticists, microbiologists, statisticians, biologists, all came together, and courts began to accept DNA.

It is submitted that in all cases where offender profiling testimony is involved, the trial judge should give a jury directive. The trial judge should inform the jury about the level of reliability and validity of offender profiling. This will assist them in determining the weight (if any) to be accorded to the testimony.

IS OFFENDER PROFILING TOO PREJUDICIAL?

Offender profiling is a technique based on probability, suspicion, assumption, and stereotypes. Stereotyping in particular creates prejudice. Offender profiling involves creating a list of characteristics or character traits against which an individual is compared to see if he or she fits a particular category. This invariably leads judges and jurors into reaching a certain conclusion.

The prejudicial effect of profile evidence usually outweighs its probative value and creates many social and legal problems. In most cases, this prejudicial effect cannot be minimized, sanitized, or removed. It has been noted that:

This clear potential to generate great prejudice triggers some familiar alarm bells. Jurors could choose to convict a defendant who is a [pedophile] for that reason alone. They may assign a disproportionate weight to the evidence of the pedophilia, or deny the accused the benefit of the doubt and convict on less than the full standard of proof. There is also a very real and even more sinister danger: that the evidence of such traits leads the police to "round up the usual suspects." If the profiler relies on a statistic that, say, pedophiles who murder are usually Caucasian and aged between 45 and 55, there is a risk that the police will only direct their inquiries toward such people, therefore leading to proportionally higher conviction rates of people who fit the bill. This in turn feeds back into and distorts the statistical data from which we began.[59]

Courts are divided on this issue. While many courts have ruled that offender profiling is too prejudicial and therefore inadmissible, many others believe that even if it is prejudicial, that the prejudicial effect does not substantially outweigh its probative value. It is submitted that the prejudicial effect of offender profiling evidence far outweighs its probative value and therefore, should be ruled inadmissible.

In *State v. Roquemore*,[60] offender profiling testimony was ruled to be too prejudicial to the accused. The Court of Appeals of Ohio stated that profile evidence is based on generalities and typical facts, and that these generalities and typical facts tend to place the defendant into a stereotype.[61] It was held that this stereotyping causes the jury to be prejudiced. As a result, the jury could decide the case based on the typical facts rather than on the actual facts.[62]

Similarly, in *Brunson v. State*,[63] the Supreme Court of Arkansas ruled that the trial court's decision allowing profiling testimony improperly mandated a legal conclusion and was prejudicial error.[64] The Supreme Court of Arkansas further stated that even if profile testimony may be relevant to the facts at issue, it may still be unfair to an accused if its prejudicial effect substantially outweighs its probative value.[65]

In *People v. Robbie*,[66] the Court of Appeals, First District, Division 3, California, also held that rapist profile testimony resulted in unfair prejudice. Walter Vincent Robbie was charged with and convicted by the Superior Court, Contra Costa County, California, of kidnapping Jane Doe, for sexual purposes, oral copulation, and penetration with a foreign object.[67]

At the trial, the defendant called several witnesses who testified that he is an honest and nonviolent man. The defendant also called Jane's ex-boyfriend and Jane's three classmates who testified that Jane was untruthful. Two other witnesses also testified that Jane used drugs. On the other hand, the prosecution called Sharon Pagaling, a special agent with the violent crime profiling unit of the California Department of Justice, to testify that the defendant's conduct was consistent with a certain type of rapist (the type alleged in this case). The defense raised an objection to the admission of this testimony. The defense argued that the testimony must be restricted to general misconceptions about sex offenders and that Pagaling should not be allowed to express her opinion on whether the defendant committed the crimes.[68] Pagaling informed the court that her testimony was "to disabuse the jury of common misconceptions about conduct of a rapist."[69]

The trial judge ruled that the testimony was admissible. It is noteworthy to point out that during her testimony, Pagaling acknowledged the fact that the behaviors and conduct she described as typical of rape cases, may also be found in nonrape cases. Robbie was convicted and sentenced to an indeterminate term of 15 years to life and he appealed.

The court of appeals held that Pagaling's testimony was profile evidence and that profile evidence is generally inadmissible to prove guilt. Justice Carol Corrigan, in the opinion, stated that:

As these cases indicate, profile evidence is inherently prejudicial because it requires the jury to accept an erroneous starting point in its consideration of the evidence. We illustrate the problem by examining the syllogism underlying profile evidence: Criminals act in a certain way; the defendant acted that way; therefore, the defendant is a criminal. Guilt flows ineluctably from the major premise through the minor one to the conclusion. The problem is the major premise is faulty. It implies that criminals, and only criminals, act in a given way. In fact, certain behavior may be consistent with both innocent and illegal behavior, as the People's expert conceded here.

This flawed syllogism lay at the heart of Pagaling's testimony. She was asked hypothetical questions assuming certain behavior that had been attributed to the defendant and was allowed to opine that it was the most prevalent kind of sex offender conduct. The jury was invited to conclude that if defendant engaged in the conduct described, he was indeed a sex offender.[70]

The court of appeals ruled that the trial court erred by admitting the expert testimony. The profile evidence was also ruled to be inadmissible. It was held that the erroneous admission of this testimony was not harmless. Therefore, the court of appeals reversed the judgment of conviction and remanded for a new trial. In reversing the judgment, the court of appeals concluded that there was a reasonable probability that the jury would have reached a decision more favorable to the defendant had the trial court excluded the highly prejudicial expert testimony.

In the above cases, profile evidence was ruled inadmissible because of its unfair prejudice. In several cases, however, some courts have admitted such evidence even though it was clear that the prejudicial effect far outweighed the probative value. For instance, in *United States v. Webb*,[71] expert testimony on *modus operandi* was admitted and ruled not prejudicial. The United States District Court for the Central District of California convicted Marty Webb of possession of ammunition by a felon. Following an informant's tip-off, Los Angeles law enforcement officers on October 17, 1995 arrested the defendant. When the officers searched the defendant's car, they found a loaded gun wrapped in a shirt and concealed in the car's engine compartment. Webb claimed that he did not know that the gun was there.

The state presented a police expert at the trial, who testified on *modus operandi* regarding the reasons why people typically hide guns in the engine compartment of cars.[72] The expert testified that people typically conceal guns in the engine compartment of a car so that they have ready access to them, so that police cannot easily find them, and also to disclaim knowledge of the gun when the police find it. The defendant objected to this testimony, arguing that it was improper and unduly prejudicial and was also inadmissible based on Evidence Rule 704(b), which prohibits an expert's opinion on the ultimate issue. The trial judge permitted the testimony and stated that the police expert witness used the word "people" instead of the word "criminals," hence it was not prejudicial. Furthermore, the trial judge ruled that the expert did not give an opinion on whether the defendant knew that a gun was in his car. Therefore, he ruled that the testimony was admissible. Webb was convicted and later appealed.

At the United States Court of Appeals, Ninth Circuit, Webb contended that the trial court erred by admitting the expert testimony. The defendant also argued that the testimony ought to have been excluded because it was similar to drug courier profile evidence and also was an opinion on the ultimate issue. The defendant further argued that the trial court ought to have applied the *Daubert* criteria, which would have ruled that the testimony was inadmissible because it was unreliable.

The court of appeals, through Justice Stephen Trott, ruled that the testimony on *modus operandi* was relevant to the facts of the case; was probative of the defendant's knowledge that the gun was in the engine compartment of the car; and provided information that was beyond the common knowledge and experience of the jury.[73] Justice Trott further stated that:

In addition, the trial court and the government took steps to mitigate the testimony's potential prejudicial effect. The government focused its questions on the practices of "persons" rather than criminals or gang members. Moreover, even if the jury drew the adverse inference that Webb was a criminal, that inference would not prejudice him because the jury already knew that Webb was a criminal: Webb had stipulated that he had been convicted of three prior felonies. In light of the above, the district court properly determined that the testimony's prejudicial effect did not substantially outweigh its probative value.[74]

On the defendant's contention that the testimony was similar to drug courier profile evidence, the court of appeals ruled that "none of the expert testimony in this case was admitted to demonstrate that Webb was guilty because he fit the characteristics of a certain drug-courier profile. Instead, the expert testimony was properly admitted to assist the jury in understanding the reasons why a person would conceal a weapon in the engine compartment of a car."[75] Justice Trott also stated that the testimony did not violate Evidence Rule 704(b) which prohibits expert opinion on the ultimate issue.

The court of appeals further ruled that the district court did not abuse its discretion in not applying the *Daubert* criteria in this case. It was held that *Daubert* did not apply in this case because the expert testimony was not scientific. In the court's view, the expert testimony was specialized knowledge of law enforcement.

The court of appeals concluded that the trial court did not abuse its discretion by admitting the testimony on *modus operandi* and therefore, affirmed the judgment of conviction. It should be noted that this case took place before the United States Supreme Court decision in *Kumho Tire Co.* in 1999, where it was held that the *Daubert* criteria applied to all forms of expert testimony.

In *Simmons v. State*,[76] offender profile testimony by a crime scene analyst was also ruled not prejudicial. In this case, Clarence Leland Simmons was convicted of intentional murder and capital murder by the Circuit Court, Jefferson County, Alabama. On January 3, 1996, the nude body of a 65-year-old woman (M.A.) was discovered by a security guard at Highland Manor Apartments in Alabama. The security guard, Alma Underwood, was instructed by the victim's daughter to check on her because she had not heard from her and was worried. When the police arrived, they discovered that M.A. had been stabbed to death and disemboweled.[77] Police investigation revealed that the last person seen with the victim was the defendant and he was arrested for the murder.

A piece of human tissue found on Simmon's pants was analyzed and the DNA from the tissue matched M.A.'s blood sample.[78] Several items were also collected from the defendant's home. The autopsy was carried out by Dr. Robert Brissie.

According to Dr. Brissie, M.A's body had been cut by the offender from the upper part of the abdomen, down the front of the abdomen, down across the pubic bone, with several extensive slicing wounds between the legs, then upward on the back of M.A's buttocks, to the back. Additionally, M.A. had been stabbed 73 times; these stab wounds were approximately an inch and half in depth and had marks indicating that the knife used to stab M.A. had a hilt. He testified that six of these incised wounds extended across the front of M.A's neck. Many of these wounds had been inflicted before M.A. died and, according to Dr. Brissie, were probably intimidation wounds and not fatal. Twenty-three of these wounds were concentrated in the chest area, at least five of these wounds did not penetrate the chest cavity and Dr. Brissie opined that some of these wounds were inflicted while M.A. was alive.[79]

Brissie also testified that most of the victim's internal organs were removed, including her intestines; her spleen and liver were cut and her left lung was split into two.

At the trial, the state called several witnesses. First, Jack Neely testified that he met the defendant and the victim the day before her murder at the South Place Pool Hall, where he had an argument with the defendant during which the defendant threatened to cut him into pieces. Loretta Chambers, a bartender at the pool hall, also testified that she witnessed the confrontation and that Simmons was with the victim on that day (January 2, 1996). Betty

Harper also testified that she saw Simmons and M.A. getting into the elevator at M.A's apartment on January 2, 1996. Jerry Trousdale and Alma Underwood, who were the maintenance person and security guard at the apartment building respectively, also testified that they saw Simmons enter the apartment with M.A. the day before her murder and that Simmons was the last person seen with M.A.

In order to bolster their claim that the defendant should be convicted of capital offense of murder committed during sexual assault, the prosecution decided to call FBI agent Thomas Neer, who testified that the crime scene analysis showed that the murder was sexually motivated. Neer was qualified by the trial court as an expert on crime scene analysis and victimology. Neer testified that his analysis of the crime scene and the autopsy report showed that the murder was sexually motivated and so the offender received sexual gratification from the acts.[80] The defendant raised an objection to the admission of this testimony but it was denied.

Simmons was convicted of intentional murder and capital murder and sentenced to death by electrocution. He appealed. Among other claims, the defendant argued that the admission of Neer's testimony by the trial court was error. The defendant also argued that Neer's expert evidence was novel scientific evidence and therefore, failed to meet *Frye* criteria, which required such testimony to have gained general acceptance in the relevant scientific community. The defendant also contended that the testimony was unduly prejudicial and violated the ultimate issue rule. In its ruling, the Court of Appeals of Alabama disagreed with the appellant. Delivering the opinion, Justice James Fry said:

We reject Simmon's argument that Neer's testimony was based on novel scientific evidence. Crime scene analysis and victimology do not rest on scientific principles like those contemplated in *Frye*; these fields constitute specialized knowledge. Specialized knowledge offers subjective observations and comparisons based on the expert's training, skill, or experience that may be helpful to the jury in understanding or determining the facts. Crime scene analysis, which involves the gathering and analysis of physical evidence, is generally recognized as a body of specialized knowledge ... Therefore, because crime scene analysis is not scientific evidence, we conclude that we are not bound by the test enunciated by *Frye*.[81]

Justice Fry further stated that Alabama Rule of Evidence 702 was the proper standard for admitting Neer's testimony. Neer testified that crime scene analysis and victimology are specialized fields of knowledge developed in the 1970s; that research in the field is published and peer reviewed, and that many law enforcement agencies use crime scene analysis and victimology in crime investigations. In its ruling, the court of appeals stated that adequate evidence has been presented to them which indicated that crime scene analysis and victimology are reliable fields of specialized knowledge. The court of appeals cited the case of *United States v. deSoto*,[82] where it was held that "a homicide and its crime scene, after all, are not matters likely to be within the knowledge of an average trier of fact."[83]

In a nutshell, the court of appeals ruled that the expert testimony assisted the jury and so its admission by the trial court was not error. The court also ruled that the testimony was more probative than prejudicial, and did not violate the ultimate rule issue. The court of appeals stated that "Neer frankly conceded the limitations of his testimony. He unequivocally testified that he was not saying that Simmons committed the murder; only that in his opinion the physical evidence from the crime scene and from M.A.'s body indicated that the offense itself was sexually motivated. Neer did not reach a 'diagnosis' of sexual abuse and certainly did not identify the offender; thus, we do not perceive Neer's testimony as testimony on the ultimate issue."[84]

Justice Fry concluded that even if the admission of the expert testimony was error, it would still be ruled as harmless error. The court of appeals affirmed the death sentence on the capital murder charge, but remanded with directions regarding the sentence for count 111. The conviction and sentence on count 11 was reversed.[85]

This case clearly demonstrates my argument that the outcome of any trial involving offender profiling testimony is determined to a great extent by the admissibility standard applied by the trial court. In this case, the court of appeals stated that Rule 702, Alabama Rule of Evidence, was the appropriate standard and applied it in this case. On the other hand, the appellant contended that the *Frye* test standard, which presumably would have excluded the testimony, was the proper standard that ought to have been applied. In this case, the reliability of the testimony seems to have been loosely interpreted by both the trial court and the court of appeals. The courts placed more emphasis on relevance and assistance to the trier of fact, without much inquiry into whether the basis of such testimony was generally accepted by the relevant community. The trial court particularly believed that crime scene analysis and victimology were reliable because "numerous law enforcement agencies relied upon crime scene analysis and victimology when conducting their investigations."[86] This is a dangerous basis to gauge the reliability of any technique. The trial court simply took the expert's words *ipse dixit* and seemed to have been seduced by Neer's impressive qualifications. The usefulness of a technique in assisting in crime investigation should not be taken as an indication that the technique will be sufficiently reliable as to be admissible in the courtroom.

State v. Sorabella[87] stands in contrast to the above case. In *Sorabella*, the court recognized the fact that profile evidence is prejudicial, but believed that the prejudicial effect could be minimized by limiting the scope of the testimony. In January 2000, the police department in New Britain, Connecticut decided to launch an undercover operation in an attempt to stop the increased violations of the state's laws regarding child pornography via the Internet. James Wardwell was one of the detectives assigned to the operation and on January 4, 2000, he logged onto an America Online (AOL) chat room posing as a 13-year-old girl, under the screen name "Danutta333.[88] He received an instant message from a man with a screen name "JoSkotr."[89] They started to exchange instant messages during which "JoeSkotr" asked the 13-year-old girl to meet with him for sexual relations, telling the girl how she should dress and what he wanted her to do to him and vice versa. He told the girl that he lived in Massachusetts but would come to Connecticut to meet her at a donut shop. "JoeSkotr" sent pornographic materials to the girl within this time. On March 8, 2000, they agreed to meet at a donut shop, but "JoeSkotr" went to the wrong shop. He arranged another meeting on March 14, 2000 at a shopping mall. On arrival at the mall, he was arrested by the police.

"JoeSkotr" was identified as John Sorabella, and he was charged with: 1) two counts of attempt to commit sexual assault in the second degree, 2) two counts of attempt to commit risk of injury to a child by sexual contact, 3) three counts of attempt to commit risk of injury to a child, 4) one count of attempt to entice a minor to engage in sexual activity, 5) one count of importing child pornography, and 6) one count of obscenity.[90]

At the trial, the state called Kenneth Lanning, a former FBI agent, who testified that the defendant possessed the psychological and behavioral characteristics of child sex offenders. In his testimony, Lanning stated that Sorabella falls under the category of sex offenders called "preferential offenders." Lanning testified about what he deemed the "customs and habits" of preferential sex offenders and situational sex offenders.[91]

According to Lanning, situational sex offenders take advantage of opportunistic situations to engage in sex offenses and are typically thought-driven, undertaking action without consideration of getting caught. Lanning testified further that preferential sex offenders are individuals who have specific sexual preferences for certain activities or victims and whose behavior is normally need-driven or fantasy-driven. Preferential sex offenders typically collect pornography, erotica, and mementos relating to their sexual interest or preference and spend a great deal of time and money in fulfilling their sexual needs or fantasies. With respect to preferential sex offenders with an interest in children, they may use child pornography to rationalize abhorrent behavior, fuel and reinforce their sexual arousal, or lower a potential victim's inhibitions by conveying the message that other children are doing it. Preferential sex offenders typically will engage in a prolonged and elaborate grooming or seduction process that is designed to exploit and manipulate vulnerable children. Preferential sex offenders may lessen the grooming time by targeting a child who is sexually experienced.[92]

The defendant filed a motion to exclude the testimony, but it was denied. The defense counsel argued that the state failed to demonstrate the admissibility of the testimony as required in the decision in *State v. Porter*,[93] when scientific evidence is being presented. The defense also argued that the testimony should not be admitted because of its prejudicial effect. Denying the motion, the trial court stated that Lanning's testimony was not scientific, and so the *Porter* rule did not apply. The court, however, instructed the expert to limit his testimony only to "customs and habits" of preferential sex offenders and that he should not state his opinion on the defendant's state of mind or whether he fits the characteristics of preferential sex offenders.

The trial court admitted the testimony and stated that its probative value outweighed its prejudicial effect. The trial court also stated that the testimony was relevant to "the defendant's intent in engaging in the behavior, his belief as to the age of Danuta333, and [to] whether his conduct was corroborative of his purpose as at least the start of a line of conduct leading naturally to the crime."[94]

The jury convicted the defendant on all counts and he was sentenced to 10 years imprisonment, with execution suspended after 5 years, and 15 years' probation.[95] The defendant appealed and the case reached the Supreme Court of Connecticut. Among other issues, the defendant argued that the trial court abused its discretion by not subjecting Agent Lanning's testimony to a *Porter* hearing. The defendant also argued that the prejudicial effect of the testimony far outweighed its probative value.

The Supreme Court of Connecticut affirmed the lower court's judgment and stated that the expert testimony was not scientific. Therefore, a *Porter* hearing was not required. The Supreme Court concluded that: 1) the testimony was relevant to the facts of the case, 2) the expert testimony assisted the jury, 3) the trial court properly limited the scope of the expert testimony to only the customs and habits of preferential sex offenders, and 4) the trial court properly gave instruction to the expert witness not to express his opinion on whether or not the defendant fits the profile of preferential sex offenders.[96] The Supreme Court of Connecticut therefore, affirmed the judgment of conviction and stated that the prejudicial effect of the expert testimony did not outweigh its probative value.

IS OFFENDER PROFILING AN OPINION ON THE ULTIMATE ISSUE?

First, what is ultimate issue rule? The "ultimate issue rule" is a rule that prohibits experts, be they laypersons or professionals, from giving an opinion on an issue of law or fact which is for the court to decide. "Ultimate

issues in criminal trials may be defined as the ultimate, sometimes called
material, facts, which must be proved by the prosecution beyond reasonable
doubt before a defendant can be found guilty of a particular offense and
those facts, if any, which must be proved by the defendant in order to avoid
guilt for that offense."[97] All witnesses are barred from testifying on the ultimate issue to be decided by the court, which is the issue of guilt or innocence. Testifying on the ultimate issue is seen as usurping the function of
the trier of fact, an invasion of the province of the jury.

The ultimate issue rule has been criticized for being "unduly restrictive;
[it] is pregnant with close questions of application, and often unfairly
obstructs the party's presentation of his case."[98] The phrase "usurping the
function of the jury" has been described as "a mere bit of empty rhetoric;"
that the witness is not trying to usurp the function of the jury by mere
expression of opinion and that jurors are not obligated to accept an expert's
opinion.[99] The ultimate issue rule "often made it unreasonably difficult for
advocates to present their cases, forcing the witnesses into verbal contor-
tions to avoid the disfavored magic phrasing."[100] The objection of undue
influence makes no allowance for cases in which the tribunal of facts is a
professional judge rather than a jury, overlooks the frequency of conflicts in
expert testimony, and is largely incompatible with the very justification for
admitting expert evidence, that the drawing of inferences from the facts in
question calls for an expertise [that] the tribunal of facts does not possess.[101]

Because of these criticisms, many jurisdictions have abolished the ultimate issue rule. Some jurisdictions added certain exceptions to the rule. In
United States, the Federal Rule of Evidence 704 provides the guideline on
the ultimate issue:

(a) Except as provided in subdivision (b), testimony in the form of an opinion or inference otherwise admissible is not objectionable because it embraces an ultimate
issue to be decided by the trier of fact.

(b) No expert witness testifying with respect to the mental state or condition of a
defendant in a criminal case may state an opinion or inference as to whether the defendant did or did not have the mental state or condition constituting an element of
the crime charged or of a defense thereto. Such ultimate issues are matters for the
trier of fact alone.[102]

Courts have been inconsistent with their decisions on the ultimate issue
when it comes to offender profiling evidence. In some cases, offender profile evidence has been ruled inadmissible based on the ultimate issue, while
in others, it has been seen as not an opinion on the ultimate issue.

In *State v. Armstrong*,[103] the Court of Appeals of Louisiana, Fourth Circuit, ruled that expert testimony regarding the "psychological dynamics" of
the defendant was "inadmissible expression of opinion as to defendant's

innocence."[104] Craigory A. Armstrong was charged with aggravated rape of his eight-year-old cousin. On the day of the rape, the girl was sleeping in her mother's house when the defendant raped her. The defendant also lived there. The victim told her 12-year-old sister about the rape but they did not tell their mother. It was reported that two days later, the girl complained of stomach cramps and was taken to Dr. Gregory Molden's clinic. The medical tests showed that the girl had gonorrhea. Molden then contacted the child protection bureau of the New Orleans police department. Interviews with the victim and her sister revealed the rape and Armstrong was arrested.

During police interrogation, Armstrong admitted having sexual intercourse with the eight-year-old girl, but claimed that the girl initiated it.[105] He also claimed that he once had gonorrhea, but thought that it had been cured. At trial, he called three witnesses who attested to his credibility. He also called a clinical psychologist who testified that his "psychological dynamics would not support the view of him being a child sexual perpetrator."[106]

The prosecution objected to the admission of this testimony. In its ruling, the Criminal District Court, Parish of Orleans, excluded the testimony. Justice George V. Perez stated that the testimony would have been an opinion on the defendant's innocence, which is for the trier of fact to decide. The petit jury convicted Armstrong of forcible rape and he was sentenced to 25 years at hard labor.[107] He appealed his conviction and contended that: 1) the trial court erred by excluding the clinical psychologist's testimony that showed he did not have the "psychological dynamics" of child sex offenders, and 2) the trial court also erred by making his confession known to the jury.

The Court of Appeals of Louisiana, Fourth Circuit, ruled that the exclusion of expert testimony by the clinical psychologist was not error. The court of appeals stated that under the Louisiana Code of Evidence Art. 704, regarding opinion on ultimate issue, "an expert shall not express an opinion as to the guilt or innocence of the accused."[108] The court of appeals affirmed the trial court's judgment and sentence.

Other cases where profile testimony was ruled inadmissible based on the ultimate issue include *State v. Haynes*,[109] where it was held that:

The testimony as to timing and panic embraced the ultimate issue of intent to be decided by the jury. Under Evid[ence] R[ule] 704, "opinion testimony on an ultimate issue is admissible if it assists the trier of the fact, otherwise it is not admissible. The competency of the trier of the fact to resolve the factual issue determines whether or not the opinion testimony is of assistance." For this reason, an ultimate issue opinion by an expert should be excluded in extreme cases where that opinion is inherently misleading or unduly prejudicial.[110]

Similarly, in *State v. Parkinson*,[111] the Court of Appeals of Idaho ruled that the admission of expert testimony on sex offender profiles was an opinion on the ultimate issue. The court of appeals upheld a trial court's ruling that the admission of expert opinion evidence on sex offender profiles is a direct comment on the guilt or innocence of the defendant and so would replace the function of the jury rather than assist the jury.[112]

The Supreme Court of Arkansas in *Brunson v. State*[113] also ruled that expert testimony on the predictability of batterers who would become murderers was an opinion on the ultimate issue. In this case, the Supreme Court of Arkansas held that the "profile testimony both mandated a conclusion and was unduly prejudicial."[114]

It should be noted however, that in *United States v. Webb*,[115] the United States Court of Appeals, Ninth Circuit, ruled that expert testimony on *modus operandi*, regarding the reasons why people conceal weapons in the engine compartment of cars, was not an opinion on the ultimate issue. In this case, the United States Court of Appeals stated that:

The expert in this case described a typical situation, and never offered any opinion about whether Webb knew the weapon was hidden in his car. The expert testified about a typical way people conceal weapons in cars and the typical reasons for their concealment. In fact, on cross-examination, the expert admitted that he had no information that Webb knew the weapon was in the engine compartment. Under these circumstances, it was left to the jury to determine whether Webb knew the gun was hidden in the car. Thus, the expert did not give an impermissible opinion under Rule 704(b).[116]

In *Simmons v. State*,[117] expert testimony by an FBI agent that the crime scene characteristics indicated that the murder was sexually motivated and so the offender received sexual gratification from the acts was ruled not a violation of the ultimate issue rule. The court said: "In this case, Neer frankly conceded the limitations of his testimony. He unequivocally testified that he was not saying that Simmons committed the murder, only that in his opinion the physical evidence from the crime scene and from M.A.'s body indicated that the offense itself was sexually motivated. Neer did not reach a "diagnosis" of sexual abuse and certainly did not identify the offender; thus we do not perceive Neer's testimony as testimony on the ultimate issue."[118]

In the final analysis, it does appear that ultimate issue is in-built in all forms of offender profile evidence. By that we mean that no matter how or in which form an offender profile is being presented, there is the overlapping tendency to touch on the ultimate issue. Offender profile testimony and its derivatives are generally geared towards one thing—pointing to the accused's guilt or innocence. In effect, profile evidence is a "leading" evidence: It leads to a certain conclusion. With appropriate jury instruction by the trial judge, however, this problem can at least be minimized. The trial judge should in all cases limit the scope of the testimony and remind the

witnesses of their role to testify and not to decide the case. We are in support of the ultimate issue rule, at least in cases involving offender profiling,
as without it witnesses will go beyond their function to assist with their testimony, and extend their role into that of final arbiters. The result will then
be a trial by witnesses rather than trial by judges and jurors.

IS OFFENDER PROFILING SUFFICIENTLY RELIABLE AS TO BE ADMISSIBLE?

Offender profiling is not sufficiently reliable as to be admissible. Offender
profiling involves gathering information from various sources—from the
crime scene, witnesses, victim statements, autopsy reports, the offender's
physical characteristics, age, race, criminal records, and so on. The question
then is: How reliable is information gathered in this manner/from these
sources? Should it be tendered in court as an indication or proof of guilt or
innocence? Offender profiling does not point to specific offenders. It cannot
determine that a given defendant committed a specific act. Offender profiling only predicts; it suggests, but it cannot prove. We should also bear in
mind the problem posed by crime scene "staging," which could lead to
profiling being based on inaccurate crime scene analysis. Fundamentally,
offender profiling is very useful in narrowing down the suspects during
crime investigation, but it has not reached the level of reliability necessary
for courtroom use. The *modus operandi* of offenders may assist judges and
jurors in understanding the behavioral patterns in some cases, but that alone
is not a sufficient basis to warrant its admission in court, nor is that an
adequate proof that the technique is reliable.

Many scholars agree that offender profiling is not a reliable technique
because its foundation or scientific basis cannot be firmly ascertained. Godwin maintained that, "Nine out of ten profiles are vapid. They play at blind
man's bluff, groping in all directions in the hope of touching a sleeve. Occasionally they do, but not firmly enough to seize it, for the behaviorists producing them must necessarily deal in generalities and types. But policemen
can't arrest a type. They require hard data: names, dates, none of which the
psychiatrists [or others involved in creating profile evidence] can offer."[119]

Alison et al. noted that there is no evidence that the technique is an accurate or reliable method of identification.[120] Risinger and Loop also maintained that even though offender profiling may be a valuable technique of
crime investigation, existing data do not show that the process is sufficiently
reliable as to be used in the courtroom as evidence.[121]

In a similar vein, it has been argued that the process of psychological
profiling is conducted in an inconsistent manner, by different groups of
people with varying degrees of training and experience, and that there is no

proper system for monitoring and reviewing the practice.[122] Snook et al. carried out a narrative review of 130 articles on criminal profiling and meta-analytic reviews and concluded that criminal profiling "appears at this juncture to be an extraneous and redundant technique for use in criminal investigations."[123]

As stated in Chapter 3, the rules guiding the admissibility of expert testimony in the United States emphasize the reliability of any expert evidence. Yet, in many cases involving offender profiling the reliability of the technique was not questioned, as in *State v. Pennell*.[124] Some courts agree, however, that offender profiling is unreliable and have ruled it inadmissible.

In *State v. Cavallo*[125] for instance, the Supreme Court of New Jersey stated that the technique is not generally accepted as being reliable. In this case, two defendants, Michael Cavallo and David R. Murro were convicted of rape, abduction, and private lewdness. On June 16, 1977 the two defendants met the victim (S.T.) at the Pittstown bar in Hunterdon, New Jersey. The victim, who was two months pregnant at the time of the alleged rape, claimed that the defendants abducted her from the bar and took her to an empty field where they raped her. The defendants on the other hand, claimed that they had a consensual sexual encounter with S.T. The two sides gave conflicting versions of events that took place that night.

At the trial, Cavallo sought to introduce testimony from a psychiatrist, Dr. Kuris which would show that he did not have the psychological traits of a rapist. Based on many years experience as a psychiatrist, Kuris stated that that the defendant did not possess the characteristics of rapists. Kuris stated that Cavallo was not a violent or aggressive person, knew the difference between right and wrong, and knew that sexual attacks are wrongful acts. He also stated that rapists are aggressive and violent and that Cavallo did not possess these characteristics.

The prosecution argued that the testimony should be excluded because it was irrelevant and not reliable. The prosecution contended that the expert character evidence was irrelevant "since, regardless of whether Cavallo has the characteristics of a 'rapist,' he may indeed have committed rape on this particular occasion."[126] The Hunterdon County Superior Court ruled that the testimony was inadmissible. The defendants were convicted. Cavallo was sentenced to 3 to 5 years for abduction, 1 to 2 years for lewdness and 10 to 20 years for rape. Murro was sentenced to 3 to 7 years for abduction, 2 to 3 years for lewdness and 12 to 20 years for rape. Their request for a new trial was denied. The case went to the Superior Court, Appellate Division.

The appellate division agreed with the trial court's decision to exclude the expert testimony. It was held that the expert character testimony was inadmissible under Rule 47, which governs the admissibility of character evidence. The appellate division stated that "the rule could not contemplate testimony of the kind proffered in this case,"[127] and that the admission of such testimony "could divert the attention of the jury from factual guilt or innocence to the defendant's propensities."[128] The appellate division affirmed the convictions but remanded the case for resentencing, as the court deemed the sentences excessive. The defendants each later received 10 to 15 years for rape and lesser sentences on the abduction and private lewdness charges.

The case reached the Supreme Court of New Jersey where the defendants argued that the exclusion of the expert character evidence was error. In its ruling, the Supreme Court of New Jersey stated that Kuris'evidence was not generally accepted as being reliable. Delivering the judgment, Justice Morris Pashman stated that the defendants "failed to persuade us that the proffered evidence has been accepted as reliable by other jurisdictions or for other purposes in the New Jersey legal system. Defendants therefore have not met their burden under Rule 56 of showing that Dr. Kuris' testimony is based on reasonably reliable scientific premises."[129] In a footnote, the supreme court noted that assuming such psychiatric testimony was generally admissible, there would still be doubts as to whether only two meetings between the defendant and Kuris was sufficient to establish proper foundation that would support Kuris's conclusions about Cavallo's psychological traits and propensities.[130]

The Supreme Court of New Jersey affirmed the appellate division's judgment and concluded that the "defendants have not met their burden of showing that the scientific community generally accepts the existence of identifiable character traits common to rapists. They also have not demonstrated that psychiatrists possess any special ability to discern whether an individual is likely to be a rapist. Until the scientific reliability of this type of evidence is established, it is not admissible."[131]

In *State v. Lowe*,[132] expert testimony on an offender's behavioral motivations was also ruled inadmissible. The defendant, Terry Lowe, was charged with two counts of aggravated murder of Phyllis Mullet and Murray Griffin. On July 5, 1986, Phyllis Mullet was at her home in Belle Center, Ohio, when she was stabbed to death, multiple times, with her throat cut.[133] Murray Griffin, a Belle Center marshall was at the scene, attending to the victim, when the perpetrator shot him. He also died at the scene. When the trial began, the state filed a notice of intention to call FBI agents who would testify on crime scene characteristics, which would assist in the identification of Lowe as the person who committed the murders. The state informed the court that the FBI agents would testify regarding the psychological profile of the offender and that FBI Agent John Douglas would testify on criminal investigative analysis, death threat analysis, and on the offender's motivation for Mullet's murder as well as the motivation behind a certain document that Lowe had written. It was reported that this document contained a list of women and the names of their immediate family members, and also contained sexual language. Mullet's name was on the list.[134]

In his testimony, Douglas stated that based on his review of the crime scene photographs, autopsy reports, police reports, and the document written by Lowe, he was of the opinion that Phyllis Mullet's murder was sexually motivated. He testified that his opinion was based on "the fact Mullet's hands and feet were bound with ligatures that had been brought to the scene by the perpetrator of the crime," the "presence of the ligatures indicated preplanning on the part of the perpetrator," and that preplanning is one of the characteristics of sexually motivated murders.[135] Douglas further stated that the document Lowe had written was sexually motivated and represented the perpetrator's plan or mission for power.[136] It should be pointed out that during cross-examination, Douglas acknowledged that his testimony on the motivations could not be "stated to a reasonable scientific certainty."[137]

The defendant presented Dr. Solomon Fulero, a psychologist, to rebut Douglas's testimony. In his testimony, Fulero also acknowledged the fact that "opinions based on criminal investigative analysis do not rise to the level of reasonable scientific certainty that is a prerequisite to consideration as expert opinion testimony."[138]

In its ruling, the trial court granted the defendant's motion to suppress Douglas's testimony. The state appealed, after certification of its inability to proceed to trial without the suppressed testimony. The state argued that the trial court erred in granting the motion to suppress the testimony.

The Court of Appeals of Ohio, Third District, reiterated the fact that a trial judge has the discretion to decide whether any evidence is relevant and will assist the trier of fact to understand the case or to determine a fact in issue. The court of appeals said:

In this case before us, the trial court suppressed the testimony of Douglas upon finding, *inter alia,* that "Mr. Douglas's opinion is an investigative tool like a polygraph; it might be used to investigate, but it does not have the reliability to be evidence." Having given careful consideration to the testimony elicited in this matter, we conclude that there is evidence in the record to support the trial court's finding that the opinion testimony of Douglas is not reliable evidence. As a whole, the record reflects that Douglas's opinion for the most part is based on the behavioral science of clinical psychology, an area in which he has no formal education, training, or license. In short, the purported scientific analytical processes to which Douglas testified are based on intuitiveness honed by his considerable experience in the field of homicide investigation. While we in no way trivialize the importance of Douglas's work in the field of crime detection and criminal apprehension, we do not find that there was sufficient evidence of reliability adduced to demonstrate the relevancy of the testimony or to qualify Douglas as an expert witness. Accordingly, the error as assigned by the state is overruled.[139]

The court of appeals therefore, affirmed the trial court's decision to suppress Douglas's testimony.

Similarly, in *State v. Stevens*,[140] the Supreme Court of Tennessee affirmed a trial court's decision to exclude expert testimony on crime scene analysis. In excluding the testimony, the trial court stated it was not "convinced that this type of analysis has been subject to adequate objective testing, or that it is based upon longstanding, reliable, scientific principles."[141] In *Stevens*, the defendant William Richard Stevens was charged with two counts of first-degree premeditated murder of his wife, Sandi Stevens and his mother-in-law Myrtle Wilson. He was also charged with one count of aggravated robbery. On December 22, 1997 the defendant called the police, who upon arrival at his mobile home in Nashville, Tennessee, found the defendant, his friend Corey Milliken, and the bodies of the victims. It was reported that Sandi Stevens's nude body was "left in a 'displayed' position, that is, lying on her back with her legs spread apart."[142] Pornographic magazines and Sandi Stevens's own nude photographs were also found around her body. Wilson's nightgown was pulled above her waist. The police found no sign of a forced entry into the apartment. The police suspected that the house showed signs of "staging" and so Stevens and Milliken were the immediate suspects. While the police were questioning Milliken, they noticed blood stains on his shirt and under his nails and gouge marks on his wrist and cheek.[143] Milliken confessed that Stevens had hired him to kill his wife and make it look like a robbery. The medical examination revealed that Sandi Stevens died as a result of ligature strangulation and that she also had a tear in her vagina. The medical examination showed that Wilson died as a result of stab wounds and manual strangulation.

At the trial, the state presented several witnesses, including Shawn Austin Milliken, Corey Milliken's younger brother, who testified that in 1997 Stevens offered him and his brother $2,500 each to kill his wife. He testified that he later decided not to go on with the plan and so Corey accepted $5,000 to carry out the murder on his own. The state also presented evidence of William Stevens's conviction in 1997 for second-degree murder. During the trial, Stevens claimed that Corey Milliken killed Sandi Stevens and Myrtle Wilson during his sexual assault on them. He argued that he did not hire Corey to kill the two women. The defense decided to call Gregg McCrary, a former FBI agent and an expert on crime scene analysis. McCrary was called to testify that "Milliken committed sexual murder as an act of aggression precipitated by an argument with his mother and stepfather the night before the crimes."[144] McCrary stated that in his opinion the display of the pornographic magazines around Sandi Stevens's body could be seen as an attempt to humiliate and degrade the victim. In his view, this relates to the motive of a sexual offense and noted that sex crimes are crimes of violence.[145] McCrary testified outside the jury and stated that the murders were sexually motivated. In his testimony, McCrary also made distinctions between the characteristics of "disorganized sexual homicide crime scene" and a "contract murder crime scene."[146] McCrary said:

The crime scene is quite sloppy and in great disarray. There is minimal use of restraints. The sexual acts tend to occur after death; so, there is postmortem injury to the victim ... indication of postmortem sexual activity. The body is left at the death scene and is typically left in view. There's a good deal of physical evidence ... that's left at the scene. And, anytime just a weapon of opportunity that the offender uses, and by that, I mean a weapon that is contained at the scene, uses it and then, it's not uncommon for the offender to leave that weapon either at or near-near the scene.[147]

McCrary further testified that "criminals usually commit disorganized violent crimes as a result of some "precipitating stressors, or stressful event" in the criminal's life. Such an event invokes a lot of anger in the offender, and that anger—transferred onto the victim—triggers this violent behavior."[148] He also stated that the crime scene analysis indicated that more than one person committed the murders and that the crime scene also showed elements of "staging." The reliability of McCrary's testimony was questioned during cross-examination.

On cross-examination, Mr. McCrary testified that the FBI had conducted a study to determine the accuracy rate of its crime scene analysis. The results of that study yielded a 75 to 80 percent accuracy rate. He presented as further evidence of the reliability of crime scene analysis the FBI's increased number of trained agents in this field from 7 to 40. Although McCrary acknowledged that crime scene analysis "is not hard science where you can do controlled experiments and come up with the ratios in all this," he said that "the proof that there is validation and reliability in the process is that it's being accepted. It's being used and the demand is just outstripping our resources to provide it.[149]

In its ruling, the trial court qualified McCrary as an expert on crime scene staging and he was allowed to testify that the murders could be the work of more than one person. The court however, ruled that McCrary's testimony would not be admitted on the issue of the motives for the murders. The trial court stated that "while the expert and many of the other FBI profilers are a tremendous asset as an investigative tool in law enforcement, the expert's testimony regarding the motivation of the suspect could not comply with the Tennessee Rule of Evidence 702 in terms of substantially assisting the trier of fact, because there is no trustworthiness or reliability."[150]

The trial court also was not convinced that this technique had been subjected to adequate objective testing, or that it was based upon well-established and reliable scientific principles. Justice Steve Dozier, delivering the judgment, also stated that the testimony could not satisfy the *McDaniel*[151] test of scientific reliability.

It should be noted that Stevens also called other witnesses, including family members, co-workers, and neighbors, who testified that he was a good father, a good and hardworking employee, and always helped his neighbors.[152]

The Criminal Court, Davidson County, Tennessee, found Stevens guilty and sentenced him to death for the murders and also sentenced him to life without parole on the aggravated robbery charge. Corey Milliken pleaded guilty to first-degree murder and was sentenced to life imprisonment.

The court of appeals affirmed the trial court's judgment of conviction and the sentence. The case automatically went to the Supreme Court of Tennessee, as it was a death sentence for first degree murder.[153] Among other issues, the supreme court addressed the issue of whether the trial court erred by limiting McCrary's testimony. The supreme court agreed with both the trial court and the court of appeals decisions and held that *McDaniel* applied to both scientific and nonscientific testimony.

On the issue of the reliability of the expert's testimony, the supreme court stated that "consequently, we are reluctant to measure the reliability of expert testimony that is not based on scientific methodology under a rigid application of the *McDaniel* factors. However, we are equally reluctant to admit nonscientific expert testimony based on an unchallenged acceptance of the expert's qualifications and an unquestioned reliance on the accuracy of the data supporting the expert's conclusions."[154] The Supreme Court of Tennessee ruled that:

This type of crime scene analysis, developed by the FBI as a means of criminal investigation, relies on the expert's subjective judgment to draw conclusions as to the type of individual who committed this crime based on the physical evidence found at the crime scene. Although we do not doubt the usefulness of behavioral analysis to assist law enforcement officials in their criminal investigations, we cannot allow an individual's guilt or innocence to be determined by such "opinion evidence connected to existing data only by the *ipse dixit*" of the expert. Essentially, the jury is encouraged to conclude that because this crime scene has been identified by an expert to exhibit certain patterns or telltale clues consistent with previous sexual homicides triggered by "precipitating stressors," then it is more likely that this crime was similarly motivated.[155]

Justice Barker also stated:

Moreover, we find that the FBI's study revealing a seventy-five to eighty percent accuracy rate for crime scene analysis lacks sufficient trustworthiness to constitute evidence of this technique's reliability. Although the frequency with which a technique leads to accurate or erroneous results is certainly one important factor to determine reliability, equally important is the method for determining that rate of accuracy or error. In this case, there is no testimony regarding how the FBI determined the accuracy rate of this analysis. For example, was accuracy determined by confessions or convictions, or both? Even then, the absence of a confession does not indicate the offender's innocence and thus an inaccuracy in the technique. Clearly, the accuracy rate alone, without any explanation of the methodologies used in the study, is insufficient to serve as the foundation for the admission of this testimony.

Therefore, because the behavioral analysis portion of Mr. McCrary's testimony does not bear sufficient indicia of reliability to substantially assist the trier of fact, we conclude that this testimony was properly excluded.[156]

The supreme court concluded that the defendant's arguments lacked merit and therefore affirmed the death sentence. The court stated that the exclusion of the unreliable expert testimony by the trial court was not error.

In *State v. Fortin*,[157] linkage analysis, signature analysis, and results of the FBI's Violent Criminal Apprehension Program [ViCAP] were ruled inadmissible. Linkage analysis was also seen as an opinion on the ultimate issue. Steven Fortin was charged with capital murder, having killed the victim in the course of a gruesome sexual assault. The victim, Melissa Padilla, aged 25, was found sexually assaulted, robbed, and strangled to death on August 11, 1994 in Avenel, Woodbridge Township, New Jersey.

Padilla's body was naked from the waist down. She was wearing a shirt, but no bra. Bags of food, a partially eaten sandwich, a store receipt, an earring, debris including cigarette butts, and a bloody one-dollar bill were found scattered near the body. Padilla's shorts, with her underwear still inside them, were found on a nearby shrub. Inside the concrete pipe was a large blood stain. The assailant had brutally beaten Padilla about her face and head. Her face was swollen and bruised, and her nose was broken. She had been killed by manual strangulation. The autopsy revealed rectal tearing and bite marks on Padilla's left breast, left nipple, and the left side of her chin.[158]

On April 3, 1995, a Maine state trooper, Vicki Gardner, aged 34, was also sexually assaulted, beaten, and strangled to unconsciousness. She survived. She was off duty that day but was traveling in a marked police vehicle, when she saw a car parked on the shoulder of Highway 95 in the state of Maine. State Trooper Gardner stopped to check what was wrong. The defendant, Steven Fortin, was inside the car. The defendant had a learner's permit issued in New Jersey. Trooper Gardner suspected that Fortin was under the influence of alcohol and gave him some sobriety tests. The tests showed that Fortin was under the influence of alcohol and Gardner placed him under arrest. She called her office and requested an officer to come to assist her. It was reported that while she was waiting for backup to arrive,

Fortin attacked. She was beaten, sexually assaulted, and strangled into unconsciousness.[159] It was reported that Fortin "then placed Gardner in the passenger's seat of the police vehicle, and drove the police vehicle down the highway. Gardner regained consciousness and partially jumped, and was partially pushed by defendant, from the vehicle."[160] Fortin lost control of the vehicle. He fled but was later arrested at a nearby rest area. Gardner's face was badly battered, and she suffered a broken nose; bite marks to her chin, to her left breast nipple and on the outer left side of her left breast; and vaginal and anal tearing and lacerations. After the defendant's attack, Gardner was naked from the waist down. Her pants were pulled off, with her underwear inside out. When interviewed later, defendant said Gardner pulled her own pants off while attempting to make sexual advances to him.[161]

At the trial for this case in the State of Maine, Fortin pleaded guilty to seven counts of kidnapping, robbery, aggravated assault, assault on an officer, attempted gross sexual assault, unlawful sexual contact, and criminal operation of motor vehicle under the influence of alcohol.[162] He was sentenced to 20 years imprisonment.

The New Jersey police were not making any progress in the investigation into Padilla's death, until April 1995 when they were informed by Maine law enforcement officials that Steven Fortin had been arrested and charged in Maine for the sexual assault of Vicki Gardner. The Maine police contacted the New Jersey police to learn if Fortin had any prior convictions, since his learner's permit showed that he lived in New Jersey. After analyzing the two cases, Lt. Lawrence Nagle who was involved with the Padilla investigation, felt Fortin might have committed both sexual assaults. He found similarities between the two crimes. Further investigations revealed that Fortin was indeed in the area where Padilla was killed on the day of the murder. Dawn Archer, Fortin's girlfriend, confirmed this.

At trial, the State of New Jersey filed a motion to admit evidence from the Maine incident to the present case in New Jersey, on the issue of identity. The state also informed the court of its intention to call former FBI agent Roy Hazelwood to testify as to the ritualistic and signature aspects of the crimes to bolster their claim that the same person committed both crimes. The defense objected to both motions and argued that the testimony should not be allowed.

Hazelwood was called as an expert on *modus operandi* and ritualistic behavior. "He is a former FBI agent, has over 32 years experience as a law enforcement professional, a 17-year affiliation with the National Center for the Analysis of Violent Crime, and has consulted on more than 7,000 crimes of violence. He has published approximately 30 articles on topics of homicide, rape, serial rape, other types of sexual assault, and various other criminal or deviant sexual behavior, and has taught at various academies and at a few universities."[163]

A pretrial hearing was conducted on the admissibility of the other-crime evidence and on the admissibility of the expert testimony. The Superior Court, Law Division, Middlesex County, New Jersey, ruled that the evidence that Fortin sexually assaulted a police officer in Maine was admissible as other-crime evidence. The court also ruled that Hazelwood was qualified as an expert on ritualistic and signature aspects of crime and so his testimony was permitted. In granting the motion to introduce the other-crimes evidence, the trial court added that the defendant's guilty plea in the State of Maine should be excluded during the state's case-in-chief.[164]

In his testimony, Hazelwood stated that he used linkage analysis in reviewing the two crimes and found that the *modus operandi* of the crimes showed 15 similarities. He was therefore of the opinion that one person committed both crimes. The 15 similarities according to Hazelwood were as follows:

1. High-risk crimes;
2. Crimes committed impulsively;
3. Victims are female;
4. Age of victims generally the same;
5. Victims crossed the path of the offender;
6. Victims were alone;
7. Assaults occurred at confrontation point;
8. Adjacent to or on well-traveled highway;
9. Occurred during darkness;
10. No weapons involved in assaults;
11. Blunt-force injuries inflicted with fists, with noses of victims broken;
12. Trauma primarily to upper face, no teeth damaged;
13. Lower garments totally removed, with panties found inside the shorts or pants of the victims;
14. Shirt left on victims and breasts free; and
15. No seminal fluid found in/on victims.[165]

Hazelwood also testified that the two crimes "were anger-motivated, and that the offender demonstrated anger through the following identified "ritualistic" or "signature" behavior in both crimes:" bites to the lower chin, bites to the lateral left breast, injurious anal penetration, brutal facial beating, and manual frontal strangulation.[166]

It should be noted that the defense on the other hand, stated that there were 16 differences between the two crimes, including differences in the age, race, weight and height of the victims, differences in the status of the victims; and the fact that Gardner was anally and vaginally assaulted, while Padilla was only anally assaulted.[167]

Apart from Hazelwood, the state also called other witnesses, including Lt. Nagle of the New Jersey police, one of the investigating officers. Nagle stated that Padilla had trauma to the head, was manually strangled, was beaten about the face, her pants pulled down, had rectal tears, and had what looked like bite marks on her left breast and on her left chin.[168] Dr. Marvin Schuster, who performed the autopsy, testified that the victim died as a result of "asphyxiation, assault, and strangulation."[169] Two police officers from the Maine State Police also testified as to the events that happened in the sexual assault of Vicki Gardner, and the type of injuries that she sustained. Dr. Lowell J. Levine, a forensic odontologist also testified. He stated that his review and comparison of the autopsy reports, the bite marks on both victims, dental casts and Fortin's bite-mark samples, showed that the bite marks found on both victims came from the defendant's teeth.

It should also be noted that DNA samples recovered from Padilla's body, a cigarette butt found at the crime scene, fingernail clippings, a dollar bill with blood stain, and blood samples from the victim and the defendant were analyzed. Some of the results were inconclusive and some could not exclude the defendant as the source of the DNA.[170] The court ruled that the other-crime evidence and Hazelwood's testimony were admissible. The defendant appealed and argued that:

1. The state should not be allowed to introduce inflammatory and severely prejudicial evidence of an allegedly similar crime under the provisions of the New Jersey Rule of Evidence 404(b) to substitute for its "paucity" of evidence;
2. The admission of evidence regarding the incident in Maine would be contrary to the established case law because the state failed to meet its burden to prove the two crimes were sufficiently identical and because the prejudicial value grossly outweighs the limited probative value; and
3. The proffered testimony of Robert Hazelwood does not meet the standard of admissibility for expert testimony as set forth by the New Jersey Supreme Court and the trial court's ruling was therefore erroneous.[171]

In its ruling, the Superior Court, Appellate Division, affirmed the trial judge's decision that the other-crime evidence can be admitted on the issue of identity. Delivering the opinion of the appellate division, Justice Robert Fall stated that "given our standard of review, we are satisfied the trial judge's decision was not "so wide off the mark that manifest denial of justice resulted," or that his ruling constitutes an abuse of discretion ... The judge carefully applied the four-prong test outlined in *Codfield* in determining whether the proffered other-crime evidence was admissible."[172] Justice Fall further stated that "the potential for prejudice by admission of the other-crime evidence in this case is great. Therefore, while we are in accord with the judge's ruling in permitting its admission, at trial the judge must 'sanitize' the other-crime evidence by confining its admissibility to those facts reasonably necessary for the probative purpose of 'identity.' To an extent, the judge ruling inadmissible defendant's guilty plea in Maine, goes to this effort of minimizing the prejudicial effect."[173] The appellate division however, ruled that Hazelwood's testimony using linkage analysis is not sufficiently reliable to be admissible as expert evidence.[174] Justice Fall said:

Here, as the judge noted, Hazelwood testified "this analysis is not based on science, but based on his training and experience with violent crime." While not based on science in the technical sense, his linkage analysis methodology is certainly founded in the area of behavioral science, in that it analyzes the conduct of the crime perpetrator in two or more crimes to determine whether there is sufficient consistency of behavior to conclude that one person committed both crimes. We conclude that the same detailed analysis regarding admission of scientific evidence is applicable and necessary in determining whether linkage analysis expert testimony is admissible. Theories or methods of explaining human conduct and behavior have consistently been subject to significant scrutiny and analysis by our courts when admission is sought.[175]

Hazelwood in his testimony stated that *modus operandi* and ritualistic behavior analysis was accepted by the law enforcement community. On that issue, Justice Fall stated that the usefulness of these methods in crime investigations are not to be doubted but they are not convinced that these methods "are sufficiently reliable for an expert in those fields to testify that the same person who committed one crime committed the other under the analysis of the facts and circumstances presented in this case."[176] Justice Fall further stated that:

Our examination of the authorities and literature authored by Hazelwood convinces us that a linkage analysis as a foundation for the expert behavior identification testimony proffered in this case is wholly inappropriate. In the recent book *The Evil that Men Do*, Stephen G. Michaud with Roy Hazelwood (1988), there is significant discussion concerning the application of linkage analysis in the identification of serial offenders. . . . Hazelwood defines therein a serial offender as one who has committed three or more offenses. Additionally, as described in this book, the use of linkage analysis leading to identification of the perpetrator also involves an evaluation of the personal history and background of the suspected perpetrator, to develop a profile.[177]

The appellate division therefore, ruled that the state has not proved that linkage analysis "is at a state of art such that an expert's testimony could be sufficiently reliable."[178] The appellate division also saw the testimony as an opinion on the ultimate issue. The appellate division affirmed the decision allowing the introduction of the other-crime evidence, after it has been 'sanitized.' The appellate division however, reversed the decision permitting Hazelwood to testify that one person was responsible for both crimes.[179]

The case reached the Supreme Court of New Jersey, on appeal and cross-appeal. On one hand, the defendant sought a review of the appellate division's ruling that the other-crime evidence was admissible. The state on the other hand, prayed the court to review the appellate division's ruling that Hazelwood's testimony was inadmissible. In its ruling, the Supreme Court of New Jersey agreed with the appellate division's ruling that linkage analysis lacks sufficient scientific reliability to establish that one person committed both crimes.[180] Delivering the opinion of the supreme court, Justice Daniel J. O'Hern added that linkage analysis is similar to the rapist profile evidence that is inadmissible and stated that Hazelwood's testimony failed to "meet the standards for the admission of testimony that relates to scientific knowledge. Although Hazelwood possessed sufficient expertise in his field and his intended testimony is beyond the ken of the average juror, the field of linkage analysis is not at a "state of the art" such that his testimony could be sufficiently reliable."[181] Justice O'Hern went on to say that "as the appellate division noted however, the authorities and literature authored by Hazelwood and others do not demonstrate that linkage analysis has attained such a state of art as to have the scientific reliability of DNA testing."[182] "Moreover, linkage analysis is a field in which only Hazelwood and a few of his close associates are involved. Concerning consensus on acceptance of "linkage analysis" in the scientific community, the other experts mentioned by Hazelwood in his testimony were either current or former co-workers. In this respect, there are no peers to test his theories and no way in which to duplicate his results.[183]

Summing up Hazelwood's linkage analysis, Justice O'Hern stated that if "stripped of its scientific mantra, the testimony is nothing more than a description of the physical circumstances present."[184] Justice O'Hern ruled that Hazelwood would have to prove the reliability of linkage analysis by producing a reliable database from which it was based. The supreme court affirmed the appellate division's judgment and remanded the matter to the law division for further proceedings. At the Superior Court, Law Division, Middlesex County, Fortin was convicted of capital murder, aggravated sexual assault, first-degree robbery, and felony murder. He was sentenced to death and appealed.

The state filed a motion for clarification of certain aspects of the judgment.[185] The Supreme Court of New Jersey held that:

1. Trial court improperly limited *voir dire* by rejecting inquiry concerning evidence of the defendant's sexual assault of law enforcement officer in another state;
2. State's expert should not have been permitted to testify on violent sexual crimes without producing a reliable database of violent sexual assault cases that he had investigated, studied, or analyzed;
3. Defendant could waive protection of *Ex Post Clause* in order to obtain instruction on life in prison without parole, if jury rejected death sentence;
4. Convictions for manslaughter several years earlier and sexual assault approximately eight months after murder were relevant and admissible at penalty phase; and
5. Aggravating factors are elements of capital murder and thus, must be submitted to a grand jury and returned in an indictment; overruling *State v. Martini*, 131 N.J. 176, 619 A.2d 1208.[186]

The Supreme Court of New Jersey reversed the judgment of conviction and remanded for a new trial. At the retrial,[187] the state presented several witnesses at the pretrial hearing, including Dr. Geetha Natarajan (the medical examiner who autopsied Padilla), who testified that in the more than 25 years she had conducted autopsies she could not remember any other case in which the autopsy revealed bite marks on the chin of the other victims.[188] Dr. Lawrence Ricci (an expert in emergency medicine and pediatrics) also "testified that both Padilla and Gardner suffered traumatic anal injuries, but could not say that those injuries were any more distinctive than similar injuries inflicted on other sexual assault victims."[189] Dr. Lowell Levine (an odontologist) also testified that in more than 30 years that he had been in the field that "he had never seen the combination of bite marks on the chin, the left nipple, and the left breast that appeared on both Gardner's and Padilla's bodies."[190] He compared the bite marks on the two victims with Fortin's dental casts and was of the opinion that there was a high degree of probability that the bite mark on Padilla's left breast was caused by the defendant's teeth. The State also called Mark Safarik, an FBI supervisory special agent, who testified that the search results of the FBI's ViCAP database showed a match between the Gardner and Padilla assaults as signature-crime. Hence, he was of the opinion that Fortin committed both crimes. It should be noted that the state decided not to call Hazelwood to testify again. They called Mark Safarik instead. In his testimony, Safarik described the Violent Criminal Apprehension Program, more commonly known as ViCAP.

Created in 1984, ViCAP is a national database of approximately 167,000 reported violent crimes (homicides, attempted homicides, and kidnappings) that the FBI maintains in Quantico, Virginia. The database represents about 3 to 7 percent of the violent crimes committed since ViCAP's inception. Nationwide participation in ViCAP is voluntary. Law enforcement agencies that complete the ViCAP form answer numerous questions about the crime for inclusion in the national database.

The general purpose of ViCAP "is to identity similarities in crimes" through a computer search isolating particular characteristics in the commission of the offense. Through such a computer search focusing on specific crime criteria, one law enforcement agency can contact and cooperate with another agency working on a "similar case with similar characteristics." According to Safarik, the "ViCAP system is looking for ... solved or unsolved homicides, or attempted homicides, missing persons cases, kidnappings, where there is a strong possibility of foul play, or unidentified dead bodies, where the manner of death is suspected to be homicide.[191]

There was a problem with the admission of Safarik's testimony, however.

Law enforcement authorities completed the ViCAP form for the Padilla murder in a timely manner for inclusion in the national database. The Maine State Police, however, did not complete a ViCAP form for the 1995 Gardner sexual assault. In 2004, in preparation for the defendant's trial, the state requested that Safarik submit a ViCAP form for the Gardner case. He did so with the assistance of a ViCAP analyst and the Maine State Police. Safarik then ran a series of searches on the ViCAP for specific criteria common to both the Padilla and Gardner crimes, such as manual strangulation, sexual assault, and bite marks on the face and chest. The searches yielded only three cases: the Padilla murder, the Gardner sexual assault, and a 1988 case from Washington State. The state argued that the searches showed that the similarities between the Padilla and Gardner crimes were so unusual as to constitute a signature. Significantly, Safarik indicated that the ViCAP database could not be released to defense counsel because of privacy concerns and that it was exempt from the Freedom of Information Act.[192]

On the other hand, the defense offered two expert witnesses. First, Dr. Norman D. Sperber (the chief forensic dentist in the San Diego medical examiner's office), stated that there were doubts as to whether the marks on Padilla's breast and chin were indeed bite marks.[193] Sperber further stated that even assuming the injuries on the breast and the chin were bite marks, he was of the opinion that they did not come from the defendant.[194] It should be noted that Sperber testified in the original trial and all parties agreed that the testimony should be used in this retrial hearing.

The defense also presented Dr. Grover Godwin, as an expert in statistical evaluation of crime scenes. Godwin stated that the reliability of the ViCAP database was questionable because of what he described as "a bias in entering the variables."[195]

The motion judge ruled that only the evidence on the bite marks, which suggested uniqueness, would be allowed. The judge also ruled that the other injuries would not be allowed because they were common to sexual crimes, and that these other injuries would be unduly prejudicial to the defendant.

The motion judge also maintained that the ViCAP database might have applicability at trial. For instance, "absent the insertion of the Maine crime, she found that the ViCAP database would be a reliable database upon which the State may rely to test the expert opinions." With regard to the Gardner ViCAP form, she observed that it was prepared for litigation purpose and therefore "failed to provide an unbiased generation of data." Alternatively, she suggested that "if the ViCAP database could be crafted to report on the uniqueness of the human bite mark criteria alone," the database would then be useful in proving "a signature-like crime." To be useful, for example, the ViCAP analysis would have "to determine how many, if any, cases involve bite marks on the chin." The judge noted, however, that the ViCAP forms do not contain a box for bite marks to the chin.[196]

The state filed a motion appealing the motion judge's decision, but it was denied by the appellate division. The state therefore, filed an interlocutory appeal at the Supreme Court of New Jersey. The state argued that there were three errors in the motion judge's ruling:

1. The motion judge conditioned the introduction of the signature-crime evidence on expert testimony explaining the uniqueness of the bite marks in the Padilla and Gardner cases;
2. The motion judge would not admit evidence of the injuries sustained by Gardner other than the bite marks, thereby denying the jury the necessary context in which to determine whether the two crimes are indeed signature crimes; and
3. The motion judge would not allow the ViCAP database to be used to show that a computer search revealed only three cases with the pattern of bite marks to the breast and chin—the Padilla and Gardner cases, and a Washington State case.[197]

In its ruling, the Supreme Court of New Jersey, through Justice Barry Albin stated that the motion judge did not err by conditioning the signature-crime evidence on the presentation of expert testimony.[198] Justice Albin further stated that the motion judge did not abuse her discretion by asking the state to provide the defense with the database of cases from which Levine and Natarajan based their opinion. Additionally, Justice Albin stated that trial courts have the authority to require an expert to provide the underlying facts or data upon which the expert based the opinion.[199] Justice Albin also stated that "significantly, although the state presented Agent Safarik to explain the functions of ViCAP, neither he nor any other expert witness vouched that a ViCAP crime match, such as the one in this case, constituted reliable signature-crime evidence."[200] Justice Albin said:

We share the judge's concern that only relevant evidence should bear on the issues that must be decided by the jury. We disagree, however, that details of the Gardner assault can be so finely parsed. Although the other injuries suffered by Gardner do not fall into the category of signature evidence, the bite marks were inflicted during a vicious sexual assault. That reality cannot be ignored or withheld from the jury without seriously distorting the import of the bite-mark evidence. By its very nature, signature-crime evidence carries the potential for prejudice. Nevertheless, signature-crime evidence may be highly probative, and in this case, we conclude that its probative value is not outweighed by its prejudicial effect. . . . Therefore, we will allow the state to present the bite-mark evidence within the general narrative of the sexual assault on Trooper Gardner.[201]

The supreme court ruled that it was necessary to place the bite-mark evidence in context because doing so would assist the jury in understanding the case and was beneficial to both the state and the defendant. Justice Albin further stated that "sanitizing the Gardner assault would keep from the jury the many differences between the two crimes that might lead it to reject the signature-crime evidence."[202] Therefore, Justice Albin stated that allowing all the material details from the Gardner assault was fair.

The Supreme Court of New Jersey affirmed the motion judge's ruling with modifications. It was held that "the State must be permitted to present the bite-mark evidence in context and therefore material details of the Gardner sexual assault cannot be censored. Testimony describing that assault, however, is subject to specific jury instructions explaining the limited use of 'other-crimes' evidence under N.J.R.E. 404(b). Finally, because the State's experts have not relied on the ViCAP database to form their opinions, the ViCAP database should not be admissible to bolster those opinions."[203]

Justice Albin acknowledged the fact that ViCAP is a very useful tool of crime investigation but stated that "ultimately, in conducting a fair trial, courts must ensure that only reliable evidence is submitted to our juries consistent with our evidentiary rules. As presented, ViCAP does not meet the standards for admissibility of evidence."[204]

The Supreme Court of New Jersey therefore, remanded the case for further proceedings.

As we can see from this case, offender profiling evidence, no matter which label is attached to it, still needs to be based on reliable facts or data. In this case, we have seen the terms linkage analysis, ritualistic behavior, signature-crime analysis, and ViCAP program all being used to show one thing—that bite marks on two victims came from one individual. This case clearly supports my argument that some profilers have the tendency to dress up their testimony in different labels so that it will be admitted. Offender profiling and its derivatives or its other labels should not be admitted as evidence until its foundation can be properly and objectively ascertained. The foundations must be proved by reliable facts and data.

The case of the Beltway snipers also helps to highlight the unreliability of offender profiling. In this case, many profilers came up with profiles of the likely offender. Many profilers predicted that the offender was likely to be a loner, a white male, possibly living near the areas of attack in Maryland. All of these turned out to be wrong. The profiles did not predict that the offender, or one of them, would be a 17-year-old black male. One of the things that made this case difficult for profiling was the choice of victims, who varied in terms of their age, gender, occupation, time of attack, place of attack, and so on. The nature of the attacks and the varied victims the offenders chose also made it difficult to draw conclusion as to the possible motives for the attacks. Some people reported seeing two white men in a white van or truck. When the snipers were caught, they turned out to be two black men. The offender was not a white male, not a loner, and not in a white van as many profilers had predicted.

The names John Allen Muhammad, aged 41, and Lee Boyd Malvo, aged 17, are not names that you should mention to people who lived in Montgomery County, Maryland, the District of Columbia, or northern Virginia in October 2002. In what became known as the Beltway Sniper attacks, Muhammad and Malvo killed 10 people and wounded three others. There are reports that 17 people were shot in total. Residents were terrified and afraid to go out. The shock, the horror, the suspense, and the fear was too much for a lot of people. Muhammad changed his last name from Williams to Muhammad in 2001 when he joined the Nation of Islam. Malvo was born in Jamaica and emigrated to the United States with his mother. The six murders that occurred in Montgomery County in Maryland began on Wednesday October 2, 2002 and ended on Tuesday October 22, 2002. All the victims were shot at various locations. The people murdered include:

1. James Martin, male, aged 55, a systems analyst, was shot around 6:30 A.M. on October 2, 2002 at the parking lot of Shoppers Food Warehouse in Wheaton;
2. James Buchanan, male, aged 39, a landscaper, was shot to death at 7:45 A.M. on October 3, 2002 while he was mowing the lawn at the Fitzgerald Auto Store in Rockville;
3. Premkumar Walekar, male, aged 54, a taxi driver, was shot to death at 8:12 A.M. on October 3, 2002 at a gas station in Aspen Hill;
4. Maria Sarah Ramos, female, aged 32, a housekeeper, was shot to death around 8:37 A.M. on October 3, 2002, while she was sitting on a bench at the Leisure World Plaza in Silver Spring;
5. Lori Lewis-Rivera, female, aged 25, a nanny, was vacuuming her minivan at a gas station in Kensington on October 3, 2002 when she was killed. She was shot to death around 10 A.M.; and

6. Conrad Johnson, male, aged 35, a bus driver, was shot to death around 6 A.M. on October 22, 2002, as he was stepping out of his vehicle in Silver Spring.

Muhammad and Malvo also shot the following people.

1. Pascal Charlot, male, aged 72, a carpenter, was shot around 9:20 P.M. while crossing the street on October 3, 2002, in the District of Columbia;
2. Caroline Seawell, female, a 43-year-old substitute teacher, was shot at 2:30 P.M. at the parking lot of Michaels' craft store in Fredericksburg, Virginia, on October 4, 2002. She survived;
3. Iran Brown, a 13-year-old boy was shot around 8 A.M. on October 7, 2002. His aunt has just dropped him off at the Benjamin Tasker Middle School in Prince George's County, Maryland. He was about to enter the school's front door when he was shot. He was rushed to the hospital and survived;
4. Dean Harold Meyers, aged 53 and an engineer, was shot to death around 8 P.M. on October 9, 2002. on his way back from work in Manassas, Virginia;
5. Kenneth Bridges, aged 53, was shot around 9:15 A.M. at a gas station off Interstate 95, near Fredericksburg, Virginia on October 11, 2002;
6. Linda Franklin, aged 47, an FBI intelligence analyst, was shot to death around 9:15 P.M. at the parking lot of Home Depot in Falls Church, Virginia on October 14, 2002; and
7. Jeffrey Hopper was shot at 8 A.M. while leaving a restaurant in Ashland, Virginia, with his wife on October 19, 2002. He survived.

Police officials in Montgomery County, Maryland led the investigation into these attacks. It was a joint operation that included law enforcement officers from other jurisdictions and agencies, including the FBI. One thing the investigators got right from the very beginning was that the attacks were linked. It was reported that about four hundred FBI agents were assigned to the case throughout the United States.[205] According to the FBI, "evidence experts were asked to digitally map many of the evolving crime scenes, and our behavioral analysts helped prepare a profile of the shooter for investigators."[206]

On October 21, 2002, investigators thought they had caught the killers when they arrested two white men with a white van outside a gas station in Richmond, Virginia. It turned that the two suspects were not the killers. The breakthrough the police needed came on October 24, 2002, when a motorist, Whitney Donahue, called the police to alert them to a car he had seen parked at a rest area on Interstate 70 in Maryland that matched the police description of the snipers' car that had just been broadcast on the radio. Around 1:30 A.M. on October 24, 2002, law enforcement agents, including FBI agents, arrested Muhammad and Malvo while they were sleeping in a blue 1990 Chevrolet Caprice sedan with New Jersey license tag NDA 21Z. Several items and highly incriminating evidence were gathered. The snipers had modified the Caprice into what the prosecuting attorney in the case called a "killing machine." They had cut a hole into the lid of the trunk, just above the license plate, through which a rifle could be projected.[207] The side and rear windows of the car were also tinted. Among several items collected from the snipers were the following:

1. A stolen Bushmaster XM-15 semiautomatic .223 caliber rifle;
2. A right-handed brown glove, which matched a left-handed brown glove that was found near the scene where Conrad Johnson was killed;
3. A rifle scope;
4. Two boxes of .338 caliber magnum ammunition;
5. Earplugs;
6. A laptop computer;
7. An AT&T calling card, which they used to make calls near the areas of attack;
8. Two identification cards from different states with different names bearing Muhammad's photo;
9. Two walkie talkies;
10. Maps, with the cities of Bethesda and Silver Spring circled;
11. A GPS device; and
12. A note containing the Beltway snipers hotline phone number and other numbers relating to the attacks.[208]

"A voice recorder found in the Caprice contained the undeleted message, 'We have given you a way out. You know our requests. You know our demands. And you know that it can be done. My advice to you is to take it because we will not deviate from what we told you to do. Thank you.' The voice on the tape was identified as the voice of John Muhammad."[209] There was overwhelming physical evidence with which to proceed with the trial of the snipers. Fingerprints and ballistic evidence were gathered. "The ballistics examination ultimately revealed that the Bushmaster had fired the shells involved in four of the six killings in Montgomery County, in the Prince George's County shooting, in the District of Columbia murder, in all five shootings in Virginia, and in the murder in Montgomery, Alabama. In the other two Montgomery County murders, the lead fragments from James Martin's body and from James Buchanan's clothing had no identifiable characteristics."[210]

It should also be noted that Malvo's DNA was found on a zip-lock bag and on the gloves recovered near the scene where Conrad Johnson was killed. A written note also was found near the scene where Conrad Johnson was killed bearing the following words: "For you, Mr. Police, Call me God."[211] "The note taunted the police for their "incompetence" and warned that "Your children are not safe. Can you hear us now? Do not play these childish games with us. You know our demands. Thank you." The note concluded, "Next person, your choice."[212]

In 2006, Muhammad was charged with six counts of first-degree murder at the Circuit Court, Montgomery, Maryland. The jury convicted him of first-degree murder of James Martin, James Buchanan, Premkumar Walekar, Maria Sarah Ramos, Lori Lewis-Rivera and Conrad Johnson. Justice James L. Ryan sentenced him to six terms of life imprisonment without the possibility of parole, to be served consecutively with each other and to be served consecutively with any previously imposed sentences in other states. Muhammad was convicted by the jury in Virginia Beach on November 17, 2003, for the murder of Dean Harold Meyer, receiving the death sentence. In *Muhammad v. Commonwealth*,[213] the Supreme Court of Virginia affirmed the death sentence. Malvo entered a guilty plea on six counts of first-degree murder for the murders in Montgomery County. Malvo was sentenced to six consecutive life sentences without the possibility of parole. Malvo also entered into guilty pleas for the crimes that occurred in Virginia.

Muhammad appealed his conviction, alleging that there were many errors in his trial. In its ruling, the Court of Special Appeals of Maryland, through Justice Charles E. Moylan, Jr., affirmed Muhammad's conviction for the murders.[214]

In this Beltway Sniper murder case, the offender profiles produced to track the suspects were wrong. Offender profilers also disagreed on the most appropriate methods or strategies the police should use in approaching the offenders. Most of the profiling comments centered on the offender's likely residential area. At one point the Beltway sniper attacks seemingly turned into an investigation by offender profilers rather than by the officially assigned investigation team. Montgomery County Police Chief Charles Moose was very critical of the comments made by some of the profilers regarding the case. He stated that some of these comments could jeopardize the investigation, and pointed out the fact that these profilers had not been briefed on the case by his investigating team. The snipers followed the news reports about the attacks and responded. As mentioned, there was overwhelming physical and incriminating evidence in this case.

Several studies have been carried out on the accuracy of profilers. In 1990, for instance, Pinizzotto and Finkel carried out a study in United States that consisted of five groups: 1) four profilers from the FBI (expert/

teachers), 2) six police detectives who had been trained by the FBI profilers, 3) six experienced police homicide and sex detectives, with no training in criminal personality profiling, 4) six clinical psychologists, and 5) six undergraduate psychology students.[215] The five groups were given two real and solved cases: a sex offense case and a homicide case. The materials the participants received for the homicide case included crime scene reports, crime scene photographs, autopsy and toxicology reports, and the victim report.[216] For the sexual offense case, the participants also received a victim statement, police reports, and victim reports.[217]

Even though it was based on a very small sample, this study generated interesting and controversial results. First, the study reported that professional profilers wrote richer profiles than did the nonprofilers in both the sex offense case and the murder case.[218]

Interestingly, the results also showed that "the profilers did not achieve higher scores than subjects in the other groups in these same categories for the homicide case."[219] In the homicide case, "profilers, however, do not appear to process this material in a way qualitatively different from any other group."[220] In the lineup rankings, the study also showed that "in the sex offense case, the experts/teachers were accurate in picking out the offender 100 percent of the time, and the profilers were accurate 83 percent of the time. As for the other groups, accuracy is lower, and declines as we move from detectives (67 percent), to psychologists (50 percent), to students (16 percent)."[221]

Based on the results of this study, Pinizzotto and Finkel concluded: "Concerning the outcome issue, professional profilers are more accurate (i.e., more correct answers, higher accuracy scores, more correct lineup identifications) for the sex offense case than nonprofilers; but these accuracy differences dissipate when we look at the homicide case. There were, however, significant outcome differences between profiler and nonprofiler groups for the homicide case in all the analyses of the written profile."[222]

The authors did acknowledge certain limitations of this study. On the small sample, the authors noted they "were unable to locate sufficient numbers of expert/teachers who were both actively engaged in profiling and willing to cooperate in this study."[223]

This goes a long way in highlighting my argument that there is a need for closer cooperation among the different professional groups involved in offender profiling.

Pinizzotto and Finkel also noted that "while the overall outcome superiority of the profilers is most likely indicative of greater expertise, it must be kept in mind that an 'investment' factor could also be invoked to explain these results. Psychologists and students may see this task as an interesting exercise, whereas profilers and detectives, perhaps, see it as the 'blood and guts' of their professions, and therefore generate lengthier profiles and spend more time on the task."[224]

Criticism of this study has argued that "only 15 items of offender information were processed by Pinizzotto and Finkel, and there was no scrutiny of the types of information on which profilers were more accurate."[225] "Pinizzotto and Finkel reanalyzed the results, giving half credit for some of the inaccurate multiple-choice answers based on the judgment of the 'expert' profiler subgroup that some wrong answers were less wrong than others; however, they never set out the results of that reanalysis, simply asserting that for both cases the only significant differences that emerged were an advantage of the profiler group compared to the student group."[226] Risinger and Loop argued that Pinizzotto and Finkel only set out the number of accurate predictions without adding the number of inaccurate predictions.[227] As such, Risinger and Loop concluded that the profilers actually got one-third of the questions wrong even in the sex offense case and got two-thirds of the questions wrong in the murder case.[228]

In 1995, FBI profilers had compiled what they called the key attributes of successful profilers. In their work, Hazelwood et al. maintained that the main attributes for successful profilers are: knowledge of the criminal mind, investigative experience, objectivity, logical reasoning/critical thinking, and a high level of intuition.[229]

In 2000, Kocsis et al. replicated the Pinizzotto and Finkel study and included the following five groups:

1. Five profilers. These profilers were those who had given some form of psychological profiling advice to a law enforcement agency;
2. Thirty-five active police officers;
3. Thirty Australian psychologists with no prior study of forensic or criminal psychology;
4. Thirty-one Australian science and economics university undergraduates; and
5. Twenty Australian psychics. These psychics believed that their paranormal abilities could be useful in constructing an offender profile.[230]

Kocsis et al. chose these groups because they are believed to possess the key attributes outlined by Hazelwood et al. Thus, the psychologists were chosen for appreciation of the criminal mind, police officers for their investigative experience, university students for objectivity and logical reasoning, and psychics for intuition. Kocsis et al. stated that this study was aimed at investigating the skills necessary for effective profiling. In order to achieve this, the study groups were presented with a solved murder case.

In the five-part survey inventory, the groups received detailed information about this solved murder case, including the following material: the crime scene report, crime scene photographs, photos of the victim's body, a forensic biologist's report, a forensic entomologist's report, a ballistics report, autopsy reports, and basic background information of the victim.[231] Study participants were asked questions about the physical characteristics, cognitive processes, offense behaviors, social history, and habits of the offender.[232]

The study results showed that the five groups differed only marginally in their total accuracy.[233] In order to answer the question specifically of whether profilers were more accurate than nonprofilers, Kocsis et al. decided to collapse the psychologists, police officers, students and psychics into one group (nonprofilers) and compared their performance with that of the profilers. The results showed that "on every measure of accuracy, the profilers answered more questions correctly than the nonprofilers. Furthermore, this difference was statistically significant on the total accuracy measure."[234]

The study results also showed that despite their training, knowledge, and experience, the profilers did not perform better than the others in the correct identification of the characteristics of the offender or the features of the offense.[235] It should be noted however, that "the profilers did descriptively outperform all other groups on the two omnibus measures of accuracy and on two of the submeasures (cognitive processes and social status and behavior). On the other two submeasures, the profilers were the second most accurate group with the difference between them and the most accurate group (psychologists) negligible and easily attributable to sampling error."[236]

The results also showed that psychologists performed better than the psychics and the police officers on most of the tasks. The study concluded that psychological knowledge is more important than intuition or investigative experience. The authors noted however, that:

In any event, the study does encourage the view that an educated insight into human behavior could play an important role in the process of psychological profiling. At the same time, it must be stressed that the psychologists' performance did not differ significantly from that of the student group, so it remains uncertain whether the psychologists' advantage over some other groups was predominately in regard to specific knowledge of the behavioral science or to a broader capacity for objective and logical analysis.[237]

The result also showed that the police officers did not perform well in the profiling task. Kocsis et al. therefore, disagreed with the earlier work by the FBI profilers, which stated that investigative experience is a key attribute of successful profilers. Kocsis et al. also showed that the psychics did not perform better than the other groups and "showed no insight into the nature of the offender beyond what reasonably could be gleaned from the prevailing social stereotype of a murderer."[238]

Kocsis et al. acknowledged the problem with the small sample of profilers in their study (only five), which they correctly noted "not only impeded the chances of statistical significance but also raised substantial doubts about this group's representativeness of profilers as a whole."[239] It should be noted that Kocsis et al. invited more than 40 profilers from several countries to participate in this study but only five agreed. This study has been criticized on the argument that the data were mere reflections of the differences in intelligence across the groups.[240]

Kocsis et al. carried out other studies in their effort to provide an empirical foundation for the key skills and abilities necessary for successful profiling. In 2002, Kocsis et al. conducted a study involving senior detectives, homicide detectives, trainee detectives, police recruits, and university students. This study also involved details of a solved murder case. The study results revealed that the university students performed better than other groups on all the submeasures except on cognitive processes and offense behaviors.[241] The result also showed that groups with postsecondary education outperformed those without postsecondary education. Kocsis et al. therefore concluded that based on this study, investigative experience is not a key attribute of effective profiling.

In 2003, Kocsis carried out yet another study involving eight groups: 1) profilers, 2) psychologists, 3) undergraduate students, 4) specialist detectives, 5) general police officers, 6) police recruits, 7) nonpolice specialists, and 8) psychics.[242] In this study, the profilers scored highest, followed by undergraduate students and psychologists. Kocsis concluded that logical reasoning ability and appreciation of the criminal mind are the key attributes.

In 2004, and using arson cases, Kocsis carried out another study involving detectives (specialists in arson), arson investigators from the fire service, professional profilers, and undergraduate university students.[243] There was a control group of community college students. The results of the study showed that profilers were more accurate than detectives, followed by undergraduate students, arson investigators, the control group, and police detectives. Based on the results of this study, Kocsis again concluded that logical reasoning ability was the key attribute for effective profiling.

Many scholars have criticized the studies by Kocsis, arguing, for instance, that Kocsis did not provide an operational definition of logical reasoning/ critical thinking and also did not test whether the participants actually possessed the skills for which they were being tested.[244] Further studies are still needed.

In this chapter, I have examined the central admissibility problems with offender profiling testimony in United States and answered such questions as: Is offender profiling impermissible character evidence? Who is qualified to give expert offender profiling evidence? Is offender profiling more prejudicial than probative? Is offender profiling an opinion on the ultimate issue? Is offender profiling sufficiently reliable as to be admissible?

It has also been noted that in some cases offender profiling is an improper subject for expert testimony. The Federal Rule of Evidence 702 being loose and too liberal has created problems for trial judges in making decisions on offender profiling cases. Under this evidence rule, almost anyone can qualify as an expert, and can give testimony either on a scientific, technical, or other specialized field of knowledge. Under a stringent application of *Frye*, it has to be shown that offender profiling has achieved widespread acceptance by the relevant community. A strict application of *Daubert* requires offender profiling evidence to satisfy the four factors, especially the requirement that the technique must be based on a reliable foundation or data.

Offender Profiling in Comparative Perspective

OFFENDER PROFILING IN THE UNITED KINGDOM

The previous chapter has shown that United States courts are inconsistent in their decisions on cases involving offender profiling. In the United Kingdom on the other hand, offender profiling evidence is generally seen as inadmissible at the moment. Several reasons account for this, but first we examine the rules governing the admissibility of expert testimony in the United Kingdom. In general terms, the English law of evidence provides that all relevant evidence is admissible so long as it is not excluded by other laws of evidence, such as the hearsay rule or opinion on character evidence rule, as well as the conduct on other occasions rule.

In the United Kingdom, the main rule governing the admission of expert evidence was arguably laid down in the case of *Folkes v. Chadd,*[1] where it was held that:

The opinion of scientific men upon proven facts may be given by men of science within their own science. An expert's opinion is admissible to furnish the court with scientific information which is likely to be outside the experience and knowledge of a judge or jury. If on the proven facts a judge or jury can form their own conclusions without help, then the opinion of an expert is unnecessary. In such a case if it is given dressed up in scientific jargon it makes judgment more difficult. The fact that an expert witness has impressive scientific qualifications does not by that fact alone make his opinion on matters of human nature and behavior within the limits of normality any more helpful than that of the jurors themselves; but there is a danger that they may think it does.[2]

In this case, the issue was whether the embankment erected by the plaintiff for the purpose of preventing the overflowing of Wells Harbor caused the decay or silting up of the harbor, by stopping the back water. The embankment was erected in 1758 and the harbor started to fill up and choke soon after that. The case was tried three times before it reached the Court of Appeal.

First, at the last Lent Assizes for the County of Norfolk, an engineer, called by the plaintiffs, testified that in his opinion that the embankment was not the cause of the decay. The plaintiffs also proffered evidence that showed that other harbors situated on similar positions on the same coast where there were no embankments had also started to fill up and choke.[3] At the trial, the jury ruled in the defendant's favor.

At the Court of Chancery, the plaintiffs called another expert, John Smeaton, a civil engineer. He stated that in his opinion the embankment did not cause the choking and filling up of the harbor. He also stated that removing the embankment would not solve the problem. An objection was raised. It was argued that "the inquiring into the site of other harbors was introducing a multiplicity of facts which the parties were not prepared to meet."[4] "It was also objected that the evidence of Mr. Smeaton was a matter of opinion, which could be no foundation for the verdict of the jury, which was to be built entirely on facts, and not on opinions."[5] The testimony was admitted, however. The Court of Chancery ruled in the plaintiffs' favor and the defendants asked for a new trial. The lower court rejected Smeaton's evidence and held that the evidence was mere opinion, based on speculation and not based on direct observation. On appeal, Lord Mansfield reversed the lower court's decision. Lord William Mansfield said:

It is objected that Mr. Smeaton is going to speak, not as to facts, but as to opinion. That opinion, however, is deduced from facts which are not disputed—the situation of banks, the course of tides and of winds, and the shifting of sands. His opinion, deduced from all these facts, is, that, mathematically speaking, the bank may contribute to the mischief, but not sensibly. Mr. Smeaton understands the construction of harbors, the causes of their destruction, and how remedied. In matters of science no other witnesses can be called. An instance frequently occurs in actions for unskillfully navigating ships. The question then depends on the evidence of those who understand such matters; and when such questions come before me, I always send for some of the brethren of the Trinity House. I cannot believe that where the question is, whether a defect arises from a natural or an artificial cause, the opinions of men of science are not to be received. Handwriting is proved every day by opinion; and for false evidence on such questions a man may be indicted for perjury. Many nice questions may arise as to forgery, and as to the impressions of seals; whether the impression was made from the seal itself, or from an impression wax. In such cases I cannot say that the opinion of seal-makers is not to be taken. I have myself received the opinion of Mr. Smeaton respecting mills, as a matter of science. The cause of the decay of the harbor is also a matter of science, and still more so, whether the removal of the bank can be beneficial. Of this, such men as Mr. Smeaton alone can judge. Therefore we are of the opinion that his judgment, formed on facts, was very proper evidence.[6]

The above decision in *Folkes v. Chadd*, was later supported by Lord Justice Frederick Lawton in *R v. Turner*.[7] The decision in *Turner*, also known as the *Turner Rule*, established the boundaries for the admissibility of expert evidence in the United Kingdom. Under the *Turner* rule, expert evidence is inadmissible unless it provides the courts with such information that is outside the common experience and knowledge of the judge or jury. *Turner* also states that expert evidence must be based on facts that can themselves be proved by admissible evidence.

In *Turner*, the defendant, Terence Stuart Turner, was charged with the murder of his girlfriend, Wendy Butterfield, by hitting her 15 times with a hammer. The defendant claimed he was provoked by the victim's statement that while he was in prison she had slept with two other men and that the child she was expecting was not his. After killing her, the defendant called the police, admitted the killing and claiming that he was provoked.

At the trial, the defendant sought to call a psychiatrist who would give evidence that he was not suffering from a mental illness and was not violent by nature, but that his personality was such that he could have been provoked under the circumstances, and was likely to be telling the truth about what happened.[8] The defense stated that the psychiatrist's opinion would be based on information from the defendant, his medical records, his family, and friend, and that the psychiatric evidence would help establish lack of intent, that Turner was likely to be easily provoked, and show that Turner was likely to have told the truth in his statements.[9] The psychiatric report stated that until the night of the crime Turner was a quiet and passive person, sensitive to other people's feelings, known by his family and friends to be even-tempered, and generally not an aggressive person.[10]

The Crown (prosecution) objected to the admission of this evidence. Mr. David Calcutt, the prosecution counsel, argued that the evidence should be excluded because, first, the defendant had not put his character in issue, and second, the report did not mention the fact that the defendant was convicted in November 1971 for unlawful possession of an offensive weapon and also convicted in May 1972 of assault with intent to rob.[11] The Crown argued that allowing the psychiatric evidence would put the defendant before the jury as possessing a character and disposition that he does not possess, based on his previous conviction for unlawful possession of an offensive weapon.[12]

The Bristol Crown Court ruled that the psychiatric evidence was irrelevant and inadmissible. It was held that the evidence was inadmissible hearsay character evidence. Turner was convicted and sentenced to life imprisonment. He appealed, arguing that the judge erred by excluding the psychiatric evidence. He also contended that it was error for the trial judge to rule that provocation was not a matter for expert medical evidence.

The Court of Appeal agreed with the trial judge that the psychiatric evidence was hearsay character evidence and therefore inadmissible. Lord

Justice Lawton, delivering the judgment, stated that "it is not for this court to instruct psychiatrists how to draft their reports, but those who call psychiatrists as witnesses should remember that the facts upon which they base their opinions must be proved by admissible evidence. This elementary principle is frequently overlooked."[13] The Court of Appeal held that:

Before a court can assess the value of an opinion it must know the facts upon which it is based. If the expert has been misinformed about the facts or has taken irrelevant facts into consideration or has omitted to consider relevant ones, the opinion is likely to be valueless. In our judgment, counsel calling an expert should in examination in chief ask his witness to state the facts upon which his opinion is based. It is wrong to leave the other side to elicit the facts by cross-examination.[14]

On the issue of whether the psychiatric evidence was relevant to the facts of the case, the Court of Appeal disagreed with the trial judge's ruling that it was irrelevant. Lord Justice Lawton stated that:

In our judgment the psychiatrist's opinion was relevant. Relevance, however, does not result in evidence being admissible: It is a condition precedent to admissibility. Our law excludes evidence of many matters which in life outside the courts sensible people take into consideration when making decisions. Two broad heads of exclusion are hearsay and opinion. As we have already pointed out, the psychiatrist's report contained a lot of hearsay which was inadmissible. A ruling on this ground, however, would merely have trimmed the psychiatrist's evidence: It would not have excluded it altogether. Was it inadmissible because of the rules relating to opinion evidence?[15]

The Court of Appeal stated that the foundation of these rules was laid down in *Folkes v. Chadd*. It was held that although the psychiatric evidence that the defendant was suffering from mental illness was admissible evidence, it had been properly excluded in this case because it was not relevant to the facts in issue. The question of whether Turner was suffering from mental illness was not at issue. Lord Justice Lawton said:

We all know that both men and women who are deeply in love can, and sometimes do, have outbursts of blind rage when discovering unexpected wantonness on the part of their loved ones: The wife taken in adultery is the classical example of the application of the defense of "provocation"; and when death or serious injury results, profound grief usually follows. Jurors do not need psychiatrists to tell them how ordinary folk who are not suffering from any mental illness are likely to react to the stresses and strains of life. It follows that the proposed evidence was not admissible to establish that the defendant was likely to have been provoked. The same reasoning applies to its suggested admissibility on the issue of credibility. The jury had to decide what reliance they could put upon the defendant's evidence. He had to be judged as someone who was not mentally disordered. This is what juries are empanelled to do. The law assumes they can perform their duties properly. The jury in this case did not need, and should not have been offered, the evidence of a psychiatrist to help decide whether the defendant's evidence was truthful.[16]

The Court of Appeal dismissed the case and concluded that "psychiatry has not yet become a satisfactory substitute for the common sense of juries or magistrates on matters within their experience of life."[17]

In the United Kingdom, a technique, method, or field of knowledge does not have to be generally accepted before it can be admitted. It must be sufficiently established to be reliable, however, before it can be admitted. This was established in *R v. Robb*,[18] where it was held that general acceptance was not a condition for the admissibility of expert testimony. In this case, a phonetics lecturer was allowed by the trial court to give expert opinion on voice identification. The expert was qualified by training and experience but in his analysis he used a method that was not generally accepted by the majority of the experts in the field unless it was supplemented by another form of acoustic analysis. The defendant objected to the admission of this evidence. The trial judge however, admitted the evidence. The defendant was convicted and he appealed.

The Court of Appeal, through Lord Justice Thomas Bingham stated that the trial judge did not err in admitting the evidence and upheld the judgment. It was also held that expert evidence does not have to be scientific to be admitted. Lord Justice Bingham said:

Expert evidence is not limited to the core areas. Expert evidence of fingerprinting, handwriting, and accident reconstruction is regularly given. Opinions may be given of the market value of land, ships, pictures, or rights. Expert opinions may be given of the quality of commodities, or on the literary, artistic, scientific, or other merit of works alleged to be obscene. Some of these fields are far removed from anything which could be called a formal scientific discipline. Yet while receiving this evidence the courts would not accept the evidence of an astrologer, a soothsayer, a witch-doctor or an amateur psychologist and might hesitate to receive evidence of attributed authorship based on stylometric analysis.[19]

It should also be noted that in *R v. Stockwell*,[20] it was held that "one should not set one's face against fresh developments, provided they have a proper foundation."[21]

Having examined the main rules guiding the admission of expert testimony in the United Kingdom, we now examine specifically the admissibility of offender profiling evidence. In contrast to the United States, offender profiling *per se* has not been admitted by any British court. The first case where the prosecution sought to introduce offender profiling evidence was in *R v. Stagg*,[22] where the trial judge refused to admit the evidence. In *Stagg*, Justice Harry Ognall stated that there was "no authority in any common law jurisdiction to the effect that such evidence has ever been treated as properly admissible in proof of identity."[23] The trial judge was highly critical of the manner in which the evidence was gathered. Justice Ognall stated there were doubts as to whether psychological profile evidence had achieved widespread acceptance or had been adequately established as to be sufficiently reliable for evidential purpose, and stated that these sort of novel techniques must satisfy admissibility standards such as *Frye* or *Daubert*. Justice Ognall further stated that he "would not wish to give encouragement either to investigating or prosecuting authorities to construct or seek to supplement their cases on this kind of basis."[24] Following the rejection of the evidence, the case collapsed. There was no full trial. There has been no attempt since then by any party to introduce such evidence in the British courtroom. How will courts in the United Kingdom receive offender profiling evidence in future?

The R. Hon. Lord Taylor of Gosforth, the former Lord Chief Justice of England, was not in support of the admission of offender profiling in the courtroom. In a lecture delivered to the British Academy of Forensic Science on November 1, 1994, Lord Taylor echoed the problems with the proliferation of experts in court and was critical of the introduction of offender profiling evidence in courts.[25] Lord Taylor called on experts to maintain integrity and clarity, and he said:

Sometimes, however, although helpful in criminal investigation, a technique may not produce admissible evidence. So-called "personality profiling" is an example: Used properly, this technique can be of great assistance in helping the police to target their investigative work upon a limited number of likely suspects.

But we must not confuse such techniques, or their results, with evidence admissible in a court of law. The rules of criminal evidence have grown up gradually over many years. Some of them, particularly the embargo on hearsay, are now of dubious value and I hope will soon be extensively reformed as the Royal Commission has recommended. But the rules have grown up in response to the essential need to ensure that the material which is considered by the jury is only that which, as a matter of logic, actually tends to demonstrate guilt or innocence, not that which creates a suspicion and therefore, invites the making of assumptions for which there is no proper basis. The rules exist to ensure that a conviction of a criminal offense is founded upon fact not guesswork or conjecture. They afford vital protection of our freedom under the law.[26]

David Ormerod maintained that if offender profiling evidence is introduced in British courts in future, that the two hurdles of the law of evidence have to be overcome—relevance and admissibility.[27] He argued that the profile must render the facts more probable or less probable before it is legally relevant. Ormerod contended that a typical profile contains much information and that not all of the information will be relevant to any given case.[28] It has also been argued that in the United Kingdom, profile evidence will be excluded as being insufficiently relevant, unreliable, prejudicial and unscientific.[29] British courts will exclude offender profiling evidence because of its extreme prejudice; courts will not accord much weight to it because of its unreliability, and its prejudicial effect will in almost all cases outweigh its probative value.[30]

In fact, there are three main areas where offender profiling evidence is likely to be ruled inadmissible if it is introduced in a future British trial. First, offender profiling is a technique without any adequate, reliable, or objective foundation at the moment. As such, British courts will likely rule it inadmissible based on the *Turner* rule, which requires that expert evidence must be based upon facts which can themselves be proved by admissible evidence. If offender profiling evidence is introduced again in a British court, the trial judge is also likely to draw on United States court decisions that have rejected the evidence. British courts will likely adopt the decision in *State v. Cavallo*,[31] where the Supreme Court of New Jersey held that "until the scientific reliability of this type of evidence is established, it is not admissible."[32]

The extreme prejudicial effect of offender profiling evidence is also another area where it is likely to be excluded in future British trials. "The prejudicial effect includes risks that the jurors could: convict a defendant on the basis of the characteristic alone (where it is reprehensible); assign a disproportionate weight to the evidence of the characteristic; deny the accused the benefit of doubt and convict on less than the full standard of proof; and the police could be inclined to 'round up the usual suspects.'"[33]

Above all, where the manner and methods of offender profiling were questionable, a trial judge will apply Section 78 of PACE (Police and Criminal Evidence Act, 1984), and exclude the evidence. Under Section 78 of PACE, a judge is allowed to exclude evidence "if it appears to the court that, having regard to all the circumstances in which the evidence was obtained, the admission of the evidence would have such an adverse effect on the fairness of the proceedings that the court ought not to admit it."

In the United Kingdom, expert testimony on any form of offender profiling is not likely to be excluded merely on the hearsay rule. There are many exceptions to the rule. In fact, in *R v. Abadom*,[34] it was held that once the primary facts on which an opinion is based have been proved by admissible evidence, the expert is entitled to draw on the work of others as part of arriving at his own conclusions. This was also supported in *English Exporters (London) v. Eldonwall Limited*.[35] It has been pointed out that where the primary information consists mainly or entirely of hearsay, the judge would be justified in warning the jury about the flimsiness of any foundation for that opinion.[36]

In the final analysis, one can safely say that in the United Kingdom there are more rules and reasons supporting the exclusion of offender profiling evidence than are rules or reasons for its admission. Offender profiling deals with character traits, is more prejudicial than probative, is not based on any reliable or objective data at the moment, and Section 78 of PACE gives judges the wide discretion to exclude such evidence that is unfair to an accused.

OFFENDER PROFILING IN CANADA

Canada is a close neighbor of United States so it is not surprising that some forms of offender profiling have been admitted in Canadian courtrooms. There is general disagreement among scholars as to whether there is a specific rule governing the admissibility of expert evidence in Canada. As David Bernstein has pointed out, some version of the reliability test has been adopted by a majority of the courts, while a few courts have adopted the general acceptance standard.[37] Arguably, the main rule governing the admissibility of expert evidence in Canada today was laid down in *R v. Mohan*,[38] where the Supreme Court of Canada laid down four factors that should be examined when faced with a decision to admit or exclude expert evidence. Prior to *Mohan*, two court rulings provided some guidelines to trial judges. The first is *R v. Beland*,[39] a case that involved the admissibility of polygraph. In this case, the defendant offered polygraph evidence but the prosecution argued that it should be excluded because it had not reached an acceptable standard of reliability. Delivering the judgment, Justice William McIntyre stated that "even the finding of a significant percentage of error in the results of a polygraph would not by itself, be sufficient to exclude it as an instrument for use in courts."[40] The second case is *R v. Lavellee*,[41] where evidence of battered woman syndrome was ruled admissible. Delivering the opinion, Justice Bertha Wilson stated that expert evidence is admissible if it was beyond the common experience and knowledge of jurors. Concurring, Justice John Sopinka said that expert opinion should be based on forms of inquiry and practice accepted within the expertise.[42]

In *Mohan*, the defendant, Chikmaglur Mohan, a pediatrician, was charged with four counts of sexual assault of four of his patients. The patients, all females, were between the ages of 13 and 16 at the time of the assaults, which took place at the defendant's medical office.[43] Mohan was alleged to have fondled the girls' breasts and engaged in extensive and intrusive questioning of their sexual life. It was also alleged that there was "digital penetration and stimulation" of the patients' vaginas and that Mohan did not wear gloves during these vaginal examinations.[44]

At the trial, the defense sought to introduce a psychiatrist, Dr. Hill to testify that the perpetrator of these sorts of sexual offenses would be part of a limited and unusual group of individuals and that Mohan did not possess the characteristics of the offenders who fall within that narrow group.[45] Hill stated that he had interviewed and treated three doctors who were accused of sexual assault of their patients. He also stated in the Mohan trial that based on a psychological profile, the likely offender in the first three sexual assaults was likely to be a pedophile, and that the perpetrator of the fourth sexual assault was likely to be a sexual psychopath.[46]

In the voir dire, Dr. Hill, the expert, began his testimony by explaining that there are three general personality groups that have unusual personality traits in terms of their psychological profile perspective. The first group encompasses the psychosexual who suffers from major mental illnesses (e.g., schizophrenia) and engages in inappropriate sexual behavior occasionally. The second and largest group contains the sexual deviation types. This group of individuals shows distinct abnormalities in terms of the choice of individuals with whom they report excitement and with whom they would like to engage in some type of sexual activity. The third group is that of the sexual psychopaths. These individuals have a callous disregard for people around them, including a disregard for the consequences of their sexual behavior towards other individuals. Another group would include pedophiles who gain sexual excitement from young adolescents, probably pubertal or postpubertal.[47]

Hill stated that pedophiles and sexual psychopaths constitute an unusual and limited class of individuals. He was further of the opinion that Mohan does not possess the characteristics of pedophiles or sexual psychopaths and so would not have sexually assaulted the four victims. The trial judge, Justice Bernstein, ruled that the testimony was inadmissible. The court stated that the testimony was unnecessary and that the jury could decide for themselves. In the trial court's view:

The evidence of Doctor Hill is not sufficient, I believe, to establish that doctors who commit sexual assaults on patients are in a significantly more limited group in psychiatric terms than are other members of society. There is no scientific data available to warrant that conclusion. A sample of three offenders is not a sufficient basis for such a conclusion. Even the allegations of the fourth complainant are not so unusual, as sex offenders go, to warrant a conclusion that the perpetrator must have belonged to a sufficiently narrow class.[48]

Therefore, the trial court concluded that the evidence was inadmissible character evidence and also did not fall within the proper sphere of expert evidence. Mohan was convicted and sentenced to nine months imprisonment on each count, concurrently and two years probation.[49]

The defendant appealed and the Crown also appealed arguing that the sentence was too light. At the Ontario Court of Appeal,[50] Justice Robin Finlayson ruled that the trial judge erred by excluding Hill's testimony. Justice Finyalson stated that the testimony was admissible on two bases. First, "given that similar fact evidence was admitted showing that the acts

compared are so unusual and strikingly similar that their similarities cannot
be attributed to coincidence, Dr. Hill's testimony was admissible to show
that the offenses alleged were unlikely to have been committed by the same
person."[51] "On the second basis, it was admissible to show that the respondent was not a member of either the unusual groups of aberrant per-
sonalities which could have committed the offenses alleged.[52]

Justice Finyalson also stated that the trial judge's conclusion was based
on a misapprehension of the evidence. He stated that in his view, the expert
did not base his opinion only on the three cases with three doctors, but
based his opinion on all of his experience.[53] The Court of Appeal therefore,
reversed the judgment and remanded for a new trial.

The case reached the Supreme Court of Canada, where Justice Sopinka
stated that this type of evidence has to be excluded based on the principles
governing the admissibility of expert evidence and the character evidence
exceptions.[54] The Supreme Court of Canada held that the admission of
expert evidence depends on the application of the following criteria: 1)
relevance, 2) necessity in assisting the trier of fact, 3) the absence of any
exclusionary rule, and 4) a properly qualified expert.[55] On the relevance of
the expert evidence, Justice Sopinka stated that:

Relevance is a threshold requirement for the admission of expert evidence as with
all other evidence. Relevance is a matter to be decided by a judge as question of law.
Although prima facie admissible if so related to a fact in issue that it tends to establish it, that does not end the inquiry. This merely determines the logical relevance of
the evidence. Other considerations enter into the decision as to admissibility. This
further inquiry may be described as a cost benefit analysis, that is "whether its value
is worth what it costs:" . . . Cost in this context is not used in its traditional economic
sense but rather in terms of its impact on the trial process. Evidence that is otherwise
logically relevant may be excluded on this basis, if its probative value is overborne
by its prejudicial effect, if it involves an inordinate amount of time which is not com-
mensurate with its value or if it is misleading in the sense that its effect on the trier
of fact, particularly a jury, is out of proportion to its reliability.[56]

Justice Sopinka summed up, stating, "it appears from the foregoing that
expert evidence which advances a novel scientific theory or technique is subjected to special scrutiny to determine whether it meets a basic threshold of
reliability and whether it is essential in the sense that the trier of fact will be
unable to come to a satisfactory conclusion without the assistance of the
expert. The closer the evidence approaches an opinion on an ultimate issue,
the stricter the application of this principle."[57] Addressing the issue of expert
evidence as to disposition, Justice Sopinka stated that in his opinion;

In order to be relevant on the issue of identity the evidence must tend to show that
the accused shared a distinctive unusual behavioral trait with the perpetrator of the

crime. The trait must be sufficiently distinctive that it operates virtually as a badge or mark identifying the perpetrator. Conversely, the fact that the accused is a member of an abnormal group some of the members which have the unusual behavioral characteristics shown to have been possessed by the perpetrator is not sufficient. In some cases it may, however, be shown that all members of the group have the distinctive unusual characteristics. If a reasonable inference can be drawn that the accused has these traits then the evidence is relevant subject to the trial judge's obligation to exclude it if its prejudicial effect outweighs its probative value. The greater the number of persons in society having these tendencies, the less relevant the evidence on the issue of identity and the more likely that its prejudicial effect predominates over its probative value.[58]

The Supreme Court of Canada also held that psychiatric evidence of the personality traits or disposition of an accused, or another is admissible if it is: relevant to the facts at issue, not a violation of any policy rule, and the evidence falls within the proper sphere of expert evidence.[59] The Supreme Court of Canada reversed the judgment of the Court of Appeal and upheld the trial court's ruling.

In *R v. Ranger,*[60] the Ontario Court of Appeal ruled that the trial judge erred by admitting expert testimony on crime scene staging, where the expert went into "criminal profiling." On August 16, 1995, two sisters Marsha, 19, and Tamara Ottey, 16, were stabbed to death in their home in Scarborough. The defendant, Rohan Ranger and his cousin Adrian Kinkead were charged with the murders. The defendants were tried and convicted separately. Marsha Ottey was Ranger's girlfriend but she ended the relationship because the defendant was very possessive and abusive. The Crown claimed that Ranger refused to accept that the relationship was over and that Ranger killed Marsha Ottey after he heard that she was moving to United States to start college. The prosecution claimed that Ranger killed her because "if he could not have her, nobody else can."[61]

The defendant claimed that he was not in the house at the time of the murders and that Kinkead committed the murders. Police investigation showed that the house was ransacked but only three items belonging to Marsha were taken. The three items were a gold necklace that the defendant had given to Marsha Ottey, a videotape of her playing soccer and her electronic organizer.[62] The Crown therefore, decided to call a crime scene reconstruction expert and criminal profiling expert, who testified that the crime scene was staged and made to look like a burglary. The expert, Detective Inspector Kathryn Lines (manager of the Behavioral Sciences Section of the Ontario Provincial Police) testified that the crime scene was staged by "someone who had an association or relationship with the victim, M., and who had a particular interest in M.'s possessions."[63] Lines stated that she based her opinion on the crime scene photographs, crime scene videotapes, police reports, and autopsy reports.

At the trial, several witnesses testified for the Crown, including Kinkead. The Crown also introduced evidence of the defendant's trip to Jamaica in January 1996, where he overstayed and was arrested. The defense argued that the evidence should be excluded because it was prejudicial. Five witnesses also testified that they saw a man fitting the description of the defendant near the victims' home around 7:30 A.M. on the day of the murder and the day before the murders. The defendant on the other hand, introduced a security videotape showing that he was at a shopping mall at 8:08 A.M. on the day of the murder. It should be noted that the time of death of the victims was given as 7:30 A.M. The prosecution contended that the defendant created a false alibi by going to the shopping mall so that he could be captured on the security video camera.[64]

The defense argued that the expert testimony by Detective Inspector Lines should not be admitted. They argued that the jury did not need expert assistance to determine whether the crime scene was staged or not, and that Lines's expert evidence was not required since the crime scene photographs and videotapes had already been provided to the court by Detective Ian Mann.

The trial judge ruled that the expert evidence was admissible, stating that the issue of whether the crime scene was staged or not was outside the common experience and knowledge of the jury and so expert assistance was necessary as long as the expert is qualified.[65] Lines was qualified by the court as an expert on crime scene staging and her testimony was admitted.

The defendants were convicted. Ranger was convicted of first degree murder for the death of Marsha Ottey and convicted of manslaughter for the death of Tamara Ottey. He appealed, arguing that he received an unfair trial. He contended that the trial judge erred by admitting Lines's unscientific expert evidence and by admitting evidence of his arrest in Jamaica; and that the trial judge's instructions to the jury were insufficient. The defendant also argued that the expert evidence did not meet the reliability or necessity criteria as required by the Supreme Court decision in *Mohan*.

At the Court of Appeal, Justice Louise Charron ruled that the trial judge erred in five areas. Delivering the opinion of the Court, Justice Charron said: "Detective Inspector Lines's testimony was not confined to the opinion that the crime scene was staged. Notwithstanding the Crown's assurance that he would not elicit evidence relating to motivation, Detective Inspector Lines' examination-in-chief included an opinion about the motivation of the perpetrator for staging the scene and a description of the most likely suspects as someone who had a particular interest in Marsha Ottey."[66]

Justice Charron restated the fact that the *Mohan* requirements must be satisfied. She went on to say that even if expert evidence meets the four *Mohan* requirements, the evidence may still be excluded if its prejudicial effect outweighs its probative value. She stated there should be an inquiry into the reliability of the expert evidence.[67]

Justice Charron also stated that the *Mohan* criteria apply on a case-by-case basis. Justice Charron further noted that Detective Inspector Lines's testimony went beyond the scope of admissible expert evidence; that the testimony went into profiling and was therefore, inadmissible. Furthermore, the judge stated that "the manner in which the crime scene evidence was packaged for the jury in this case exemplifies the usual dangers associated with expert opinion evidence."[68] Justice Charron said:

In this case, Detective Inspector Lines' opinions about the perpetrator's likely motivation for staging the crime scene and his characteristics as a person associated with the victims and having a particular interest in Marsha constituted evidence of criminal profiling. Criminal profiling is a novel field of scientific evidence, the reliability of which was not demonstrated at trial. To the contrary, it would appear from her limited testimony about the available verification of opinions in her field of work that her opinions amounted to no more than educated guesses. As such, her criminal profiling evidence was inadmissible. The criminal profiling evidence also approached the ultimate issue in this case and, hence, was highly prejudicial. The prejudice was further heightened by the limits placed on defense counsel's cross-examination and by the prominence that the trial judge gave to Detective Inspector Lines' evidence in his charge.[69]

Justice Charron also ruled that the evidence about the defendant's trip and arrest in Jamaica was of no probative value and was very prejudicial. The Court of Appeal concluded that the errors were harmful and remanded for a new trial.

In *R v. Clark*,[70] the Court of Appeal for Ontario ruled that expert evidence on crime scene staging was admissible even though it went into criminal profiling. This is quite in contrast with its prior decision in *Ranger* discussed above. On December 26, 1995, the bodies of William Tweed and his wife Phyllis were found in their home in Thornhill, Ontario. They had been stabbed to death. Police investigators suspected that the perpetrator had staged the crime scene to show forced entry and burglary. The defendant, Joel Clark, was the main suspect. Investigations showed that a few weeks before the murders, Clark had stolen the victims' credit card and used it to buy an engagement ring for his girlfriend.[71] It should be noted that the defendant lived with his grandmother near the Tweeds and that his grandmother was very close to them. The defendant also visited the Tweeds regularly to help them out with odd jobs. They were so close that the Tweeds gave his grandmother a duplicate key to their house to keep in case of emergency.[72]

Blood stains found on the defendant's pants matched Mr. Tweed's DNA. Furthermore, while he was in custody, the defendant confided in his cell mate (an undercover police officer), Sergent Ian Matthews, that he stabbed the Tweeds and could not understand how the police were still able to detect blood on his pants because he had washed the pants after the murders.[73]

The defendant admitted stealing the credit card but denied the murders. He stated that another man, Marcel Whyte, committed the murders.[74] At the trial, the Crown called a crime scene reconstruction expert to testify. Detective Inspector Kathryn Lines stated that the crime scene examination revealed elements of crime scene staging and that one individual was responsible for the murders. She based her opinion on the crime scene photographs, crime scene videotapes, personal visit to the house, police reports, and autopsy reports. Lines testified that the crime scene had been staged to look like a burglary, and that the killer was someone who knew the victims and knew the layout of their apartment.[75] She also stated that it was a blitz-attack and that the victims were sleeping at the time they were killed. Justice Peter Howden admitted the evidence. The defendant was convicted of two counts of murder and he appealed.

Among other claims, the defendant argued that Lines's expert testimony should not have been admitted because it was unnecessary, unreliable, and more prejudicial than it was probative. The defendant also argued that much of her testimony was inadmissible criminal profiling evidence.

Delivering the opinion of the Court of Appeal, Justice Michael Moldaver ruled that the trial judge did not err in admitting the expert evidence. Justice Moldaver however, stated that a small amount of the evidence was impermissible criminal profiling evidence, but the small amount could not have affected the outcome. The Court of Appeal held that:

A properly qualified expert in crime scene analysis can offer opinion evidence about what occurred at the crime scene and how the crime was committed (crime scene reconstruction evidence). Crime scene reconstruction evidence is potentially admissible. Its ultimate acceptance or rejection will depend on whether it conforms ... [to] the rules that govern the admissibility of expert evidence in general. In respect of crime scene reconstruction evidence, the following three areas will generally require close attention: whether the evidence is necessary in the sense that it is likely to fall outside the knowledge or normal experience of the average juror; whether the opinion is reliable in the sense that it is anchored in the evidence and not the product of guesswork or speculation; and whether there is a real danger that the jury will be overwhelmed by the evidence and give it more weight than it deserves. Crime scene reconstruction evidence is to be contrasted with expert evidence offered to explain why the crime was committed in a particular manner (the perpetrator's motivation), more particularly, who is more likely to have committed the crime ("criminal profiling evidence"). Criminal profiling evidence will generally be inadmissible, as criminal profiling is a novel field of scientific evidence and often appears to be based on nothing more than educated guesses. In this case, the police officer's evidence that the crime scene was staged was properly admitted, as was her evidence as to how the crime was committed.

She was qualified to express an opinion about staging and her evidence fell outside the knowledge and experience of the average juror. Her opinion was reliable in the sense that it was anchored in the evidence and not the product of guesswork or speculation, and the evidence of staging was not so complex or technical that the jury was likely to be overwhelmed by it and give it more weight than it deserved.[76]

Justice Moldaver went on to say that the expert evidence was not an opinion on the ultimate issue and that there was overwhelming evidence against the defendant that some amount of criminal profiling could not have affected the outcome.[77]

In dismissing the appeal, Justice Moldaver stated that the crime scene reconstruction evidence was properly admitted even though it contained some amount of criminal profiling evidence. This is quite in contrast with the Court's earlier ruling in *Ranger* on the admissibility of criminal profiling evidence. This case also supports the call for extra judicial control in all cases involving offender profiling or its derivatives.

OFFENDER PROFILING IN OTHER COUNTRIES

Offender profiling is still in its infancy but it has been used in criminal investigations in a few countries, including Australia, Finland, Italy, Japan, the Netherlands, Russia, and South Africa. This does not mean that it has been admitted in the courtroom. In Australia, offender profiling *per se* has not been admitted in any court. There has been no major court decision banning the reception of offender profiling evidence in courts. Under the Australian rules of evidence, expert testimony is admissible if it is relevant to the facts at issue and not excluded by other evidence rules, such as the expertise rule, the common knowledge rule, the factual basis rule, and the ultimate issue rule. In Finland, offender profiling is mainly used in crime investigations. Courts generally see offender profiling and its derivatives as an aid to crime investigation. In the Netherlands, the Offender Profiling Unit of the National Intelligence Division of the National Police Agency conducts offender profiling activities.

As we mentioned earlier, offender profiling technique is still in its infancy, hence the technique is not used in many countries, especially in the developing countries. For instance, in countries like Nigeria, the technique has not been used in crime investigation. As such, the evidential implications of such evidence have not arisen. It is important, however, to examine how the courts will receive such evidence if offered in future trials. Offender profiling deals with the character traits of an individual. In Nigeria, it is likely to be seen by the courts as permissible character evidence. In Nigeria, "the general rule is that the fact an accused has committed some other offenses or other misconduct on other previous occasions or is of bad character or reputation is not relevant in subsequent proceedings. The rationale behind this rule is that the accused person's guilt has to be independently proved by the prosecution. The admissibility of previous misconduct will only go to prejudice the mind of a court."[78] The Nigerian Evidence Act,[79] section 69(1) states that the fact that an accused person is of bad character is irrelevant in subsequent proceedings. There are certain exceptions, however, which are contained in Section 69(2) of the Evidence Act. It says the fact that an accused person is of bad character is relevant: 1) when the bad character of the accused person is a fact in issue; and 2) when the accused person has given evidence of his good character.

It is noteworthy to point out that Nigeria is a former British colony, hence the Nigerian legal system is based on British common law tradition. In fact, the Nigerian rules of expert evidence are virtually the same as that of Great Britain. Thus, a witness must be qualified as an expert and the opinion must be outside the common experience and knowledge of the judge or jury.[80] In Nigeria, the general principle is that the facts upon which an expert based his or her opinion must be provided. This is where offender profiling evidence will likely be ruled inadmissible if it is to be introduced in a Nigerian court today. The Nigerian Supreme Court will likely draw from the position of British courts on the admissibility of offender profiling. They are likely to state that such evidence should not be admitted until its reliability can be established. Thus, in *Dickson Arisa v. The State*,[81] the Supreme Court of Nigeria ruled that opinion evidence by an expert on mental illness had no evidential weight because the expert failed to provide the basis for his opinion. Justice Abdul Agbaje stated that the law required that for expert evidence to be admitted, the facts upon which the opinion was based must be provided. Nigerian courts may not accord much weight to expert evidence where the factual basis was not produced.[82] Furthermore, in cases where two expert witnesses gave conflicting expert opinions, the court will rely on the opinion of the expert who provided the facts or data upon which the opinion was based.[83] It should also be noted that in Nigeria, a technique, method, or field of knowledge does not have to be scientific before it can be admitted. In a nutshell, the main area where offender profiling evidence is likely to be excluded in Nigeria, in future cases, is the lack of reliable data upon which the technique is based. The prejudicial effect of offender profiling will probably be another strong area for exclusion of offender profiling evidence.

In all jurisdictions examined in this work, the trial judge has enormous latitude to decide who is qualified to give expert evidence and when such evidence is needed. Similarly, no jurisdiction examined here requires an expert to have gained the expertise in a certain way. An expert can be qualified by education, skill, training, or knowledge. All jurisdictions appear to be liberal in deciding who is qualified to give expert testimony.

Conclusion

Offender profiling is a crime investigation technique normally used when an offender did not leave any physical traces at the scene of crime. It aims to predict the likely characteristics of the unknown offender by looking at behavioral patterns and other nonphysical clues. Profiling in general was not originally intended to be used for crime investigation or for courtroom purpose. Offender profiling began from early attempts by criminologists to explain criminality and to predict criminal behavior. It then moved on to the next stage of using it to profile heads of states (for intelligence purposes only). Later, psychiatrists and psychologists started offering psychological profiles to assist the police to find unknown killers. Following this stage, the FBI discovered that psychological profiles were indeed helpful in its pursuit of unknown serial killers, and the Bureau devised its own crime scene analysis approach. Today offender profiling has become one of the most controversial, useful, but worrying techniques of crime investigation. It is submitted that we should now move on to the next stage of using offender profiling as a crime prevention technique.

There is an uneasy relationship among the different segments of law enforcement involved with offender profiling. Each approach to offender profiling takes a parochial view. Each segment of the law enforcement community sees offender profiling as its own monopoly or exclusive club. As a result, the potential of offender profiling has been limited. The sharing of knowledge and experience is suggested. We need an integrated approach, where all groups can come together as a team. Psychiatrists, psychologists, criminologists, and law enforcement agents all have a role to play, not only in crime investigations, but also in coming up with crime prevention measures and programs. These professionals have knowledge of the kind of individuals likely to commit certain types of crime, knowledge of the location a particular crime is likely to happen, and knowledge about the type of individual that is likely to be a victim of a certain type of crime. Therefore, by pulling resources together, the future of offender profiling looks very exciting and will prove to be an invaluable technique of crime investigation and crime prevention. As we have seen, offender profiling has not yet reached the level to be called a hard science, but in time it will be. It has been pointed out elsewhere that "if a technique cannot be proved, then it is not science."[1] Offender profiling at the moment cannot be proved, therefore, it is not science.

The current lack of unity and cooperation and absence of information sharing among the different profiling communities creates a further legal dilemma—how much can one convince the courts as to the reliability and validity of offender profiling? Until the profiling communities come together as a team, the search for the scientific basis and for general acceptance of this technique will continue to be a mirage. A way forward in the United States, for instance, would be the establishment of a professional body for offender profilers that would draw upon various professions. The well-established professional bodies can play an important role in this issue by organizing well-publicized interdisciplinary conferences and presenting papers. Such professional bodies, as the American Psychological Association, the Academy of Forensic Sciences, and the Society for Police and Criminal Psychology, are best suited for this function. There is no gainsaying the fact, however, that offender profiling at the moment is a "specialized field of knowledge," that is very useful in crime investigation. At the moment, professional offender profilers tend to publish their work in their own journals. This is also hampering the potential of offender profiling.

Currently, all the different approaches base their arguments on assumptions, inferences, probabilities, personal intuition, and on their clinical practice experience. Suffice it to say that none of these approaches can properly be described as sufficiently reliable for proving a defendant's guilt or innocence. We have also seen that offender profiling at best should be described as a multidisciplinary practice that calls for knowledge and experience in such fields as criminology, psychiatry, psychology, and law enforcement.

This book supports the idea put forward by David Ormerod that for offender profiling to be easily admitted in courts, the profile should be produced by a "profiling team" rather than by individual profilers. We believe courts are reluctant to accept a profiler's expert opinion because much of it is based on personal intuition.

The three main rules governing the admissibility of expert testimony in United States have their various strengths and weaknesses. Arguably, the *Frye* test offers ease of application. Trial judges do not have to become scientists in order to decide on scientific evidence. The Federal Rule of Evidence 702 is too loose and too liberal: Almost anything can be admitted as expert evidence—be it scientific, technical, or other specialized knowledge. Similarly, almost anyone can qualify as an expert under the Federal Rule of

Evidence 702, either by way of knowledge, skill, experience, training, or education. *Daubert* has proved very problematic in application, and is arguably not favored by many trial judges. *Daubert* has raised more questions than answers.

This examination of these three rules of scientific admissibility has shown the confusion and inconsistencies resulting from their adoption. This leads to one obvious question—is it possible to adopt one particular rule? The *Frye* test, the Federal Rules of Evidence, and *Daubert* are not constitutional constructions. As such they are not binding on the individual states. The United States operates a federal system of government; hence, the states have always enjoyed the freedom to choose the rule they prefer. Above all, the United States Supreme Court has not given any reason why states should adopt one particular rule.

I submit that *Frye*, combined with the Federal Rules of Evidence, offers the most appropriate standard for the admissibility of expert testimony. Its success has been noted in the case of *Christophersen v. Allied–Signal Corp.*[2] It is submitted that the United States Supreme Court should revisit the issue and give the lower courts and the states reasons justifying the need for the adoption of one rule. Then we may see some sort of uniformity in judicial decisions. Then the lower courts will not face the risk of having their decisions reversed, simply because their state has adopted a rule different from the one adopted by the federal courts.

One of the main issues surrounding the admissibility of expert testimony has been on general acceptance. Many states are in favor of the *Frye* test. Interestingly, many trial judges generally accept and prefer the *Frye* test. Several research studies have supported this argument.[3] Dahir et al., for instance, carried out a study of 325 state trial judges (from the 50 states and the District of Columbia) and found that there is "a strong tendency for judges to continue to rely on more traditional standards, such as general acceptance and qualifications of the expert, when assessing psychological syndrome and profile evidence."[4] Their study also suggests that "judges do understand some of the less technical guidelines (i.e., general acceptance and peer review and publication) but not the more technical ones (i.e., falsifiability and error rate), and that they prefer general acceptance and qualifications of the expert as guidelines when determining the admissibility of psychological evidence."[5] The study therefore, concluded that "judges are relying on criteria and habits of analysis familiar to them (mainly *Frye v. United States' [1923]* general acceptance standard, relevance, and qualifications and credibility of the expert) even as they struggle with new ideas foisted on them from above."[6] It makes sense therefore, to adopt a standard that is generally accepted by trial judges as being the appropriate standard, bearing in mind that these trial judges are the "gatekeepers."

Offender profiling is a multidisciplinary practice, largely based on intuition, guesswork, and speculation. At the moment it can best be described as an art with the potential of becoming a science. Offender profiling should be generally accepted as being sufficiently reliable by the general profiling community, not just the law enforcement community. Arguably, it is only those in the law enforcement community who see offender profiling or its derivatives as reliable techniques for courtroom purposes at the moment. Until the different segments come together as a team, offender profiling should not be taken as a technique that has achieved widespread recognition as to be introduced into the courtroom as evidence.

Many experts who testify on offender profiling have the tendency to flaunt their qualifications in front of the courts. The result is that courts tend to be seduced by these impressive and sometimes "intimidating credentials." This also results in many of these experts testifying beyond their expertise. What is happening today is that many of the profilers who are supposed to be criminal investigators now think that they are criminal prosecutors. They tend to forget that their role is to testify and not to decide cases. It is therefore, submitted that there should be extra judicial control when dealing with expert testimony on offender profiling. In all cases involving offender profiling, the trial judge should inform the jury at the onset that offender profiling evidence does not identify a specific offender; that it is not identification evidence; and that its reliability cannot be objectively ascertained at the moment. The trial judge should limit the testimony to patterns of behavior and crime scene characteristics, which in some cases may assist the trier of fact in understanding the circumstances of a case.

It is worrying that in some cases, profile testimony has even been admitted by trial courts, when it was clearly irrelevant to the case, as in *United States v. Baldwin*.[7] There should be a jury instruction in all cases involving offender profiling and its derivatives. The trial judge should inform the jury about the level of reliability and validity of this technique. This will help them to determine the weight (if any) that should be accorded to the testimony.

The above problem has been compounded by the Federal Rule of Evidence 702. Offender profiling as we have seen falls under a specialized field of knowledge, but Rule 702 has created problems for trial judges when deciding who is qualified to give expert offender profiling testimony.

Offender profiling testimony is more effective when it is being proffered by the defendant to show innocence, than when it is being offered by the prosecution to show the defendant's guilt. Further research on this argument is suggested. Offender profiling is also effective when there are codefendants and it is being offered to show that one defendant is less likely to have committed the crime. With offender profiling evidence, it is easier to prove innocence than guilt, but this does not mean that it is reliable.

Offender profiling *per se*, is supposedly inadmissible in many jurisdictions, including the United States and Canada. When it is labeled differently and dressed up in other terms, however, courts have admitted it. Is this because many people including judges do not understand what offender profiling is and the different forms or shapes of offender profiling? Or is it that some criminal profilers are playing on the intelligence of judges, lawyers, and jurors? More research is needed in this area. If an expert witness says that he or she is going to testify on "offender profiling," it will not be allowed, but if the same expert says he or she is going to testify on the same thing under a different label, then it will be allowed. Two of the Canadian cases have highlighted this issue. In other cases an expert was allowed to testify on crime scene staging, and then eventually touched on the ultimate issue. Whether any form of offender profiling will be admitted depends on the label the expert is using, not on the content or issue involved. In the United States, profiling evidence on motivational analysis has been allowed in some cases and excluded in others. In Canada, on the other hand, expert testimony on motivational analysis is supposedly not allowed, but when it is presented as testimony on crime scene reconstruction analysis, it may be admitted. Who is fooling whom?

I say again that offender profiling is not sufficiently reliable as to be admissible. It is also submitted that offender profiling is more prejudicial than it is probative. The findings of this work also support my claim that there is an uneasy relationship among the different professions involved with offender profiling. As a result, the potential of this technique has been limited. There are doubts as to the reliability and validity of this technique. It is submitted that offender profiling should not be used in the courtroom until its reliability can be properly and objectively ascertained. The guessing game of offender profiling should not be played in the courtroom. Offender profiling and its derivatives should not be admitted until their reliability can be objectively ascertained. Offender profiling is a technique based on probabilities and no individual should be convicted on probability.

Notes

CHAPTER 1

1. Ronald. M. Holmes & Stephen T. Holmes, Profiling Violent Crimes: An Investigative Tool 3 (1996).

2. *Id.*

3. *Id.,* at 4.

4. *Id.,* at 5.

5. Vernon J. Geberth, Practical Homicide Investigation: Tactics, Procedures, and Forensic Techniques 22 (4th ed. 2006).

6. John Douglas & L. K. Douglas, *Modus Operandi and Signature Aspects of Violent Crime, in* Crim. Classification Man. 260 (Douglas et al. eds., 2006).

7. Geberth, *supra* note 5, at 824.

8. Michael D. Risinger & Jeffrey L. Loop, *Three Card Monte, Monty Hall, Modus Operandi and 'Offender Profiling': Some Lessons of Modern Cognitive Science for the Law of Evidence,* 24 Cardozo L. Rev. (Nov. 2002) at 193, 254.

9. Holmes & Holmes, *supra* note 1, at 2.

10. J. T. McCann, *Criminal Personality Profiling in the Investigation of Violent Crime: Recent Advances and Future Directions* 10 Behav. Sci. & L. 476 (1992).

11. Peter B. Ainsworth, Offender Profiling and Crime Analysis 9 (2001).

12. Deborah Schurman-Kauflin, Vulture: Profiling Sadistic Serial Killers 10 (2005).

13. Cesaro Lombroso, L'uoma Delinquente (The Criminal Man) (1876).

14. Charles Goring, The English Convict: A Statistical Study 174 (1913).

15. R. Garofalo, Criminology 110 (trans. 1914).

16. Earnest A. Hooton, The American Criminal: An Anthropological Study 309 (1939).

17. Earnest A. Hooton, Crime and Man 301 (1939).

18. George B. Vold, Theoretical Criminology 62 (1958).

19. Elmer H. Johnson, CRIME, CORRECTION, AND SOCIETY 211 (1974).

20. Hans Gross, CRIMINAL INVESTIGATION: A PRACTICAL TEXTBOOK FOR MAGISTRATES, POLICE OFFICERS AND LAWYERS, 478 (1924) Sweet & Maxwell.

21. Hans Gross, CRIMINAL PSYCHOLOGY 55 (1934).

22. From THE COMPLETE JACK THE RIPPER by Donald Rumbelow, published by W. H. Allen. Reprinted by permission of The Random House Group Ltd. 111 (1975).

23. Walter C. Langer, THE MIND OF ADOLF HITLER: THE SECRET WARTIME REPORT, 19 (1972).

24. *Id.*, at 215–216.

25. William H. Sheldon, VARIETIES OF DELINQUENT YOUTH 36, 105–107 (1949).

26. Sheldon Glueck, and E. Glueck, PHYSIQUE AND DELINQUENCY 286 (1956).

27. Ernst Kretschmer, PHYSIQUE AND CHARACTER: AN INVESTIGATION OF THE NATURE OF CONSTITUTION AND THE THEORY OF TEMPERAMENT (1925).

28. James A. Brussel, CASEBOOK OF A CRIME PSYCHIATRIST 1X (1968).

29. *Id.*

30. *Id.*, at 47.

31. *Id.*, at 3.

32. R. K. Ressler, A. W. Burgess & J. E. Douglas, SEXUAL HOMICIDE: PATTERNS AND MOTIVES 122 (1992).

33. *Id.*

34. David Canter, CRIMINAL SHADOWS: INSIDE THE MIND OF THE SERIAL KILLER 14 (1994).

35. Paul Britton, THE JIGSAW MAN 49 (1997).

36. R v. Stagg, Central Criminal Court, 14 September, 1994.

37. http://www.bps.org.uk/media-centre/press-releases/releases$/disciplinary-matters$/outcome-of-preliminary-proceedings-for-disciplinary-hearing-for-mr-paul-britton$.cfm (accessed 01/01/2008).

38. David Canter & Lawrence Alison, *Profiling in Policy and Practice*, *in* PROFILING IN POLICY AND PRACTICE 8 (D. Canter & A. Lawrence eds., 1999).

39. *Id.*

40. Canter, *supra* note 34, at 52–57.

CHAPTER 2

1. Richard J. Badcock, *Developmental and Clinical Issues in Relation to Offender Profiling in the Individual*, *in* OFFENDER PROFILING: THEORY, RESEARCH AND PRACTICE, 26 (Janet L. Jackson & Debra A. Bekerian eds., 1997).

2. Steven A. Egger, *Psychological Profiling: Past, Present, and Future* 15 J CONTEMP. CRIM. JUST. 250 (1999).

3. Paul Wilson, Robyn Lincoln & Richard Kocsis, *Validities, Utility and Ethics of Profiling for Serial Violent and Sexual Offenders* 4 PSYCHIATRY, PSYCHOL. & L. 4 (1997).

4. http://www.fbi.gov/hq/isd/cirg/ncavc.htm (accessed January 16, 2007).

5. Richard N. Kocsis, CRIMINAL PROFILING: PRINCIPLES AND PRACTICE X111 (2006).

6. Ainsworth, *supra* note 11 (Chap. 1), at 100.

7. Ressler et al., *supra* note 32, (Chap. 1), at 121, 123.

8. *Id.*, at 130.

9. Joseph A. Davies, *Criminal Personality Profiling and Crime Scene Assessment: A Contemporary Investigative Tool to Assist Law Enforcement Public Safety*, 15 J. Contemp. Crim. Just. (August 1999) at 296.

10. Robert R. Hazelwood, *Analyzing the Rape and Profiling the Offender*, in Practical Aspects of Rape Investigation: A Multidisciplinary Approach 169 (Robert R. Hazelwood & Ann W. Burgess eds., 3rd ed., 2001).

11. *Id.*, at 175.

12. Ainsworth, *supra* note 11 (Chap. 1), at 105.

13. *Id.*

14. Holmes & Holmes, *supra* note 1 (Chap. 1), at 120.

15. *Id.*, at 122.

16. *Id.*, at 120.

17. *Id.*, at 121.

18. *Id.*, at 122.

19. Ainsworth, *supra* note 11 (Chap. 1), at 105.

20. Holmes & Holmes, *supra* note 1 (Chap. 1), at 126.

21. *Id.*, at 128.

22. *Id.*, at 123.

23. Ainsworth, *supra* note 11 (Chap. 1), at 106.

24. Holmes & Holmes, *supra* note 1 (Chap. 1), at 124.

25. *Id.*, at 123.

26. *Id.*

27. Ainsworth, *supra* note 11 (Chap. 1), at 106.

28. Holmes & Holmes, *supra* note 1 (Chap. 1), at 130.

29. Ainsworth, *supra* note 11 (Chap. 1), at 107.

30. Holmes & Holmes, *supra* note 1 (Chap. 1), at 129.

31. *Id.*, at 131.

32. The following discussion draws from the work of Douglas et al., *Criminal Profiling from Crime Scene Analysis* 4 Behav. Sci. & L. 401–421 (1986), to whom I am grateful.

33. *Id.*

34. Ainsworth, *supra* note 11 (Chap. 1), at 102.

35. *Id.*, at 114.

36. David Canter & L. Alison eds., Profiling in Policy and Practice (1999), at 6.

37. Damon A. Muller, *Criminal Profiling: Real Science or Just Wishful Thinking?* 4 Homicide Studies (August 2000), at 248.

38. *Id.*, at 249.

39. David Canter—Biography, http://www.liv.ac.uk/psychology/staff/dcanter.html (last accessed February 11, 2007).

40. David Canter, Criminal Shadows: Inside the Mind of the Serial Killer 29 (1994).

41. *Id.*, at 33.

42. *Id.*

43. *Id.*, at 5.

44. *Id.*, at 35.

45. The following discussion draws from the work of David Canter, to whom I am indebted.

46. Muller, *supra* note 37, at 241.

47. *Id.*

48. *Id.*, at 242.

49. Egger, *supra* note 2, at 247.

50. David Canter & P. Larkin *The Environmental Range of Serial Rapists* 13 JOURNAL OF ENVIRONMENTAL PSYCHOLOGY 63–69 (1993).

51. Maurice Godwin & David Canter, *Encounter and Death: The Spatial Behavior of U. S. Serial Killers* 20 POLICING: AN INTERNATIONAL JOURNAL OF POLICE STRATEGY AND MANAGEMENT 24–38 (1997).

52. Maurice Godwin & David Canter, *Encounter and Death: The Spatial Behavior of U. S. Serial Killers*, POLICING: AN INTERNATIONAL JOURNAL OF POLICE STRATEGY AND MANAGEMENT, Volume 20, Number 1, 27 (1997).

53. *Id.*, at 27.

54. *Id.*, at 29.

55. *Id.*, at 35.

56. *Id.*, at 36.

57. G. B. Palermo & R. N. Kocsis, OFFENDER PROFILING: AN INTRODUCTION TO THE SOCIOPSYCHOLOGICAL OF VIOLENT CRIME ANALYSIS 158 (2005).

58. Muller, *supra* note 37, at 251.

59. Ainsworth, *supra* note 11 (Chap. 1), at 118.

60. Egger, *supra* note 2, at 252.

61. Ainsworth, *supra* note 11 (Chap. 1), at 132.

62. Wilson, Lincoln & Kocsis, *supra* note 3, at 6.

63. Ainsworth, *supra* note 11 (Chap. 1), at 123.

64. D. Kim Rossmo, *Geographic Profiling in* OFFENDER PROFILING: THEORY, RESEARCH AND PRACTICE 174 (Janet L. Jackson & Debra A. Bekerian eds., 1997).

65. *Id.,* at 161.

66. D. Kim Rossmo, *Geographic Profiling in* OFFENDER PROFILING: THEORY, RESEARCH AND PRACTICE 162 (Janet L. Jackson & Debra A. Bekerian eds., 1997). Copyright 1997 John Wiley & Sons Limited. Reproduced with permission.

67. *Id.*, at 161.

68. Michael G. McGrath, *Criminal Profiling: Is there a Role for the Forensic Psychiatrist?* 28 J. AMER. ACADEMY PSYCHIATRY & LAW 319 (2000). Copyright American Academy of Psychiatry and the Law. Reprinted with Permission.

69. *Id.*

70. Brent Turvey, CRIMINAL PROFILING: AN INTRODUCTION TO BEHAVIORAL EVIDENCE ANALYSIS 29 (1999).

71. Brent Turvey, CRIMINAL PROFILING: INTRODUCTION TO BEHAVIORAL EVIDENCE ANALYSIS 686 (2nd ed., 2002).

72. Turvey, *supra* note 70, at 28.

73. *Id.*, at 35.
74. *Id.*, at 36.
75. *See,* Kocsis, *supra* note 5, at xiv.
76. *Id.*, at xvi.
77. Palermo & Kocsis, *supra* note 56, at 183.
78. *Id.*, at 220.

CHAPTER 3

1. Joseph L. Peterson, John P. Ryan, Pauline J. Houlden & Steven Mihajlovic, *The Use and Effects of Forensic Science in the Adjudication of Felony Case* 32 J. FORENSIC SCI. 1730, 1748 (1987).

2. Steve Uglow, EVIDENCE: TEXT AND MATERIALS 619 (1997).

3. Frye v. United States, 293 F. 1013, 1014 (D.C. Cir. 1923).

4. *Id.*

5. *Id.*

6. *Id.*

7. *Id.*

8. Melissa M. Horne, *Novel Scientific Evidence: Does* Frye *Require that General Acceptance within the Scientific Community be Established by Disinterested Scientists?* 65 U. DET. L. REV. 147 (Fall 1987).

9. James E. Starrs, *A Still-Life Watercolor:* Frye v. United States 27 JOURNAL OF FORENSIC SCIENCES 686 (July 1982).

10. Cornet v. State, 450 N.E. 2d 498 (Ind. 1983).

11. Thaddeus Murphy, *The Admissibility of Scientific Evidence in Illinois* 21 LOY. U. CHI. L. J. 935, 943 (Spring 1990). Copyright, 1990 Loyola University Chicago School of Law, Law Journal. This was originally published in the Loyola University Chicago Law Journal Vol. 21. Reprinted with permission.

12. Andre A. Moenssens, *Admissibility of Scientific Evidence–An Alternative to the* Frye *Rule* 25 WM. & MARY L. REV. 545, 548 (Summer 1984).

13. *Id.*, at 549.

14. United States v. Addison, 498 F.2d 741 (D.C. Cir. 1974).

15. *Id.*, at 743.

16. *Id.*, at 744.

17. People v. Kelly, 17 Cal.3d 24, 549 P.2d 1240 (1976).

18. *Id.*, at 1244.

19. United States v. Addison, 498 F.2d 741 (D.C. Cir. 1974).

20. People v. Kelly, 17 Cal.3d 24, 549 P.2d 1244, 1245 (1976).

21. *Id.*, at 1245.

22. Reed v. State, 283 Md. 374, 393 A.2d 364 (1978).

23. *Id.*

24. *Id.*

25. Edward J. Imwinkelried, *The Importance of* Daubert *in* Frye *Jurisdictions* 42 CRIM. LAW BULLETIN 5 (March–April 2006).

26. David Faigman, David H. Kaye, Michael J. Saks & Joseph Sanders, Sci-ence in the Law: Standards, Statistics and Research Issues 8 (2002). Copyright 2002 Thomson West. Reprinted with permission.

27. *Id.*, at 9.

28. Constantine J. Maletskos & Stephen J. Spielman, *Introduction of New Scientific Methods in* Court, Law Enforcement Science and Technology 957, 958 (S.A. Yefsky, ed. 1967).

29. Faigman, Kaye, Saks & Sanders, *supra* note 26, at 8.

30. Coppolino v. State, 223 So.2d 68 (Fla. App. 1968).

31. *Id.*, at 69.

32. *Id.*, at 72.

33. *Id.*, at 75.

34. Moenssens, *supra* note 12, at 545.

35. Mark McCormick, *"Scientific Evidence: Defining a New Approach to Admissibility,"* 67 Iowa L. Rev. 879, 915 (1981–1982).

36. Paul C. Giannelli, *The Admissibility of Novel Scientific Evidence:* Frye v. United States, *a Half-Century Later* 80 Colum. L. Rev. 1197, 1226 (1980).

37. *Id.*

38. Charles T. McCormick, Handbook of the Law of Evidence 363 (1954).

39. Reed v. State, 283 Md. 371. A.2d 364 (1978).

40. *Id.*

41. James R. Richardson, Modern Scientific Evidence: Civil and Criminal 24 (2nd ed. 1974).

42. Murphy, *supra* note 11 at 967.

43. Arthur Kantrowitz, *Controlling Technology Democratically* 63 Am. Sci. 505 (1975).

44. James A. Martin, *The Proposed "Science Court"* 75 Mich. L. Rev. 1058, 1059 (1977).

45. *Id.*

46. Giannelli, *supra* note 36, at 1232.

47. Justice David L. Bazelon, *Coping with Technology Through the Legal Process* 62 Cornell Law Review 817, 827 (June 1977).

48. *Id.*

49. For full details of all the states and the rules they have adopted, please *see;* David E. Bernstein & Jeffrey D. Jackson, *The* Daubert *Trilogy in the States* 44 Jurimetrics (2004), 351, 351–366; Joseph R. Meaney, *From* Frye *to* Daubert*: Is a Pattern Unfolding?* 35 Jurimetrics J. (1995), 191, 191–199; and Heather G. Hamilton, *The Movement from* Frye *to* Daubert*: Where Do the States Stand?* 38 Jurimetrics (1998), 201, 201–213.

50. Fed. R. Evid. 702

51. Fed. R. Evid. 401

52. Fed. R. Evid. 402

53. Fed. R. Evid. 403

54. Fed. R. Evid. 703

55. Fed. R. Evid. 704

56. Fed. R. Evid. 705

57. United States v. Smith, 869 F.2d 348 (7th Cir. 1989).

58. *Id.*, at 351.

59. United States v. Downing, 753 F.2d 1224, 1224 (3rd Cir. 1985).

60. *Id.*, at 1232.

61. *Id.*, at 1233.

62. *Id.*, at 1237.

63. State v. Kersting, 50 Or. App. 461, 623 P.2d 1095 (1981).

64. *Id.*

65. *Id.*

66. Christophersen v. Allied-Signal Corp., 939 F.2d 1106 (5th Cir. 1991).

67. *Id.*, at 1110.

68. Glen Weissenberger, *The Supreme Court and the Interpretation of the Federal Rules of Evidence* 53 Ohio St. L. J. 1307, 1309 (1992).

69. Glen Weissenberger, *The Elusive Identity of the Federal Rules of Evidence* 40 Wm. & Mary L. Rev. 1613 (May 1999).

70. Edward J. Imwinkelried, *Whether the Federal Rules of Evidence Should Be Conceived as a Perpetual Index Code: Blindness Is Worse than Myopia* 40 Wm. & Mary L. Rev. 1595, 1596 (1999).

71. Daubert v. Merrell Dow Pharmaceuticals, Inc., 509 U.S. 579 S. Ct. 2786 (1993).

72. Daubert v. Merrell Dow Pharmaceuticals, Inc., 509 U.S. 579 S. Ct. 2794 (1993).

73. *Id.*, at 2793.

74. The three additional requirements are noted in italics. Fed. R. Evid. 702.

75. Daubert v. Merrell Dow Pharmaceuticals, Inc., 509 U.S. 579, 113 S. Ct. 2786 (1993).

76. *Id.*, at 2791.

77. Daubert v. Merrell Dow Pharmaceuticals, 727 F. Supp. 570, 572, (S.D. Cal. 1989).

78. *Id.*, at 575.

79. *Id.*

80. Daubert v. Merrell Dow Pharmaceuticals, 951 F.2d 1128, 1129 (9th Cir. 1991)

81. *Id.*, at 1130.

82. *Id.*, at 1131.

83. *Id.*

84. Daubert v. Merrell Dow Pharmaceuticals, Inc., 509 U.S. 579, 113 S. Ct. 2792 (1993).

85. *Id.*, at 2792-94.

86. *Id.*, at 2796-9.

87. *Id.*, at 2794.

88. *Id.*

89. Martin L. C. Feldman, *May I Have the Next Dance, Mrs. Frye?* 1969 Tul. L. Rev. 793 (February 1995).

90. *Id.*

91. *Id.*, at 802.

92. Martin L. C. Feldman, *May I Have the Next Dance, Mrs.* Frye?, originally published in 1969 TUL. L. REV. 806 (1995). Reprinted with the permission of the Tulane Law Review Association, which holds the copyright.

93. Paul S. Milich, *Controversial Science in the Courtroom:* Daubert *and the Law's Hubris*, 43 EMORY L. J. 913, 917 (1994).

94. Randolph N. Jonakait, *The Meaning of* Daubert *and What that Means for Forensic Science* 15 CARDOZO L. REV. (April 1994), at 2103.

95. *Id.*, at 2106.

96. *Id.*, at 2111.

97. *Id.*

98. Michael C. Polentz, *Post-*Daubert *Confusion with Expert Testimony*, 36 SANTA CLARA L. REV. 1187, 1202 (1996).

99. Andre A. Moenssens, *Novel Scientific Evidence in Criminal Cases: Some Words of Caution* 84 J. CRIM. L. & CRIMINOLOGY (Spring 1993), at 1, 4.

100. *Id.*, at 5–20.

101. People v. Leahy, 8 Cal.4th 587, 882 P.2d 321 (1994).

102. *Id.*, at 592.

103. *Id.*, at 591.

104. *Id.*, at 594.

105. *Id.*, at 604.

106. *Id.*

107. General Electric Co. v. Joiner, 522 U.S. 136, 118 S. Ct. 512 (1997).

108. *Id.*, at 518.

109. *Id.*

110. General Electric Co. v. Joiner, 864 F. Supp. 1310 (N.D. Ga. 1994).

111. *Id.*, at 1326.

112. General Electric Co. v. Joiner, 78 F.3d 524 (1996).

113. General Electric Co. v. Joiner, 522 U.S. 136, 118 S. Ct. 512 (1997).

114. *Id.*, at 143.

115. *Id.*, at 146.

116. Paul C. Giannelli, Daubert *Revisited* 41 CRIM. LAW BULLETIN 5 (June 2005).

117. *Id.*

118. Kumho Tire Co. v. Carmichael, 526 U.S. 137, 119 S. Ct. 1167 (1999).

119. *Id.*, at 138.

120. *Id.*, at 137.

121. *Id.*, at 144.

122. *Id.*, at 143.

123. Carmichael v. Samyang Tire, Inc., 923 F. Supp. 144 (SD Ala. 1997).

124. Kumho Tire Co. v. Carmichael, 526 U.S. 137 (1999).

125. 131 F.3d 1433, 1435 (11th Cir. 1997).

126. Kumho Tire Co. v. Carmichael, 526 U.S. 137, 138 (1999).

127. *Id.*

128. *Id.*, at 151.

129. *See,* Glen Weissenberger, WEISSENBERGER'S FEDERAL EVIDENCE: 2006 COURT-ROOM MANUAL 227 (2005).

CHAPTER 4

1. Fed. R. Evid. 404
2. Fed. R. Evid. 405
3. Fed. R. Evid. 406
4. State v. Haynes, 1988 WL 99189 (Ohio App. 9 Dist).
5. *Id.*, at 2.
6. *Id.*
7. *Id.*, at 3.
8. *Id.*
9. *Id.*
10. *Id.*, at 5.
11. *Id.*
12. *Id.*
13. *Id.*
14. *Id.*, at 6.
15. State v. Roquemore, 85 Ohio App.3d 448, 620 N.E.2d 110 (1993).
16. *Id.*, at 115.
17. *Id.*, at 112.
18. *Id.*
19. *Id.*, at 113.
20. *Id.*, at 112.
21. *Id.*, at 113.
22. *Id.*
23. *Id.*, at 115.
24. *Id.*
25. *Id.*, at 116.
26. *Id.*
27. *Id.*
28. *Id.*
29. State v. Parkinson, 128 Idaho 29, 909 P.2d 647 (1996).
30. *Id.*, at 32.
31. *Id.*
32. *Id.*
33. *Id.*, at 35.
34. *Id.*
35. *Id.*
36. Penson v. State, 222 Ga. App. 253, 474 S.E.2d. 104 (Ga. 1996).
37. *Id.*, at 106.
38. *Id.*
39. Sanders v. State, 251 Ga. 70, 76 (3), 303 S.E.2d 13 (1983).

40. Penson v. State, 222 Ga. App.253, 474 S.E.2d. 104, 106 (Ga. 1996).

41. *Id.*

42. *Id.*, at 107.

43. CAL. EVID. CODE § 1101 (West. Supp. 1992).

44. Fed. R. Evid. 702.

45. Brunson v. State, 349 Ark. 300, 79 S.W.3d 304 (2002).

46. *Id.*, at 307.

47. *Id.*

48. *Id.*

49. *Id.*

50. *Id.*, at 306.

51. *Id.*

52. *Id.*, at 310.

53. Dillion v. State, 317 Ark. 384, 394, 877 S.W.2d. 915, 920 (1994).

54. Brunson v. State, 349 Ark. 300, 310, 79 S.W.3d 304 (2002).

55. *Id.*

56. Risinger & Loop, *supra* note 8 (Chap. 1), at 257.

57. *Id.*, at 284.

58. *Id.*

59. David Ormerod, *The Evidential Implications of Psychological Profiling*, CRIM. L. REV. Volume 92, 873, 874 (1996). Copyright 1996 Criminal Law Review. Reprinted with kind permission of Sweet & Maxwell.

60. State v. Roquemore, 85 Ohio App. 3d 448, 620 N.E.2d 110 (1993).

61. *Id.*

62. *Id.*

63. Brunson v. State, 349 Ark. 300, 79 S.W.3d 304 (2002).

64. *Id.*

65. *Id.*, at 314.

66. People v. Robbie, 92 Cal.App.4th 1075 (2001).

67. *Id.*

68. *Id.*, at 1081.

69. *Id.*

70. *Id.*, at 1085.

71. United States v. Webb, 115 F.3d 711 (1997).

72. *Id.*

73. *Id.*

74. *Id.*, at 715.

75. *Id.*

76. Simmons v. State, 797 So.2d 1134 (Ala. 2000).

77. *Id.*, at 1147.

78. *Id.*, at 1148.

79. *Id.*

80. *Id.*, at 1150.

81. *Id.*, at 1151.

82. United States v. deSoto, 885 F.2d 354, 359 (7th Cir. 1989).

83. Simmons v. State, 797 So.2d 1134, 1147 (2000).

84. *Id.*, at 1158.

85. *Id.*

86. *Id.*, at 1155.

87. State v. Sorabella, 277 Conn. 155, 891 A.2d 897 (2006).

88. *Id.*, at 163.

89. *Id.*

90. *Id.*, at 160.

91. *Id.*, at 212.

92. *Id.*, at 213.

93. State v. Porter, 241 Conn. 57, 698 A.2d 739 (1997). *Cert. denied*, 523 U.S. 1058, 118 S. Ct. 1384, 140 L. Ed. 2d 645 (1998).

94. State v. Sorabella, 277 Conn. 155, 212, 891 A.2d 897 (2006).

95. *Id.*, at 162.

96. *Id.*, at 217.

97. Colin Tapper, Cross and Tapper on Evidence 551 (1995).

98. McCormick, *supra* note 38 (Chap. 3), at 26.

99. 7 John H. Wigmore, Evidence in Trials at Common Law 18 (Revised by James H. Chadbourn, 1978) (1920).

100. Steven I. Friedland, Paul Bergman & Andrew E. Taslitz, Evidence Law and Practice 262 (2000).

101. Adrian Keane, The Modern Law of Evidence 407 (1989).

102. Fed. R. Evid. 704.

103. State v. Armstrong, 587 So.2d 168 (La. 1991).

104. *Id.*

105. *Id.*, at 169.

106. *Id.*, at 170.

107. *Id.*, at 169.

108. *Id.*, at 170.

109. State v. Haynes, 1988 WL 999189, 3, (Ohio App. 9 Dist).

110. *Id.*, at 4.

111. State v. Parkinson, 128 Idaho 29, 909 P.2d 647, 650 (1996)

112. *Id.*, at 32.

113. Brunson v. State, 349 Ark. 300, 79 S.W.3d 304 (2002).

114. *Id.*, at 312.

115. United States v. Webb, 115 F.3d 711 (1997).

116. *Id.*, at 715.

117. Simmons v. State, 797 So.2d 1134 (2000).

118. *Id.*, at 1158.

119. J. Godwin, Murder USA: The Ways We Kill Each Other 276 (1978).

120. L. Alison, A. West & A. Goodwill, *The Academic and the Practitioner Pragmatists' Views of Offender Profiling* 10 Psychol. Pub. Pol'y & L. 78 (2004).

121. Risinger & Loop, *supra* note 8 (Chap. 1), at 252.

122. David C. Ormerod & Jim Sturman, *Working with the Courts: Advice for Expert Witnesses*, in THE FORENSIC PSYCHOLOGIST'S CASEBOOK: PSYCHOLOGICAL PROFILING AND CRIMINAL INVESTIGATION 191 (L. Alison ed., 2005).

123. Brent Snook, Joseph, Eastwood, Paul Gendreau, Claire Goggin & Richard M. Cullen, *Taking Stock of Criminal Profiling: A Narrative and Meta-Analysis* 34 CRIMINAL JUSTICE AND BEHAVIOR 437, 448 (2007).

124. State v. Pennell, 602 A.2d 48 (Del. 1991).

125. State v. Cavallo, 88 N.J 508, 443 A.2d 1020 (1982).

126. *Id.*, at 515.

127. *Id.*

128. *Id.*, at 514.

129. *Id.*, at 526.

130. *Id.*

131. *Id.*, at 529.

132. State v. Lowe, 75 Ohio App.3d 404, 599 N.E.2d 783 (Ohio. 1991).

133. *Id.*

134. *Id.*

135. *Id.*

136. *Id.*

137. *Id.*, at 407.

138. *Id.*

139. *Id.* at 408.

140. State v. Stevens, 78 S.W.3d 817 (Tenn. 2002).

141. *Id.*, at 831.

142. *Id.*, at 826.

143. *Id.*, at 825.

144. *Id.*, at 827.

145. *Id.*, at 828.

146. *Id.*

147. *Id.*

148. *Id.*

149. *Id.*, at 831.

150. *Id.*

151. McDaniel v. CSX Transportation, Inc., 955 S.W.2d 257, 264–65 (Tenn. 1997); which held that the *Daubert* factors also applied to nonscientific testimony.

152. State v. Stevens, 78 S.W.3d 817, 828 (Tenn. 2002).

153. In accordance with Tenn. Code. Anns 39-13-206(a)(1)(1997).

154. State v. Stevens, 78 S.W.3d 817, 833 (Tenn. 2002).

155. *Id.*, at 835.

156. *Id.*, at 836.

157. State v. Fortin, 162 N.J. 517, 745 A.2d 509 (2000).

158. State v. Fortin, 162 N.J. 517, 510, 745 A.2d 509 (2000).

159. State v. Fortin, 318 N.J. Super. 577, 588, 724 A.2d 818 (1999).

160. *Id.*

161. *Id.*

162. *Id.*, at 589.
163. *Id.*, at 590.
164. *Id.*, at 581.
165. *Id.*, at 591.
166. *Id.*, at 592.
167. *Id.*, at 609.
168. *Id.*, at 584.
169. *Id.*, at 586.
170. *Id.*, at 587.
171. *Id.*, at 582.
172. *Id.*, at 597.
173. *Id.*, at 598.
174. *Id.*, at 600.
175. *Id.*
176. *Id.*, at 609.
177. *Id.*
178. *Id.*, at 610.
179. *Id.*
180. State v. Fortin, 162 N.J. 517, 525, 745 A.2d 509 (2000).
181. *Id.*, at 526.
182. *Id.*, at 527.
183. *Id.*
184. *Id.*, at 533.
185. State v. Fortin, 178 N.J. 540, 843 A.2d 974 (2004).
186. *Id.*
187. State v. Fortin, 189 N.J. 579; 917 A.2d 746; (2007).
188. *Id.*, at 589.
189. *Id.*
190. *Id.*
191. *Id.*
192. *Id.*, at 590.
193. *Id.*, at 591.
194. *Id.*
195. *Id.*
196. *Id.*, at 754.
197. *Id.*, at 593.
198. *Id.*, at 597.
199. *Id.*, at 598.
200. *Id.*, at 603.
201. *Id.*, at 599.
202. *Id.*, at 600.
203. *Id.*, at 585.
204. *Id.*, at 606.
205. http://www.fbi.gov/page2/oct07/snipers102407.html (last visited March 23, 2008).

206. *Id.*

207. Muhammad v. State, 177 Md. App. 188, 934 A.2d 1059, 1075 (2007).

208. *Id.*

209. *Id.*, at 1076.

210. *Id.*, at 1075.

211. *Id.*, at 1069.

212. *Id.*

213. *Muhammad* v. Commonwealth, 269 Va. 451, 619 S.E.2d 16 (2005), *cert denied,* 547 U.S. ———, 126 S.Ct. 2035, 164 L.Ed.2d 794 92006).

214. Muhammad v. State, 177 Md.App. 188, 934 A.2d 1059, 1139 (2007).

215. Anthony J. Pinizzotto & Norman J. Finkel, *Criminal Personality Profiling: An Outcome and Process Study* 14 LAW AND HUMAN BEHAVIOR (1990), at 215–233.

216. *Id.*, at 219.

217. *Id.*

218. *Id.*, at 222.

219. *Id.*, at 224.

220. *Id.*, at 215.

221. Anthony J. Pinizzotto & Norman J. Finkel, *Criminal Personality Profiling: An Outcome and Process Study* 14 LAW AND HUMAN BEHAVIOR 224 (1990). Copyright 1990 Law and Human Behavior. Reprinted with kind permission of Springer Science and Business Media.

222. Anthony J. Pinizzotto & Norman J. Finkel, *Criminal Personality Profiling: An Outcome and Process Study* 14 LAW AND HUMAN BEHAVIOR 227 (1990). Copyright 1990 Law and Human Behavior. Reprinted with kind permission of Springer Science and Business Media.

223. *Id.*, at 218.

224. Anthony J. Pinizzotto & Norman J. Finkel, *Criminal Personality Profiling: An Outcome and Process Study* 14 LAW AND HUMAN BEHAVIOR 227 (1990). Copyright 1990 Law and Human Behavior. Reprinted with kind permission of Springer Science and Business Media.

225. Richard N. Kocsis, Harvey J. Irwin, Andrew F. Hayes & Ronald Nunn, *Expertise in Psychological Profiling: A Comparative Assessment* 15 J. OF INTERPERSONAL VIOLENCE (2000), at 314.

226. Footnote 320, in Michael D. Rissinger & Jeffrey L. Loop, *Three Card Monte, Monty Hall, Modus Operandi and "Offender Profiling:" Some Lessons of Modern Cognitive Science for the Law of Evidence,* 24 CARDOZO L. REV. 193, 320 (Nov. 2002).

227. Footnote 322, in Michael D. Risinger & Jeffrey L. Loop, *Three Card Monte, Monty Hall, Modus Operandi and "Offender Profiling:" Some Lessons of Modern Cognitive Science for the Law of Evidence* 24 CARDOZO L. REV. 193, 320 (Nov. 2002).

228. Risinger and Loop, *supra* note 8 (Chap. 1), at 249.

229. R. R. Hazelwood, R. K. Ressler, R. L. Dupue & J. C. Douglas, *Criminal Investigative Analysis: An Overview, in* PRACTICAL ASPECTS OF RAPE INVESTIGATION: A MULTIDICIPLINARY APPROACH (R. R. Hazelwood & A. W. Burgess eds., 2nd ed., 1995).

230. Kocsis et al., *supra* note 225, at 316.

231. *Id.*, at 317.

232. *Id.*, at 319.

233. *Id.*, at 320.

234. *Id.*

235. *Id.*, at 321.

236. *Id.*

237. *Id.*

238. *Id.*

239. *Id.*, at 327.

240. *Id.*, at 326.

241. R. N. Kocsis, A. F. Hayes & H. J. Irwin, *Investigative Experience and Accuracy in Psychological Profiling of a Violent Crime* 17 JOURNAL OF INTERPERSONAL VIOLENCE 811–823 (2002).

242. Richard N. Kocsis, *Criminal Psychological Profiling: Validities and Abilities* 47 INTERNATIONAL JOURNAL OF OFFENDER THERAPY AND COMPARATIVE CRIMINOLOGY 126–144 (2003).

243. Richard N. Kocsis, *Psychological Profiling of Serial Arson Offenses: An Assessment of Skills and Accuracy* 31 CRIMINAL JUSTICE AND BEHAVIOR 341–361 (2004).

244. Craig Bennell, Shevaun Corey, Alyssa Taylor & John Ecker, What Skills Are Required for Effective Offender Profiling? An Examination of the Relationship between Critical Thinking Ability and Profile Accuracy, Paper Presented at the 35th Annual Conference of the Society for Police and Criminal Psychology, Chevy Chase, Md. (October 26, 2006).

CHAPTER 5

1. Folkes v. Chadd, (1782) 3 Doug KB 157.

2. *Id.*

3. *Id.*

4. *Id.*, at 159.

5. *Id.*

6. *Id.*

7. R v. Turner, (1975) Q.B. 834 (C.A).

8. *Id.*, at 840.

9. *Id.*

10. *Id.*, at 839.

11. *Id.*

12. *Id.*, at 834.

13. *Id.*, at 840.

14. *Id.*

15. *Id.*, at 841.

16. *Id.*, at 841.

17. *Id.*, at 843.

18. R v. Robb, (1991) 93 Cr. App. R. 161.

19. *Id.*, at 164.

20. R v. Stockwell, (1993) Cr. App.R. 260.

21. Lord Taylor C. J., in R v. Stockwell, (1993) CR. APP. R. 260, 264.

22. R v. Stagg, Central Criminal Court, 14 September, 1994.

23. *Id.*

24. *Id.*

25. Rt. Hon. Lord Taylor of Gosforth, *The Lund Lecture* 35 MEDICINE, SCIENCE AND THE LAW (January 1995), at 3.

26. Rt. Hon. Lord Taylor of Gosforth, *The Lund Lecture* 35 MEDICINE, SCIENCE AND THE LAW (January 1995), at 3. Reprinted with permission.

27. Ormerod, *supra* note 59 (Chap. 4), at 867.

28. *Id.*

29. Ormerod & Sturman, *supra* note 122 (Chap. 4), at 182.

30. Ormerod, *supra* note 59 (Chap. 4), at 877.

31. State v. Cavallo, 88 N.J. 508, 443 A.2d 1020 (1982)

32. *Id.*, at 529.

33. Ormerod & Sturman, *supra* note 122 (Chap. 4), at 185.

34. R v. Abadom, [1983] 1 WLR 126.

35. English Exporters (London) v. Eldonwall Limited, [1973] Ch. 415, Chancery Division.

36. Uglow, *supra* note 2 (Chap. 3), at 623.

37. David E. Bernstein, *Junk Science in the United States and the Commonwealth* 21 YALE J. INT'L L. (Winter 1996) at 123, 140.

38. R v. Mohan, 89 C.C.C. 3d 402 (1994); 114 D.L.R. (4th) 419; 1994 D.L.R. LEXIS 1297.

39. R v. Beland, [1987] 2 S.C.R. 398.

40. *Id.*, at 417.

41. R v. Lavallee, 55 C.C.C. 3d 97 (1990).

42. *Id.*, at 132.

43. R v. Mohan, 114 D.L.R. (4th) 419; 1994 D.L.R. LEXIS 1297.

44. *Id.*

45. *Id.*

46. R v. Mohan, 89 C.C.C. 3d 402 (1994);114 D.L.R. (4th) 419, 423; 1994 D.L.R. LEXIS 1297.

47. *Id.*

48. *Id.*, at 425.

49. *Id.*, at 423.

50. R v. Mohan, (1992) 8 O.R. 3d 173.

51. R v. Mohan, 89 C.C.C. 3d 402 (1994); 114 D.L.R. (4th) 419, 426; 1994 D.L.R. LEXIS 1297.

52. *Id.*

53. *Id.*, at 426.

54. *Id.*, at 427.

55. *Id.*

56. *Id.*

57. *Id.*, at 431.

58. *Id.*

59. *Id.*, at 435.

60. R v. Ranger, 178 C.C.C. (3d) 375; 2003 C.C.C. LEXIS 265.

61. *Id.*, at 378.

62. *Id.*

63. *Id.*

64. *Id.*, at 379.

65. *Id.*, at 388.

66. *Id.*, at 390.

67. *Id.*, at 394.

68. *Id.*, at 398.

69. *Id.*, at 405.

70. R v. Clark, 69 O.R. (3d) 321; 2004 Ont. Rep. LEXIS 25.

71. *Id.*, at 325.

72. *Id.*, at 326.

73. *Id.*, at 327.

74. *Id.*, at 331.

75. *Id.*, at 322.

76. *Id.*, at 323.

77. *Id.*

78. Adah C. Eche, THE NIGERIAN LAW OF EVIDENCE, 115 (2000).

79. Evidence Act, Laws of the Federation, 1990. Federal Republic of Nigeria, Supreme Court of Nigeria, Abuja (1990).

80. There is a legal provision for a jury in Nigerian, but jurors are not used. The trier of fact is the judge and whether expert opinion will assist him is not an issue to be contested by the parties.

81. Dickson Arisa v. The State, [1988] 7 S.C.N.J. (Pt.1) 76, 84.

82. Eche, *supra* note 78, at 126.

83. *Id.*

CONCLUSION

1. Norbert Ebisike, AN APPRAISAL OF FORENSIC SCIENCE EVIDENCE IN CRIMINAL PROCEEDINGS 93 (2001).

2. Christophersen v. Allied Signal Corp., 939 F.2d 1106 (5th Cir. 1991).

3. *See generally*, Veronica B. Dahir, James T. Richardson, Gerald P. Ginsburg, Sophia I. Gatowski, Shirley A. Dobbin, & Mara L. Merlino, *Judicial Application of* Daubert *to Psychological Syndrome and Profile Evidence* 11 PSYCHOL. PUB. POL'Y & L. 62, 74 (March 2005).

4. Veronica B. Dahir, James T. Richardson, Gerald P. Ginsburg, Sophia I. Gatowski, Shirley A. Dobbin & Mara L. Merlino, *Judicial Application of* Daubert *to Psychological Syndrome and Profile Evidence* 11 PSYCHOL. PUB. POL'Y & L. 62, 73 (March 2005).

5. *Id.*, at 75.

6. *Id.*, at 78.

7. United States v. Baldwin, 418 F.3d 575 (Ohio. 2005).

Bibliography

Ainsworth, P. B., *Offender Profiling and Crime Analysis*, Devon, Willan Publishing, (2001).

Alison, L. (ed.), *The Forensic Psychologist's Casebook: Psychological Profiling and Criminal Investigation*. Devon, Willan Publishing, (2005).

Alison, L., C. Bennell, A. Mokros, and D. Ormerod, "The Personality Paradox in Offender Profiling: A Theoretical Review of the Process Involved in Deriving Background Characteristics from Crime Scene Actions," *Psychology, Public Policy and Law,* Volume 8, 115–135 (2002).

Alison, L., M. Smith, O. Eastman, and L. Rainbow, "Interpreting the Accuracy of Offender Profiles," *Psychology, Crime and Law,* Volume 9, 185–195 (2003).

Alison, L. J., M. Smith, O. Eastman, and L. Rainbow, "Toulmin's Philosophy of Argument and its Relevance to Offender Profiling," *Psychology, Crime and Law,* Volume 9, 173–183, (2003).

Alison, L., A. West, and A. Goodwill, "The Academic and the Practitioner: Pragmatists' Views of Offender Profiling," *Psychology, Public Policy and Law*, Volume 10, 71–100, (March/June 2004).

Allen, R. J., "Expertise and the Daubert Decision," *The Journal of Criminal Law and Criminology*, Volume 84, Number 4, 1157–1175, (1993–94).

Atikian, M. K., "Nasty Medicine: Daubert v. Merrell Dow Pharmaceuticals, Inc. Applied to a Hypothetical Medical Malpractice Case," *Loyola Los Angeles Law Review*, Volume 27, 1513–1557, (June 1994).

Ault, R. L., and J. T. Reese, "A Psychological Assessment of Crime Profiling," *FBI Law Enforcement Bulletin*, Volume 49, Number 3, 22–25 (March 1980).

Badcock, R. J., "Developmental and Clinical Issues in Relation to Offending in the Individual," in *Offender Profiling: Theory, Research and Practice* (J. L. Jackson and D. A. Bekerian, eds.) Chichester, John Wiley (1997).

Bartol, C., *Criminal Behavior: A Psychosocial Approach*, New Jersey, Prentice Hall, (5th ed., 1999).

Bartol, C., "Police Psychology: Then, Now and Beyond," *Criminal Justice and Behavior*, Volume 23, 70–79 (1996).

Bazelon, D. L., "Coping with Technology through the Legal Process," *Cornell Law Review*, Volume 62, Number 5, 817–828, (June 1977).

Becker, E. R., and A. Orenstein, "The Federal Rules of Evidence After Sixteen Years–The Effect of 'Plain Meaning' Jurisprudence, The Need for an Advisory Committee on the Rules of Evidence, and Suggestions for Selective Revision of the Rules," *George Washington Law Review*, Volume 60, Number 4, 857–914, (1992).

Bennell, C., S. Corey, A. Taylor, and J. Ecker, "What Skills are Required for Effective Offender Profiling? An Examination of the Relationship between Critical Thinking Ability and Profile Accuracy," Paper Presented at the 35th Annual Conference of the Society for Police and Criminal Psychology, Washington/Chevy Chase Maryland, (October, 2006).

Bennell, C., and J. N. Jones, "Between a ROC and a Hard Place: A Method for Linking Serial Burglaries by Modus Operandi," *Journal of Investigative Psychology* and *Offender Profiling*, Volume 2, 23–41, (2005).

Bennell, C., J. N Jones, P. J. Taylor, and B. Snook, "Validities and Abilities in Criminal Profiling: A Critique of the Studies Conducted by Richard Kocsis and his Colleagues," *International Journal of Offender Therapy and Comparative Criminology*, Volume 50, Number 3, 344–360, (June 2006).

Bernstein, D. E., "Frye, Frye, Again: The Past, Present, and the Future of the General Acceptance Test," *Jurimetrics Journal*, Volume 41, 385–407, (Spring 2001).

Black, B., "A Unified Theory of Scientific Evidence," *Fordham Law Review*, Volume 56, 595–694, (1988).

Blau, T. H., *The Psychologist as Expert Witness*, New York, John Wiley, (1984).

Bleil, C., "Evidence of Syndromes: No Need for a 'Better Mousetrap,'" *South Texas Law Review*, Volume 32, 27–76, (1990).

Blinka, D. D., "Expert Testimony and the Relevancy Rule in the Age of Daubert." *Marquette Law Review*, Volume 90, Number 2, 173–226, (Winter 2006).

Boon, J., "Contribution of Personality Theories to Psychological Profiling", in *Offender Profiling: Theory, Research* and *Practice* (J. L. Jackson., and D. A. Bekerian, eds.), Chichester, John Wiley (1997).

Boon, J. C. W., "Offender Profiling: Distinguishing the Media Prurience from Real-Life Science," *1 Inter Alia*, 31–35, (1995).

Boon, J., and G. Davies, "Criminal Profiling," *Policing*, Volume 9, 218–227 (1993).

Booth, W. C., C. G. Colomb, and J. M. Williams, *The Craft of Research*, Chicago, IL, The University of Chicago Press, (1995).

Borders, J. D., "Fit to be Fryed: *Frye v. United States* and the Admissibility of Novel Scientific Evidence," *Kentucky Law Journal*, Volume 77, 849–879 (Sept/Oct. 1989).

Boyce, R. N., "Judicial Recognition of Scientific Evidence in Criminal Cases," *Utah Law Review*, Volume 8, 313–327 (1964).

Bretz, R. J., "Scientific Evidence and the Frye Rule: The Case for a Cautious Approach," *Cooley Law Review*, Volume 4, 506–521 (1987).

Britton, P., "Editorial: Articulating a Systematic Approach to Clinical Crime Profiling," *Criminal Behaviour and Mental Health*, Volume 70, 13–17 (1997).

Britton, P., *The Jigsaw Man*, London, Bantam Press, (1997).

Britton, P., *Picking up the Pieces*, London, Bantam Press, (2000).

Brussel, J. A., *Casebook of a Crime Psychiatrist*, New York, Simon and Schuster, (1968).

Burgess, A., J. Douglas, R. D'Agostino, C. Hartman, and R. Ressler, "Sexual Killers and their Victims: Identifying Patterns through Crime Scene Analysis," *Journal of Interpersonal Violence*, Volume 1, Number 3, 288–308 (September 1986).

Cameron, E., "Some Psychoanalytic Aspects of Serial Homicide," *Cardozo Law Review*, Volume 24, 2267–2285 (August 2003).

Canter, D., *Criminal Shadows: Inside the Mind of the Serial Killer*, London, HarperCollins, (1994).

Canter, D., "Offender Profiling," *Psychologist*, Volume 2, 12–16 (1989).

Canter, D., "Offender Profiling and Investigative Psychology," *Journal of Investigative Psychology and Offender Profiling*, Volume 1, Number 1, 1–15 (December 2003).

Canter, D., "Profiling as Poison." *Inter Alia*, Volume 2, Number 1, 10–11 (1998).

Canter, D., and L. Alison (eds.), *Profiling in Policy and Practic*, Ashgate, Aldershot, (1999).

Canter, D., and L. Alison (eds.), *Profiling Property Crimes,* Ashgate, Aldershot, (2000).

Canter, D., and L. Alison (eds.), *Profiling Rape and Murder*, Ashgate, Aldershot, (2000).

Canter, D., L. J. Alison, E. Alison, and N. Wentink, "The Organized/Disorganized Typology of Serial Murder," *Psychology, Public Policy and Law*, Volume 10, 293–320 (September 2004).

Canter, D., and R. Heritage, "A Multivariate Model of Sexual Offence Behaviour: Developments in Offender Profiling," *Journal of Forensic Psychiatry*, Volume 1, Number 2, 185–212 (1990).

Canter, D., and P. Larkin "The Environmental Range of Serial Rapists," *Journal of Environmental Psychology*, Volume 12, 63–69 (1993).

Chisum, J. W., and B. E. Turvey, *Crime Reconstruction,* San Diego, Academic Press, (2007).

Christian, V., "Admissibility of Scientific Expert Testimony: Is Bad Science Making Law? *Northern Kentucky Law Review,* Volume 18, 21–40 (Fall 1990).

Cleary, E. W., "Preliminary Notes on Reading the Rules of Evidence," *Nebraska Law Review*, Volume 57, 908–919 (1978).

Cleary, E. W., S. K. Brown, E. G. Dix, E. Gellhorn, H. D. Kaye, R. Meisenholder, E. F. Roberts, and W. J. Strong, *McCormick on Evidence*, St. Paul, MN., West Publishing, (3rd ed., 1984).

Cochran, D. Q, "*Alabama v. Clarence Simmons*: FBI "Profiler" Testimony to Establish an Essential of Capital Murder," *Law and Psychiatry Review*, Volume 23, 69–89 (1999).

Cook, E. P., and D. L. Hinman, "Criminal Profiling: Science and Art," *Journal of Contemporary Criminal Justice*, Volume 15, Number 3, 230–241 (August 1999).

Copson, G., *Coals to Newcastle? Part 1: A Study of Offender Profiling*, London: Police Research Group Special Series, Home Office, (1995).

Curran, W. J., "Expert Psychiatric Evidence of Personality Traits," *University of Pennsylvania Law Review*, Volume 103, Number 8, 999–1019 (1955).

Dabney, A., L. D. Dean, V. Topalli, and R. C. Hollinger, "The Impact of Implicit Stereotyping on Offender Profiling: Unexpected Results from an Observational Study of Shoplifting," *Criminal Justice and Behavior*, Volume 33, Number 5, 646–674 (October 2006).

Dahir, V. B., J. T. Richardson, G. P. Ginsburg, S. I. Gatowski, S. A. Dobbin, and M. L. Merlino, "Judicial Application of Daubert to Psychological Syndrome and Profile Evidence," *Psychology, Public Policy and Law*, Volume 11, 62–82 (March 2005).

Davies, A., "Editorial: Offender Profiling," *Medicine, Science and Law*, Volume 34, Number 3, 185–186 (1994).

Davies, A., "Rapists Behaviour: A Three-Aspect Model as a Basis for Analysis and Identification of a Serial Crime," *Forensic Science International*, Volume 55, 173–194 (1992).

Davies, D., and W. C. Follette, "Rethinking the Probative Value of Evidence: Base Rates, Intuitive Profiling, and the "Postdiction" of Behavior," *Law and Human Behavior*, Volume 26, Number 2, 133–158 (April 2002).

Davies, J. A., "Criminal Personality Profiling and Crime Scene Assessment: A Contemporary Investigative Tool to Assist Law Enforcement Public Safety," *Journal of Contemporary Criminal Justice*, Volume 15, Number 3, 292–301 (August 1999).

DeNevi, D., and J. Campbell, *Into the Minds of Madmen: How the FBI's Behavioral Science Unit Revolutionized Crime Investigation*, New York, Prometheus Books (2003).

Dietz, P., *Criminal Investigative Analysis ('Profiling') in Civil Litigation*, Association of Trial Lawyers of America, Annual Convention Reference Materials, Volume 2 (July 2003).

Dietz, P. E., and J. T. Reese, "The Perils of Police Psychology: 10 Strategies for Minimizing Role Conflicts when Providing Mental Health Services and Consultation to Law Enforcement Agencies," *Behavioral Sciences and the Law*, Volume 4, 385–400 (1986).

Douglas, J. E., and A. E. Burgess, "Criminal Profiling: A Viable Investigative Tool Against Violent Crime," *FBI Law Enforcement Bulletin*, Issue [?] 12, 1–5 (1986).

Douglas, J. E., A. W. Burgess, A. G. Burgess, and R. K. Ressler, *Crime Classification Manual: A Standard System for Investigating and Classifying Violent Crimes*, San Francisco, Jossey-Bass, (2nd ed. 2006).

Douglas, J. E., and L. K. Douglas, "Modus Operandi and the Signature Aspects of Violent Crime," in *Crime Classification Manual* (E. J. Douglas, A. W. Burgess, A. G. Burgess, and R. K. Ressler, eds.) San Francisco, CA, Jossey-Bass (2nd ed. 2006).

Douglas, J. E., and C. Munn, "Violent Crime Scene Analysis: Modus Operandi, Signature, and Staging," *FBI Law Enforcement Bulletin*, Volume 61, 1–10 (1992).

Douglas, J. E., and M. Olshaker, *Anatomy of Motive*, New York, Scribner (1999).

Douglas J. E., and M. Olshaker, *Journey into Darkness*, New York, Scribner, (1997).

Douglas, J. E., and M. Olshaker, *Mindhunter: Inside the FBI's Elite Serial Crime Unit*, New York, Pocket Books, (1996).

Douglas, J. E., R. K. Ressler, A. W. Burgess, and R. C. Hartman, "Criminal Profiling from Crime Scene Analysis," *Behavioral Sciences and the Law*, Volume 4, Number 4, 401–421 (1986).

Duncan, K. L., "Lies, Damned Lies, and Statistics: Psychological Syndrome Evidence in the Courtroom After Daubert," *Indiana Law Journal*, Volume 71, 753–771 (1996).

Duruigbo, E. A, *Multinational Corporations and International Law: Accountability and Compliance in the Petroleum Industry*, New York, Transnational Publishers, (2003).

Dwyer, D., "Evidence–Federal Rules of Evidence Supersede General Acceptance Standard for Admissibility of Scientific Evidence–*Daubert v. Merrell Dow Pharmaceuticals, Inc.*, *Suffolk University Law Review*, Volume 28, 252–260 (Spring 1994).

Ebisike, N., *An Appraisal of Forensic Science Evidence in Criminal Proceedings*, London, Greenway Press, (2001).

Eche, A. C., *The Nigerian Law of Evidence*, Lagos, Malthouse Press, (2000).

Egger, S. A. "Psychological Profiling: Past, Present, and Future," *Journal of Contemporary Criminal Justice*, Volume 15, Number 3, 242–261 (1999).

Faigman, L. D., D. H. Kaye. M. J. Saks, and J. Sanders, *Science in the Law: Standards, Statistics, and Research Issues*, St. Paul, MN, Westgroup, (2002).

Faigman, L. D., E. Porter, and M. J. Saks, "Check your Crystal Ball at the Courthouse Door, Please: Exploring the Past, Understanding the Present, and Worrying about the Future of Scientific Evidence," *Cardozo Law Review*, Volume 15, 1799–1835 (1994).

Farrell, M. G., "Daubert v. Merrrell Dow Pharmaceuticals, Inc.: Epistemiology and Legal Prosess," *Cardozo Law Review*, Volume 15, 2183–2217 (1994).

Farrell, N. S., "Congressional Action to Amend Federal Rule of Evidence 702: A Mischievous Attempt to Codify Daubert v. Merrell Dow Pharmaceuticals, Inc., *Journal of Contemporary Health Law and Policy*, Volume 13, 523–551 (Spring 1997).

Farrington, D., and S. Lambert, "Statistical Approaches to Offender Profiling", in *Profiling Property Crimes* (D. Canter, and L. Allison eds.), 233–273, Aldershot, Ashgate (2000).

Faukner, F. J., and Steffen, T. D., "Evidence of Character: From the Crucible of the Community" to the "Couch of the Psychiatrist," *University of Pennsylvania Law Review*, Volume 102, 980–994 (1954).

Federal Rules of Evidence, U.S. Government Printing Office, Washington, DC, (2006).

Feehan, J. G., "Life After Daubert and Kumho Tire: An Update on Admissibility of Expert Testimony," *Illinois Bar Journal*, Volume 88, 134–142 (March 2000).

Feldman, M. L. C., "May I Have the Next Dance, Mrs. Frye?" *Tulane Law Review,* Volume 69, 793–807 (February 1995).

Fenicato, M. A., "PA Supreme Court Unable to Rule on Daubert and/or Frye Rules," *Lawyers Journal,* Volume 3, Number 3, 3 (February 2001).

Foster, K. R., and P. W. Huber, *Judging Science: Scientific Knowledge and the Federal Courts,* Cambridge, MA, The MIT Press, (1997).

Fradella, H. F., A. Fogarty, and L. O'Neill, "The Impact of Daubert on the Admissibility of Behavioral Science Testimony," *Pepperdine Law Review,* Volume 30, 403–444 (2003).

Friedland, S. I., P. Bergman, and A. E. Taslitz, *Evidence Law and Practice,* New York, Matthew Bender & Co. (2000).

Friedman, R. D., "The Death and Transfiguration of Frye," *Jurimetrics Journal,* Volume 34, 133–148 (Winter 1994).

Friedman, R. D., *The Elements of Evidence,* St. Paul, MN, West Group, (2nd ed. 1998).

Garofalo, R., *Criminology,* trans. R. W. Millar, Boston, Little, Brown and Company, (1914).

Geberth, V. J., *Practical Homicide Investigation: Tactics, Procedures and Forensic Techniques,* Boca Raton, CRC Press/Taylor and Francis, (4th ed. 2006).

Geberth, V. J., "The Signature Aspect in Criminal Investigations," *Law and Order,* Volume 43, Number 11 (November 1995).

Giannelli, P. C., "The Admissibility of Novel Scientific Evidence: Frye v. United States, A Half-Century Later," *Columbia Law Review,* Volume 80, 1197–1250 (1980).

Giannelli, P. C., "Daubert: Interpreting the Federal Rules of Evidence," *Cardozo Law Review,* Volume 15, 1999–2026 (1994).

Giannelli, P. C., and E. Imwinkelried, "Scientific Evidence: The Fallout from Supreme Court's Decision in Kumho Tires," *Criminal Justice,* Volume 14, 12–19 (Winter 2000).

Gildea, L. S., "Sifting the Dross: Expert Witness Testimony in Minnesota after the Daubert Trilogy," *William Mitchell Law Review,* Volume 26, 93–116, (2000).

Glueck, S., and E. Glueck, *Physique and Delinquency,* New York, Harper and Bros. (1956).

Godwin, G. M.(ed.), *Criminal Psychology and Forensic Technology: A Collaborative Approach to Effective Profiling,* Boca Raton, CRC Press (2001).

Godwin, G. M., *Hunting Serial Predators: A Multivariate Approach to Profiling Violent Behavior,* Boca Raton, CRC Press (1999).

Godwin, G. M., and Canter, D., "Encounter and Death: The Spatial Behavior of US Serial Killers," 20 Policing: *An International Journal of Police Strategy and Management,* Volume 20, Number 1, 24–38, (1997).

Godwin, J., *Murder USA: The Ways We Kill Each Other,* New York, Ballantine (1978).

Gonzalez, L., "The Admissibility of Scientific Evidence: The History and Demise of Frye v. United States," *University of Miami Law Review,* Volume 48, 371–397 (November 1993).

Goring, C., *The English Convict: A Statistical Study*, London, His Majesty's Stationery Office (1913).

Gottfreddson, M. R, and T. Hirschi, *A General Theory of Crime*, Stanford, Calif., Stanford University Press (1990).

Graham, L. C., *An Introduction to the Law of Evidence*, St. Paul, MN, West Publishing, (3rd ed. 1996).

Graham, M. H., *Handbook of Federal Evidence,* 3, St. Paul, MN, Thomson West, (6th ed. 2006).

Gross, H., *Criminal Investigation,* London, Sweet and Maxwell, (1924).

Gross, H., *Criminal Psychology,* New Jersey, Patterson Smith, (4th ed. 1934).

Grubin, D., "Offender Profiling," *Journal of Forensic Psychology*, Volume 6, Number 2, 259–263 (1995).

Gudjonsson, G., "The Admissibility of Expert Psychological and Psychiatric Evidence in England and Wales," *Criminal Behaviour and Mental Health*, Volume 2, 245–252 (1992).

Gudjonsson, G., "The Implications of Poor Psychological Evidence in Court," *Expert Evidence*, Volume 2, 12–24 (1992).

Gudjonsson, G. H., and G. Copson, "The Role of the Expert in Criminal Investigation," in *Offender Profiling: Theory, Research* and *Practice* (J. L. Jackson and D. A. Bekerian, eds.), Chichester, John Wiley, (1997).

Hagan, F. E., *Introduction to Criminology*, Chicago, Nelson-Hall Publishers, (3rd ed. 1994).

Hagen, M. A., *Whores of the Court: The Fraud of Psychiatric Testimony and Rape of American Justice*, New York, Regan Books, (1997).

Hakkanen, H., "Finnish Research Team Applies Psychological Science to Police Work," *Psychology International*, Volume 14, Number 1, 1, 4–5 (Winter 2003).

Hakkanen, H., P. Lindlof, and P. Santtila, "Crime Scene Actions and Offender Characteristics in a Sample of Finnish Stranger Rapes," *Journal of Investigative Psychology and Offender Profiling*, Volume 1, Number 1, 17–32, (December 2003).

Hand, L., "Historical and Practical Considerations Regarding Expert Testimony," *Harvard Law Review*, Volume 15, 40–58 (1902).

Hanson, S. R., "James Alphonzo Frye Is Sixty-Five Years Old: Should He Retire?" *Western State University Law Review*, Volume 16, Number 2, 357–460 (Spring 1989).

Hazelwood, R. R., and J. E. Douglas, "The Lust Murderer," *FBI Law Enforcement* Bulletin, Volume 49, 18–22 (1980).

Hazelwood, R. R., P. E. Dietz, and J. Warren, "The Criminal Sexual Sadist," *FBI Law Enforcement Bulletin*, Volume 61, 12–20 (February 1992).

Hazelwood, R. R., and A. W. Burgess (eds.), *Practical Aspects of Rape Investigation: A Multidisciplinary Approach*, Boca Raton, CRC Press, (2nd ed. 1995).

Hazelwood, R. R., and J. I. Warren, "Linkage Analysis: Modus Operandi, Ritual, and Signature in Serial Sexual Situations," *Aggression and Violent Behavior*, Volume 8, 587–598 (2003).

Hickey, E. W., *Serial Murderers and Their Victims*, Belmont, CA, Wadsworth Publishing, (4th ed. 2005).

Hicks, S. J., and B. D. Sales, *Criminal Profiling: Developing an Effective Science and Practice*, Washington, DC, American Psychological Association, (2006).

Hilton, K., and A. Irons, "A "Criminal Personas" Approach to Countering Criminal Creativity," *Crime Prevention and Community Safety*, Volume 8, 248–259 (2006).

Holcomb, W. R., and Daniel, A. E., "Homicide without an Apparent Motive," *Behavioral Sciences and the Law*, Volume 6, 429–437 (1988).

Holmes, R. M., and T. S. Holmes, *Profiling Violent Crimes: An Investigative Tool*, Thousand Oaks, CA, Sage Publications, (2nd ed. 1996).

Homant, R. J., and D. B. Kennedy, "Psychological Aspects of Crime Scene Profiling: Validity Research," *Criminal Justice and Behavior*, Volume 25, Number 3, 319–343 (September 1998).

Hooton, E. A., *The American Criminal: An Anthropological Study*, Volume 1, Cambridge, Harvard University Press, (1939).

Hooton, E. A., *Crime and Man*, Cambridge, Harvard University Press, (1939).

Horne, M. M., "Novel Scientific Evidence: Does Frye Require that General Acceptance within the Scientific Community be Established by Disinterested Scientists?" *University of Detroit Law Review*, Volume 65, 147–162 (Fall 1987).

Horton, M. T., "The Debate is Over: Frye Lives No More," *Thurgood Marshall Law Review*, Volume 19, 379–400 (Spring 1994).

Howlett, J., K. Hanfland, and R. Ressler, "The Violent Criminal Apprehension Program," *FBI Law Enforcement Bulletin*, Volume 55, 14–18 (1986).

Imwinkelried, E. J., "A Brief Defense of the Supreme Court's Approach to the Interpretation of the Federal Rules of Evidence," *Indiana Law Review*, Volume 27, 267–294 (1994).

Imwinkelried, E. J., "Daubert Revisited: Disturbing Implications," *Champion*, Volume 22, 18–27 (May 1998).

Imwinkelried, E. J., "Evaluating the Reliability of Nonscientific Expert Testimony: A Partial Answer to the Questions left Unresolved by Kumho Tire Co. v. Carmichael," *Maine Law Review*, Volume 52, 19–41 (2000).

Imwinkelried, E. J., *Evidentiary Foundations*, New Jersey, LexisNexis, (6th ed. 2005).

Imwinkelried, E. J., "Federal Rule of Evidence 402: The Second Revolution," *The Review of Litigation*, Volume 6, 129–174 (1987).

Imwinkelried, E. J., "The Importance of Daubert in Frye Jurisdictions," Criminal Law Bulletin, Volume 42, Number 2, 5–17 (March–April 2006).

Imwinkelried, E. J., *The Methods of Attacking Scientific Evidence*, New Jersey, LexisNexis, (4th ed. 2004).

Imwinkelried, E. J., "Moving Beyond 'Top Down' Grand Theories of Statutory Construction: A 'Bottom Up' Interpretive Approach to the Federal Rules of Evidence," *Oregon Law Review*, Volume 75, 389–427 (1996).

Imwinkelried, E. J., "A New Era in the Evolution of Scientific Evidence–A Primer on Evaluating the Weight of Scientific Evidence," *William and Mary Law Review*, Volume 23, 261–290 (1981).

Imwinkelried, E. J., "The Next Step after Daubert: Developing a Similarly Epistemological Approach to Ensuring the Reliability of Nonscientific Expert Testimony," *Cardozo Law Review*, Volume 15, 2271, 2294 (1994).

Imwinkelried, E. J. (ed.), *Scientific and Expert Evidence*, New York, Practicing Law Institute, (2nd ed. 1981).

Imwinkelried, E. J., "The Standard for Admitting Scientific Evidence: A Critique from the Perspective of Juror Psychology," *Villanova Law Review*, Volume 28, 554–571 (1983).

Imwinkelried, E. J., "Whether the Federal Rules of Evidence Should be Conceived as a Perpetual Index Code: Blindness is Worse than Myopia," *William and Mary Law Review*, Volume 40, 1595–1612 (1999).

Imwinkelried, E. J., P. C. Giannelli, Gilligan, F. A. and F. I. Lederer, *Courtroom Criminal Evidence*, Virginia, The Michie Co., (2nd ed. 1993).

Ingram, S., "If the Profile Fits: Admitting Criminal Psychological Profiles into Evidence in Criminal Trials," *Washington University Journal of Urban and Contemporary Law*, Volume 54, 239–266 (1998).

Innes, M., N. Fielding, and N. Cope, "The Appliance of Science? The Theory and Practice of Criminal Intelligence Analysis," *British Journal of Criminology*, Volume 45, 39–57 (2005).

Jackson, J. D., "The Ultimate Issue Rule: One Rule too Many," *Criminal Law Review*, 75–86 (1984).

Jackson J. L., and D. A. Bekerian (eds.), *Offender Profiling: Theory, Research and Practice*, Chichester, John Wiley, (1997).

James, S. H., and J. J. Nordby (eds.) *Forensic Science: An Introduction to Scientific Investigative Techniques*, Boca Raton, FL, CRC Press/Taylor and Francis, (2nd ed. 2005).

Jenkins, P., *Using Murder: The Social Construction of Serial Homicide*, New York, Aldine De Gruyter, (1994).

Jensen, J. P., "Frye V. Daubert: Practically the Same? *Minnesota Law Review*, Volume 87, 1577–1619 (May 2003).

Johnson, E. H., *Crime, Correction, and Society*, Illinois, The Dorsey Press, (3rd ed. 1974).

Jonakait, R. N., "The Meaning of Daubert and What that Means for Forensic Science," *Cardozo Law Review*, Volume 15, 2103–2117 (April 1994).

Kantrowitz, A., "Controlling Technology Democratically," *American Scientist*, Volume 63, 505–509 (1975).

Kaye, D. H., D. E. Bernstein, and J. L. Mnookin, *The New Wigmore: A Treatise on Evidence*, New York, Aspen Publishers, (2004).

Keane, A., *The Modern Law of Evidence*, London, Butterworth, (1989).

Keane, P., Ethical Issues and Role of the Judge, Paper Presented at the 2004 ABA Judicial Division's Traffic Court Seminar, San Francisco, October 13, 2004.

Kennedy, D. B., and R. J. Homant, "Problems with the Use of Criminal Profiling in Premises Security Litigation," *Trial Diplomacy Journal*, Volume 20, 223–229 (1997).

Keppel, R., *Signature Killers*, New York, Pocket Books, (1997).

Keppel, R., "Signature Murders: A Report of Several Related Cases," *Journal of Forensic Sciences*, Volume 40, Number 4, 670–674 (July 1995).

Kiely, T. F., *Forensic Evidence: Science and the Criminal Law*, Boca Raton, FL, Taylor and Francis, (2nd ed. 2006).

Knight, R. A., J. I. Warren, R. Reboussin, and B. J. Soley, "Predicting Rapist Type from Crime-Scene Variables," *Criminal Justice and Behavior*, Volume 25, Number 1, 46–80, (March 1998).

Kocsis, R. N., *Criminal Profiling: Principles and Practice*, New Jersey, Humana Press, (2006).

Kocsis, R. N., "Criminal Psychological Profiling: Validities and Abilities," *International Journal of Offender Therapy and Comparative Criminology*, Volume 47, Number 2, 126–144 (2003).

Kocsis, R. N., "Validities and Abilities in Criminal Profiling: The Dilemma for David Canter's Investigative Psychology," *International Journal of Offender Therapy and Comparative Criminology*, Volume 50, Number 4, 458–477 (August 2006).

Kocsis, R. N., R. W. Cooksey, and H. J. Irwin, "Psychological Profiling of Offender Characteristics from Crime Behaviors in Serial Rape Offence," *International Journal of Offender Therapy and Comparative Criminology*, Volume 46, Number 2, 144–169 (2002).

Kocsis, R. N., Cooksey, W. R., and Irwin, J. H., "Psychological Profiling of Sexual Murders: An Empirical Model," *International Journal of Offender Therapy and Comparative Criminology*, Volume 46, Number 5, 532–554 (2002)

Kocsis, R. N., G. Z. Heller, and A. Try, "Visual Versus Narrative Case Material: The Impact on Criminal Psychological Profiling," *International Journal of Offender Therapy and Comparative Criminology*, Volume 47, Number 6, 664–676 (2003).

Kocsis, R. N., and J. Middledorp, "Believing is Seeing 111: Perceptions of Content in Criminal Psychological Profiles," *International Journal of Offender Therapy and Comparative Criminology*, Volume 48, Number 4, 477–494 (2004).

Kretschmer, E., *Physique and Character: An Investigation of the Nature of Constitution and the Theory of Temperament*, New York, Harcourt, (1925).

Lane, B., *The Encyclopedia of Forensic Science*, London, Headline, (1992).

Langer, W. C., *The Mind of Adolf Hitler*, New York, Basic Books, (1972).

Leiter, B., "The Epistemology of Admissibility: Why Even Good Philosophy of Science Would Not Make for Good Philosophy of Evidence," *Brigham Young University Law Review*, Volume 1997, Issue 4, 803–820 (1997).

Lester, J. D., *Writing Research Papers: A Complete Guide*, New York, Harper-Collins, (8th ed. 1996).

Levin, J., and Fox, J. A., *Mass Murder*, New York, Plenum, (1985).

Liebert, J., "Contributions of Psychiatric Consultation in the Investigation of Serial Murder," International Journal of Offender Therapy and Comparative Criminology, Volume 29, Number 3, 187–199 (1985).

Lipson, S. A., *Is it Admissible?*, Costa Mesa, CA., James Publishing, (2007).

Lombroso, C., *L'Uoma Delinquente*, Turin, Italy, Fratella Bocca, (1876).

Lombroso, C., *Crime: Its Causes and Remedies*, Boston, Little, Brown and Company, (1918).

Makros, A., and Alison, L. J., "Is Offender Profiling Possible? Testing the Predicted Homology of Crime Scene Actions and Background Characteristics in a Sample of Rapists," *Legal and Criminological Psychology*, Volume 7, 25–43 (2002).

Maletskos, C., and Spielman, S., Introduction of New Scientific Methods in Court, Law Enforcement Science, and Technology, 957–958, (S. S. Yefsky, ed.) Washington, DC, Thompson, (1967).

Maliver, D., "Out of the FRYE ING Pan and into Daubert: Trial Judges at the Gate will not Spell Relief for Plaintiffs," *University of Pittsburgh Law Review*, Volume 56, 245–269 (Fall 1994).

Mair, K., "Can a Profile Prove a Sex Offender Guilty?" *Expert Evidence*, Volume 3, 139 (1995).

Markle, A., *Criminal Investigation and Presentation of Evidence*, St. Paul, MN, West Publishing, (1976).

Martin, J. A., "The Proposed "Science Court," *Michigan Law Review*, Volume 75, 1058–1091 (1977).

Maskin, A., "The Impact of Daubert on the Admissibility of Scientific Evidence: The Supreme Court Catches Up with a Decade of Jurisprudence," *Cardozo Law Review*, Volume 15, 1929–1943 (1994).

Mauch, J. E., and J. W. Birch, *Guide to Successful Thesis and Dissertation: A Handbook for Students and Faculty,* New York, Marcel Dekker, Inc., (3rd ed. 1993).

McCaghy, C. H., and T. A. Capron, *Deviant Behavior: Crime, Conflict and Interest Groups*, New York, (3rd ed. 1994).

McCann, J. T., "Criminal Personality Profiling in the Investigation of Violent Crime: Recent Advances and Future Directions," *Behavioral Sciences and the Law*, Volume 10, 475–481 (1992).

McCord, D., "Syndromes, Profiles and Other Mental Exotica: A New Approach to the Admissibility of Nontraditional Psychological Evidence in Criminal Cases," *Oregon Law Review*, Volume 66, 19–108 (1987).

McCormick, C. T., *Handbook of the Law of Evidence,* St. Paul, MN, West Publishing, (1954).

McCormick, M., "Scientific Evidence: Defining a New Approach to Admissibility," *Iowa Law Review*, Volume 67, 879–916 (1982).

McCrary, G., Telephone Interview, October 27, 2006.

McCrary, G., and K. Ramsland, *The Unknown Darkness: Profiling the Predators Among Us,* New York, HarperTorch, (2004).

McGrath, M. G., "Criminal Profiling: Is there a Role for the Forensic Psychiatrist?" *The Journal of the American Academy of Psychiatry and the Law*, Volume 28, Number 3, 315–324 (2000).

McLeod, K. A., "Is Frye Dying or is Daubert Doomed? Determining the Standard of Admissibility of Scientific Evidence in Alabama Courts," *Alabama Law Review*, Volume 51, 883–905 (Winter 2000).

Michaud, G. S., and R. Hazelwood, *The Evil that Men Do*, New York, St. Martin's Press, (1998).

Milich, P. S., "Controversial Science in the Courtroom: Daubert and the Law's Hubris," *Emory Law Journal*, Volume 43, 913–926 (1994).

Mogck, D. L., "Are We there Yet? Refining the Test for Expert Testimony through Daubert, Kumho Tire and Proposed Federal Rule of Evidence 702," *Connecticut Law Review*, Volume 33, 303–336 (Fall 2000).

Moenssens, A. A., "Admissibility of Scientific Evidence–An Alternative to the Frye Rule," *William and Mary Law Review*, Volume 25, 545–575 (Summer 1984).

Moenssens A. A., "Novel Scientific Evidence in Criminal Cases: Some Words of Caution," *Journal of Criminal Law and Criminology*, Volume 84, 1–21 (Spring 1993).

Moenssens, A. A., Inbau, F. E., and J. E. Starra, J., *Scientific Evidence in Criminal Cases*, New York, The Foundation Press, (3rd ed. 1986).

Mueller, C. B., and L. C. Kirkpatrick, *Evidence*, New York, Aspen Law Publishers, (2nd ed. 1999).

Muller, D. A, "Criminal Profiling: Real Science or Just Wishful Thinking?, *Homicide Studies*, Volume 4, Number 3, 234–264 (August 2000).

Murphy, T., "The Admissibility of Scientific Evidence in Illinois," *Loyola University of Chicago Law Journal*, Volume 21, 935–972 (Spring 1990).

Murphy, W. D., and J. M. Peters, "Profiling Child Sexual Abusers: Psychological Considerations," *Criminal Justice and Behavior*, Volume 19, Number 1, 24–37 (March 1992).

Myers, J., *Evidence in Child Abuse and Neglect Cases*, Vol. 1, New York, John Wiley, (3rd ed. 1997).

Neal, B. S., "Into the Minds of Madmen: How the FBI's Behavioral Science Unit Revolutionalized Crime Investigation," (Book Review) *Trial*, Volume 40, 89–90 (May 2004).

Neufeld, J. P. "Admissibility of New or Novel Scientific Evidence in Criminal Cases, DNA Technology and Forensic Science," *The Banbury Report*, Coldspring Harbor, Laboratory Press, (1989).

Nowikowski, F., "Psychological Offender Profiling: An Overview," Criminologist, Volume 19, 225–226 (1995).

O'Connor, S., "The Supreme Court's Philosophy of Science: Will the Real Karl Popper Please Stand Up? *Jurimetrics Journal*, Volume 35, 263–276 (1995).

Okeke C. N., *Controversial Subjects of Contemporary International Law: An Examination of the New Entities of International Law and their Treaty-Making Capacity,* Boston, Little, Brown and Company (1973).

Okeke, C. N., "International Law in the Nigerian Legal System," *California Western International Law Journal*, Volume 27, 311–355 (1997).

Okeke, C. N., *The Theory and Practice of International Law in Nigeria*, Enugu, Fourth Dimension Press, (1986).

Oleson, J., "Psychological Profiling: Does it Actually Work? *Forensic Update*, Volume 46, 11–14 (1996).

Ormerod, D., "Criminal Profiling: Trial by Judge and Jury, Not Criminal Psychologist," in *Profiling in Policy and Practice* (D. Canter, and L. Alison, eds.) Aldershot, Ashgate Publishing, (1999).

Ormerod, D. C., "The Evidential Implications of Psychological Profiling," *Criminal Law Review*, Volume 92, 863–877 (1996).

Ormerod, D., and Sturman, J., "Working with the Courts: Advice for Expert Witnesses," in *The Forensic Psychologist's Casebook: Psychological Profiling and Criminal Investigation* (L. Alison ed.), 170–243 (2005).

Osborn, A. S., "Reasons and Reasoning in Expert Testimony," *Law and Contemporary Problems*, Volume 2, 490–494 (1935).

Osborne, J. W., "Judicial/Technical Assessment of Novel Scientific Evidence," *University of Illinois Law Review*, Volume 1990, Issue 2, 497–546 (1990).

O'Toole, M., "Criminal Profiling: The FBI Use Criminal Investigative Analysis to Solve Crimes," *Corrections Today*, Volume 6, 44–47 (1999).

Owen, D., *Criminal Minds: The Science and Psychology of Profiling*, New York, Barnes and Noble, (2004).

Palermo, G. B., "Criminal Profiling: The Uniqueness of the Killer," *International Journal of Offender Therapy and Comparative Criminology*, Volume 46, Number 4, 383–385 (2002).

Palermo, G. B., and R. N. Kocsis, *Offender Profiling: An Introduction to the Sociopsychological Analysis of Violent Crime*, Springfield, IL, Charles C. Thomas Publishers, (2005).

Park, R. C., D. P. Leonard, and S. H. Goldberg, *Evidence Law: A Student's Guide to the Law of Evidence as Applied in American Trials*, St. Paul, MN, Westgroup, (1998).

Peterson, J. L., P. J. Ryan, P. J. Houlden, and S. Mihajlovic, S., "The Use and Effects of Forensic Science in the Adjudication of Felony Cases," *Journal of Forensic Science*, Volume 32, 1730–1748 (1987).

Petherick, W., *The Science of Profiling*, New York, Barnes and Noble, (2005).

Petherick, W. (ed.), *Serial Crime: Theoretical and Practical Issues in Behavioral Profiling*, Burlington, MA, Academic Press, (2006).

Petherick, W., "What's in a Name? Comparing Applied Profiling Methodologies," *Journal of Law and Social Challenges*, Volume 5, 173–188 (Summer 2003).

Pinizzotto, A. J., "Forensic Psychology: Criminal Personality Profiling," *Journal of Police Science and Administration*, Volume 12, Number 1, 32–40 (1984).

Pinizzotto, A. J., and N. J. Finkel, "Criminal Personality Profiling: An Outcome and Process Study," *Law and Human Behavior*, Volume 14, Number 3, 215–233 (1990).

Pistorius, M., *Profiling Serial Killers and Other Crimes in South Africa*, South Africa, Penguin Books, (2005).

Polentz, M. C., "Post-Daubert Confusion with Expert Testimony," *Santa Clara Law Review*, Volume 36, 1187–1218 (1996).

Porter, B., "Mindhunters: Tracking Down Killers with the FBI's Psychological Profiling Team," *Psychology Today*, 44–52 (April 1983).

Prater, D. D., D. J. Capra, S. A. Saltzburg, and C. M. Arguello, *Evidence: The Objection Method*, New Jersey, LexisNexis, (2nd ed. 2002).

Reese, J., "Obsessive Compulsive Behavior: The Nuisance Offender," *FBI Law Enforcement Bulletin*, Volume 48, 6–12 (August 1979).

Ressler, R. K., A. W. Burgess, and J. E. Douglas, *Sexual Homicide: Patterns and Motives*, New York, The Free Press, (1992).

Ressler, R. K., and T. Shachtman, *Whoever Fights Monsters,* New York, Pocket Books, (1992).

Richardson, J. R., *Modern Scientific Evidence: Civil and Criminal*, Cincinnati, The W. H. Anderson Co., (2nd ed. 1974).

Risinger. M. D., and J. L. Loop, "Three Card Monte, Monty Hall, Modus Operandi and "Offender Profiling:" Some Lessons of Modern Cognitive Science for the Law of Evidence," *Cardozo Law Review*, Volume 24, 193–285 (November 2002).

Rogers, W. H., *The Law of Expert Testimony*, St. Louis, Central Law Journal, (2nd ed. 1891).

Rossi, D., "Crime Scene Behavioral Analysis: Another Tool for the Law Enforcement Investigator," *The Police Chief*, 152–155 (January 1982).

Rossi, F. F., *Expert Witnesses*, Chicago, American Bar Association, (1991).

Rossmo, D. K., "Geographic Profiling," in *Offender Profiling: Theory, Research and Practice,* (J. L. Jackson, and D. A. Bekerian, eds.), Chichester, John Wiley, (1997).

Rossmo, D. K., *Geographic Profiling*, Boca Raton, FL, CRC Press, (2000).

Rudd, R. G., *The Nigerian Law of Evidence*, London, Butterworths, (1964).

Rumbelow, D., The Complete Jack the Ripper, London, Penguin, (1975).

Saccuzzo, D. P., "Still Crazy After All These Years: California's Persistent Use of the MMPI as Character Evidence in Criminal Cases" *University of San Francisco Law Review*, Volume 33, 379–400 (1999).

Saferstein, R., *Criminalistics: An Introduction to Forensic Science*, Englewood Cliffs, N.J., Prentice Hall, (9th ed. 2006).

Salfati, C. G., and Canter, D. V., "Differentiating Stranger Murders: Profiling Offender Characteristics from Behavioral Styles," *Behavioral Sciences and the Law*, Volume 17, 391–406 (1999).

Salfati, C. G., and A. L. Bateman., "Serial Homicide: An Investigation of Behavioral Consistency," *Journal of Investigative Psychology and Offender Profiling*, Volume 2, 121–144 (2005).

Sanders, J., S. S. Diamond, and E. Vidmar, "Legal Perceptions of Science and Expert Knowledge," *Psychology, Public Policy and Law*, Volume 8, 139–153 (June 2002).

Santtila, P., A. Ritvanen, and A. Mokros, "Predicting Burglar Characteristics from Crime Scene Behavior," *International Journal of Police Science and Management*, Volume 6, 136–154 (2004).

Santtila, P., Fritzon, K., and Tamelander, A. L., "Linking Arson Incidents on the Basis of Crime Scene Behavior," *19 Journal of Police and Criminal Psychology*, 1–16 (2005).

Scallen, A. E., "Classical Rhetoric, Practical Reasoning, and the Law of Evidence," *American University Law Review*, Volume 44, 1717–1749 (1994–1995).

Scallen, A. E., "Interpreting the Federal Rules of Evidence: The Use and Abuse of the Advisory Committee Notes," *Loyola Los Angeles Law Review*, Volume 28, 1283–1302 (1995).

Schurman-Kauflin, D., *Vulture: Profiling Sadistic Serial Killers*, Boca Raton, Universal Publishers, (2005).

Schwartz, A., "A 'Dogma of Empiricism' Revisited: Daubert v. Merrell Dow Pharmaceuticals, Inc., and the Need to Resurrect the Philosophical Insight of Frye v. United States," *Harvard Journal of Law and Technology*, Volume 10, Number 2, 149–237 (Winter 1997).

Shehab, J. M., "The Future of the Davis-Frye Test in Michigan: Rumors of Its Demise Have Been Greatly Exaggerated," *University of Detroit Mercy Law Review*, 113–134 (Fall 1996).

Sheldon, W. H., *Varieties of Delinquent Youth*, New York, Harper Brothers Publishing, (1949).

Shuman, D. W., *Psychiatric and Psychological Evidence*, St. Paul, MN, Thomson West, (3rd ed. 2005).

Skaggs, C. C., "Evidence: Say Good-Bye to the Frye 'General Acceptance' Test: Daubert v. Merrell Dow Pharmaceuticals," *Washburn Law Journal*, Volume 33, 450–465 (Spring 1994).

Smith, C., "Psychological Offender Profiling," *The Criminologist*, Volume 17, 244–250 (1993).

Snook, B., J. Eastwood, P. Gendreau, C. Goggin, and R. M. Cullen, "Taking Stock of Criminal Profiling: A Narrative Review and Meta-Analysis," *Criminal Justice and Behavior*, Volume 34, Number 4, 437–453 (April 2007).

Starrs, J. E., "'A Still-Life Watercolor', Frye v. United States," *Journal of Forensic Sciences*, Volume 27, Number 3, 684–694 (July 1982).

Strano, M., "A Neural Network Applied to Criminal Psychological Profiling: An Italian Initiative," *International Journal of Offender Therapy and Comparative Criminology*, Volume 48, Number 4, 495–503 (2004).

Sucharitkul, S., *State Immunities and Trading Activities in International Law*, London, Stevens and Sons, (1959).

Sucharitkul, S., "The Future of International Law," Paper Presented at the 16th Regional Meeting of the American Society of International Law, at Golden Gate University School of Law, San Francisco, CA, on April 6, 2007.

Sutherland, E. H., and Cressey, D. R., *Principles of Criminology*, Philadelphia, PA, J.B. Lippincott, (7th ed. 1966).

Sutherland, E., and Cressey, D., *Criminology*, Philadelphia, PA, J.B. Lippincott, (1970).

Tapper, C., *Cross and Tapper on Evidence*, Oxford, Oxford University Press, (1995).

Tarantino, J. A., *Strategic Use of Scientific Evidence*, New York, Kluwer Law Book Publishers, (1988).

Taslitz, A. E., "Myself Alone: Individualizing Justice through Psychological Character Evidence," *52 Maryland Law Review*, 1–120 (1993).

Taylor, Lord Taylor of Gosforth, Lord Chief Justice of England, "The Lund Lecture," *Medicine, Science and the Law*, Volume 35, Number 1, 3–8 (January 1995).

Teten, H., "Offender Profiling" in *The Encyclopedia of Police Science* (B. William ed.), New York, Garland, 365–367 (1989).

Torres, A. N., M. T. Boccaccini, and H.A. Miller, "Perceptions of the Validity and Utility of Criminal Profiling Among Forensic Psychologists and Psychiatrists," *Professional Psychology: Research and Practice*, Volume 37, Number 1, 51–58 (February 2006).

Tuerkheimer, F., "The Daubert Case and Its Aftermath: Shot-Gun Wedding of Technology and Law in the Supreme Court," *Syracuse Law Review*, Volume 51, 803–840 (2001).

Turco, R., "Psychological Profiling," *International Journal of Offender Therapy and Comparative Criminology*, Volume 34, 47–154 (1990).

Turvey, B., *Criminal Profiling: An Introduction to Behavioral Evidence Analysis*, San Diego, CA, Academic Press, (1999).

Turvey, B., *Criminal Profiling: An Introduction to Behavioral Evidence Analysis*, San Diego, CA, Academic Press, (2nd ed. 2002).

Uglow, S., *Evidence; Text and Materials*, London, Sweet and Maxwell, (1997).

Van Den Wyngaert, C., *Criminal Procedure Systems in the European Community*, London, Butterworth Publishers, (1993).

Vandiver, J., "Crime Profiling Shows Promise," *Law and Order*, Volume 30, Number 10, 33–78 (1982).

Vold, G. B., *Theoretical Criminology*, New York, Oxford University Press, (1958).

Vorpagel, R. E., "Painting Psychological Profiles: Charlatanism, Coincidence, Charisma, Chance or New Science?, *Police Chief*, 156–159 (January 1982).

Walsh, J. T., "Keeping the Gate: The Evolving Role of the Judiciary in Admitting Scientific Evidence," *Judicature Genes and Justice*, Volume 83, Number 3, 140–144 (Nov/Dec. 1999).

Waltz, J. R, and Park, R.C., *Evidence: Cases and Materials*, New York, Foundation Press, (10th ed. 2003).

Ward, J., *Crime Busting: Breakthroughs in Forensic Science*, London, Blandford Press, (1998).

Warren, R. A., *The Effective Expert Witness*, Lightfoot, Va., Gaynor Publishing, (1997).

Wecht, C. H., and J. T. Rago, (eds.), *Forensic Science and Law: Investigative Applications in Criminal, Civil and Family Justice*, Boca Raton, FL, CRC Press, (2006).

Weissenberger, G., "The Elusive Identity of the Federal Rules of Evidence," *William and Mary Law Review*, Volume 40, 1613–1622 (May 1999).

Weissenberger, G., "Evidence Myopia: The Failure to See the Federal Rules of Evidence as a Codification of the Common Law," *William and Mary Law Review*, Volume 40, 1539–1593 (May 1999).

Weissenberger, G., "The Supreme Court and the Interpretation of the Federal Rules of Evidence," *Ohio State Law Journal*, Volume 53, 1307–1339 (1992).

Weissenberger, G., *Weissenberger's Federal Evidence: 2006 Courtroom Manual*, New Jersey, LexisNexis/Mathew Bender, (2005).

Weissenberger, G., and J. J. Duane, *Weissenberger's Federal Evidence*, New Jersey, LexisNexis, (5th ed. 2006).

West, A., "Clinical Assessment of Homicide Offenders: The Significance of Crime Scene Analysis in Offence and Offender Analysis," *Homicide Studies*, Volume 4, 219–233 (2000).

White, P. (ed.), *Crime Scene to Court: The Essentials of Forensic Science*, Cambridge, The Royal Society of Chemistry, (1998).

Wigmore, J. H., *Evidence in Trials at Common Law*, Vol. 7 (revised by James H. Chadbourn) Boston, MA, Little Brown and Company, (1978).

Wigmore, J. H., *Wigmore on Evidence*, Boston, MA, Little Brown and Company, (1983).

Wilson, P., and K. Soothhill, "Psychological Profiling: Red, Green or Amber?, *The Police Journal*, Volume 69, Number I, 12–20 (1996).

Wilson, P., R. Lincoln, and R. Kocsis, "Validity, Utility and Ethics of Profiling for Serial Violent and Sexual Offenders," *Psychiatry, Psychology and Law*, Volume 4, Number 1, 1–12 (1997).

Winerman, L., "Does Profiling Really Work?, *Monitor on Psychology*, Volume 35, Number 7, 67 (July/August 2004).

Winslow, R. W., and S. X. Zhang, *Criminology: A Global Perspective*, Englewood Cliffs, NJ, Prentice Hall, (2007).

Woodhams, J., and K. Toye, "An Empirical Test of the Assumptions of Case Linkage and Offender Profiling with Serial Commercial Robberies," *Psychology, Public Policy and Law*, Volume 13, 59–85 (February 2007).

Younger, I., M. Goldsmith, and D. A. Sonenshein, *Principles of Evidence*, Cincinnati, OH, Anderson Publishing, (4th ed. 2000).

Table of Cases

Index

ABOUT THE AUTHOR

NORBERT EBISIKE is a graduate of Golden Gate University School of Law, San Francisco, California; University of Kent, Canterbury, England; and the University of Westminster, London, England. He is the author of the book *An Appraisal of Forensic Science Evidence in Criminal Proceedings*. His peer-reviewed journal articles include "The Evidence of Children: An Evaluation of the Core Problems and Dilemmas with Children's Testimony" in *Criminal Law Bulletin* (2008). His research interests include forensic science evidence, criminology, comparative criminal justice, children and the law, sociolegal studies, and crime scene investigations.